# BONDS LOST

## SUBORDINATION, CONFLICT AND MOBILISATION IN RURAL SOUTH INDIA *c.* 1900–1970

# BONDS LOST

*Subordination, Conflict and Mobilisation in Rural South India c. 1900–1970*

GUNNEL CEDERLÖF

MANOHAR
2026

First published 1997
Reprinted 2021, 2022, 2023, 2024, 2025, 2026



ISBN 978-81-7304-193-8

*Published by*
Ajay Kumar Jain *for*
Manohar Publishers & Distributors
4753/23 Ansari Road, Daryaganj
New Delhi 110 002

*Printed at*
Replika Press Pvt. Ltd.

# Contents

# List of Illustrations

Jacket photograph: Gunnel Cederlöf

# List of Tables, Graph and Maps

*List of Tables*



*Graph*



*List of Maps*

# Preface

We were standing at the top of the steps admiring the front of the large building. The warm, south Indian night embraced us as the powerful Goundar landlord related his father's and grandfather's history. It was clear to anyone listening that this was their village in the deepest sense of the word. It had been a pleasant evening, the landlord had been generous with his time, and, as we stood talking, we could hear the women in the house preparing an evening meal.

Suddenly, looking out towards the front gate, we observed someone moving. The man had been standing there for quite some time, and now that the landlord set eyes on him, he slipped out of his shoes and walked across the front yard towards us. Both landlord and visitor were dressed in similar western styles and could easily have been taken for government employees in the streets of Tiruppur. Here, in front of the house, the man approaching kept his head low. As he stopped in front of the steps, we came to stand four or five steps higher up, looking down at him.

The visitor was a leading person of the Madhari community of the village, the community that had laboured in the Goundars' fields for generations. He was the real host for our visit that night but he had been away when we had arrived at his house. Now he came to enquire about his guests. Would we honour him by sharing a meal with him and his family in his home? The landlord, turning his back to the man and pointing with his left hand; asked, 'Do you want to go with him or stay where you are?'

The irresolution I felt in making the decision was later that night replaced by a growing understanding of history. I am part of it, it is part of me. Travelling to the other side of the globe does not change this fact.

During my work on this study, I have greatly benefited from discussions, advice and support from many persons. I have been fortunate in having inspiring supervision. Professor Rolf Torstendahl has supervised my work in the Department of History at Uppsala

University ever since my course dissertations as an undergraduate student. In a similar way, Olle Törnquist, Associate Professor in the Department of Government and working at the Unit of Development Studies, has been closely involved in the entire process of the present work. I am very grateful to them both for their generous support.

Lars Berge, Inga Brandell, Bipan Chandra, Torbjörn Engdahl, Barbara Harriss White, Beppe Karlsson, Christer Krokfors, Anu Mai Köll, Staffan Lindberg, M.M.S. Pandian, Pamela Price, Lars Rudebeck, David Washbrook, Ingrid Widlund and Maria Ågren have read and commented on different parts of the text and suggested many improvements. Ingrid Widlund has shared her time with me and we have had many laughs about everyday frustrations during some of my journeys to India. Rolf Torstendahl, Torkel Jansson and Jan Lindegren read and commented on the final version of the manuscript. I am grateful to them all.

Invaluable as interpreter, knowledgeable companion and friend, Ranjini accompanied me for the interviews with villagers of the Coimbatore district. I have also benefited much from the time and assistance that have been given to me by the Swedish Lutheran missionaries, as I have gone through their material. Important material has also been made available with the help of V. Tangadurai, S. J. Christopher Masillamani, P. Jeyapaul, D. Daniel Jayaraj and E. Jacob, the pastors in Tiruppur, Palladam, Mandiripalayam, Pollachi and Madras respectively. The work has benefited much from my stays at the Tamil Nadu Theological Seminary in Madurai, the Madras Institute for Development Studies in Madras and Bharathiar University in Coimbatore. The staffs of these seminaries and of all the different archives I have worked in have been most helpful.

The members of Rolf Torstendahl's and Stellan Dahlgren's seminars at the Department of History and of the Seminar for Development Studies, both seminars within Uppsala University, have made many fruitful comments on texts I have presented to them. I am grateful for the opportunities to develop further some parts of the present work in a project on estrangement and outsiders in society, *Främlingsprojektet*, at the Department of History. The warm and generous atmosphere I feel at my workplace, the Unit of Development Studies at Uppsala University, is an atmosphere that any researcher might envy.

With much knowledge and a father's concern, Karl Inge Sandred corrected my English. Neil Tomkinson corrected the final version of the manuscript. Klas Hagren corrected the list of transcribed Tamil. I owe them a lot. Needless to say, any remaining mistakes are entirely mine. Photographs have been generously provided by Karin Andrén and Elisabeth Bergman.

Without funding, this project would never have materialised. I am most grateful for the support given by the Swedish Agency for Research Cooperation with Developing Countries (SAREC), the Nordic Institute of Asian Studies, the Swedish Institute in Stockholm and the Royal Swedish Academy of Letters, History and Antiquities (*Kungliga Vitterhets Historie och Antikvitets Akademien*).

Finally, and nearest to my heart, come the three persons with whom I share my life. My sons Erik and Gustav are the best young travellers I can think of. They taught me to see India from a perspective much nearer to the ground and never to forget all the basic questions. My husband Leif was the one who asked me to join him to go to India fifteen years ago, and, together with him, I have shared also that part of India that words cannot grasp.

*Lundbacken, 1997* GUNNEL CEDERLÖF

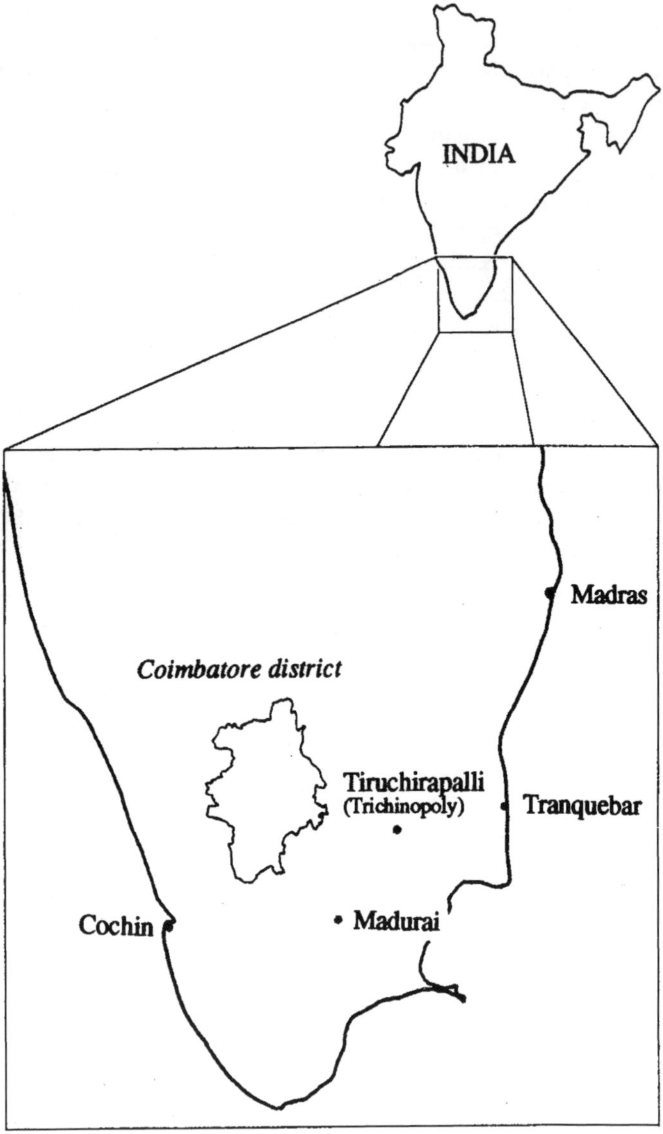


The external boundaries of India depicted in this map are neither correct nor authentic

MAP 1: INDIA AND THE COIMBATORE DISTRICT

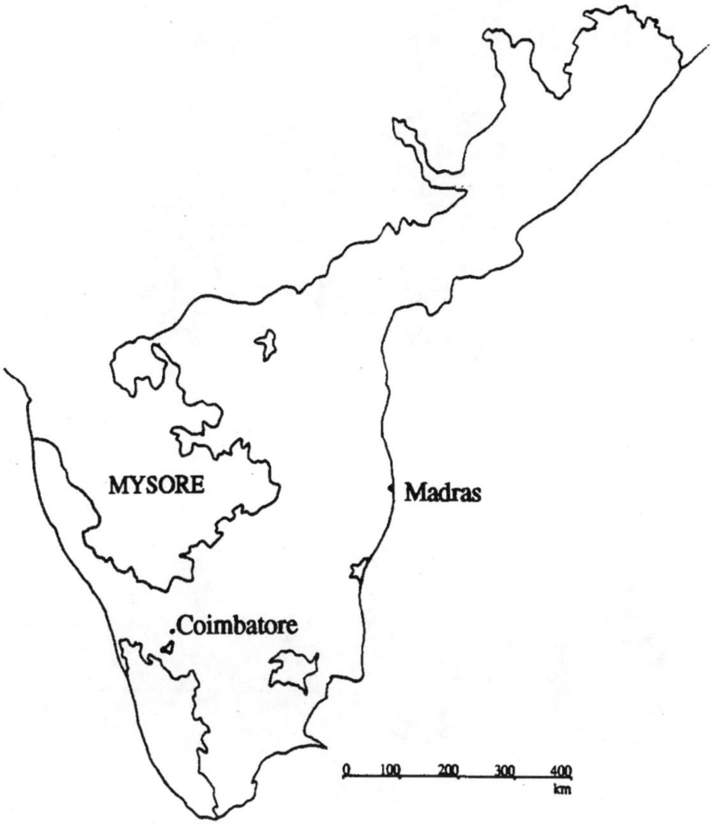


The external boundaries of India depicted in this map are neither correct nor authentic

MAP 2: THE MADRAS PRESIDENCY *c.* 1910

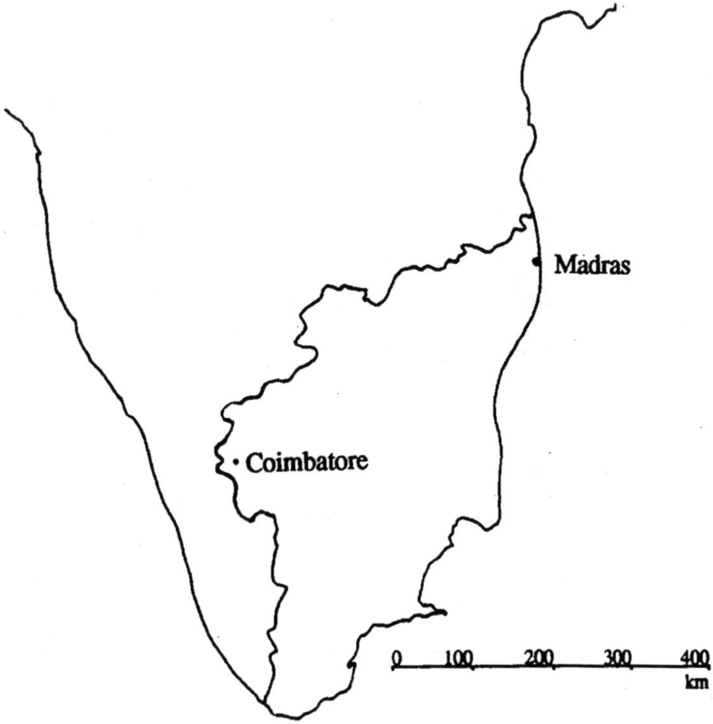


The external boundaries of India depicted in
this map are neither correct nor authentic

MAP 3: THE STATE OF TAMIL NADU

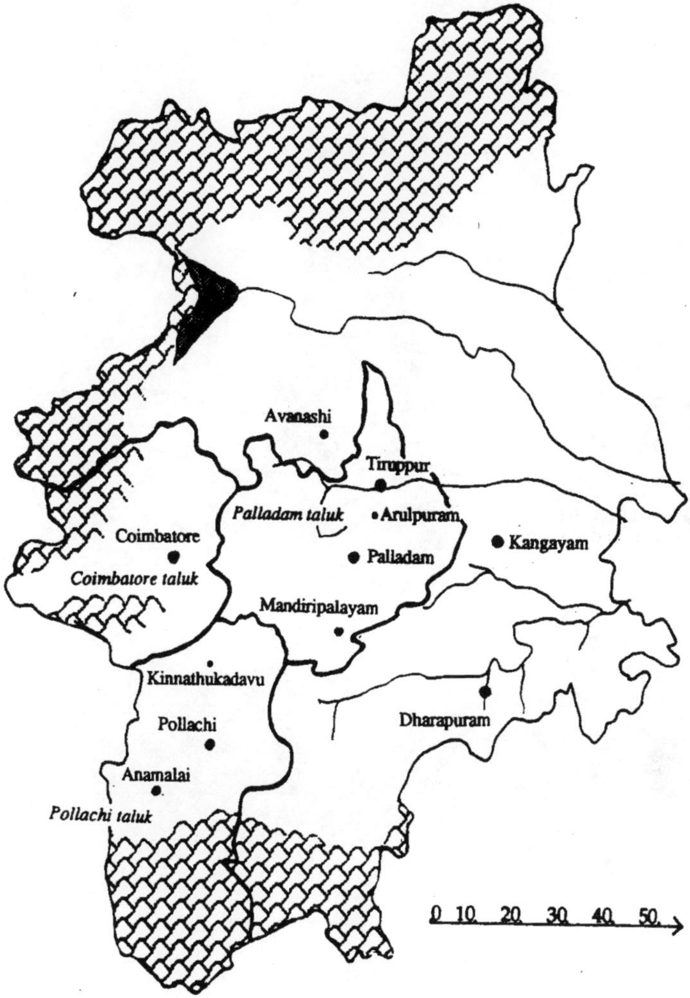


The external boundaries of India depicted in this map are neither correct nor authentic

MAP 4: THE COIMBATORE DISTRICT

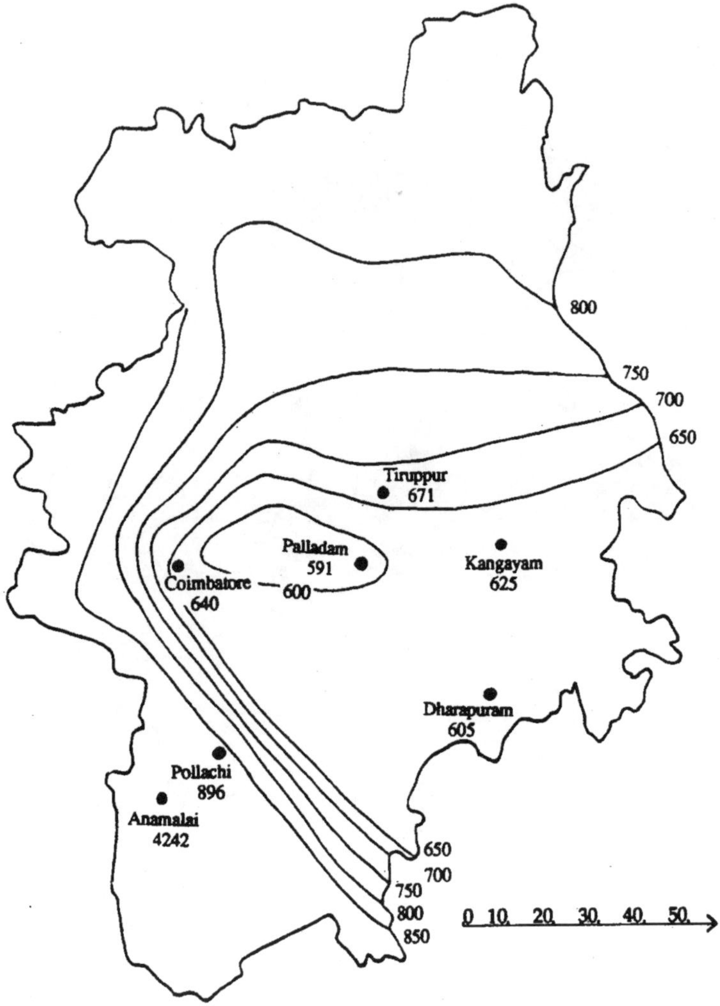


The external boundaries of India depicted in
this map are neither correct nor authentic

**MAP 5: AVERAGE ANNUAL RAINFALL IN THE COIMBATORE DISTRICT (MM)**

*(Compiled from R.K. Sivanappan/P.K. Aiyasamy 1978, p. 15)*

CHAPTER 1

# Introduction

The bulls were worked from 7-10 a.m. & 3-6 p.m. They had to walk up the [missing word] inching backwards, which is tiring & they were blowing and panting. These bulls cost 150 Rupees: waterbuffalos, ugly creatures (asuttamāka is a good word for them, ugly and unclean) only cost Rs 50 & are good for their milk. The well system is called kavalai—the bucket system.[1]

On the evening of one of his daily visits to the nearby village of Saveripalayam, the young ICS officer made some notes in his diary about the impressive hard work that brought the water out of the wells to the fields. The year was 1937, and he was only twenty-three years old, on his first assignment in India as Assistant Collector in Coimbatore to apply the justice of the British Crown.[2] The *kavalai* was impressive to watch and on different dates in the diary there are figures of depth and width of wells and costs of cattle. Hour after hour, the draught animals pulled the heavy bags from the deep wells to let them discharge into the irrigation canals and bring water to the dry soils. Thereafter, the cattle backed up the little slope and let the bag drop back into the water again. Three to four hours in the morning before the midday heat, and again in the evening. No wonder that the young man was impressed.

Knowledge and skills were associated with the *kavalai.* The wooden construction and the leather bags had to stand the pressure of tons of water. In every village, skilled leather-workers lived, whose task was to flay dead cattle, tan the skin by a process that took more than a month, and stitch the bags. The skin from one buffalo made one bag, and this bag would last for about half a year. In the dry lands of the Coimbatore district, no farmer could make a profit from his field's without relying on the work of a leather-worker. One of the main reasons why a farmer employed first and foremost a man of the leather-working community as an agricultural labourer at the farm was to ensure irrigation for his lands. The labourer was employed on contracts that in practice turned out to be permanent and to last as long as the farmer needed the labourer in his service.

But even though agriculture united the farmer and the leather-worker, there was a deep divide between them. An area that was segregated from the main village housed the leather-working community. Informal rules of social behaviour kept them apart. To deal with death and the unclean was unthinkable for anyone but a member of the leather-working community, and the village community kept them in their place. The *kavalai* thereby not only implied skills, but also bore witness to social barriers between high and low.

However, it is not the purpose of this study to trace the progress of the *kavalai*. Equipment does not change the route of history. In the highlands of south India, the *kavalai* technique was a tool in the hands of people who strove to achieve certain goals. The purpose here is to reconstruct the relationship between those who worked on the farms, but, so to speak, met on opposite sides of the *kavalai*: the owner, employer and dominant, on the one side, and the labourer, skilled and dependent, on the other.

Throughout the last century, the leather-workers of the highlands of Tamilnad[3] were rarely at the centre of interest when official records were written. Not owning land, they did not leave traces in settlement registers, and living up to a mile away from the main villages, a visitor could leave a village without ever setting eyes on them. Here and there, they were recorded in descriptive texts as stitching the leather bags that lifted water out of the wells. In these cases, they were mentioned by the name for Tamil leather-workers, Chakkiliyar, and not by their own name originating from Telugu, Madhari. Apart from such passages, they were mentioned occasionally as farm labourers in government documents or were described in letters home to Europe as dirty and extremely poor, living under pitiable conditions.

The reverse is the case with the dominant farming community that took on Madhari labourers. The Goundar were praised by the British officials for their spirit of enterprise and will to work hard under difficult climatic conditions. These farmers seem to have fulfilled the rulers' dreams of the industrious small farmer, bringing good crops from dry soils to the market and revenue to the public treasury.

However, both the Madhari and the Goundar were key actors in the agricultural production of the highlands. They were not the only communities represented in agriculture, either as landowners or as labourers. Nor did economic divisions strictly follow caste lines. But in influence and exercise of power in the villages, the Goundar appear hard to match. At the same time, the Madhari had skills that no farmer cultivating lands of any substantial size could do without. This situation explains why members of the Goundar and the Madhari communities are the key-persons also in the present study.

This is a study of social relationships between rural-based groups of people over a period of seventy years from the beginning of the twentieth century until the late 1960s. The area is situated in the highlands of the southern part of the peninsula, surrounded by mountains from the Nilgiris in the north to the Anamalais in the south. Today the region is divided into two districts, Periyar and Coimbatore. However, Periyar is a new district, and during the period studied the major part of this region came under the Coimbatore district. The region sometimes carries its old name, Kongu, which refers to an area that better corresponds to the geographically defined, highland region. The two communities lived in the same villages but were segregated in space by social codes of behaviour and taboos. They were related by labour but divided by access to the produce and by control over the resources that brought wealth to some and survival to others. They joined in the ceremonies and festivals that marked the village year, but even here segregation between the two determined the level of participation. They were interrelated and interdependent, as regards their survival, but at the same time were socially segregated by caste and were economically on the most uneven terms.

At first sight, this seems to have been the condition throughout the period under study. However, a change in the preconditions for agriculture was already under way at the date when the present study begins. Cotton was becoming the most profitable of crops, and a textile industry had been established in the major towns of the region. The economy was shifting from subsistence cultivation and the breeding of cattle for the cultivators' needs and for sale to a situation in which new crops were being cultivated for commercial purposes. The Coimbatore district, which was one of the earliest in the Presidency to develop industries, was drawn into the larger market for textile exports. The wealthier farmers made investments in agriculture and were able to expand. Communications were improved, factories erected, and commercial crops became increasingly important in the farmer's economy. At the tea estates and the urban-based factories, the demand for labour increased, and there were labourers—most of them coming from the socially and economically lowest sections of society—who could to a limited extent benefit from growing employment opportunities.

Coinciding with this major transformation of the economy, there was a movement among the 'untouchable' castes organising along caste-lines to change their religion on a grand scale. 'Mass conversion' to either Islam or Christianity took place in many parts of Tamilnad, as regarded Christianity, under the aegis of several, predominantly Protestant, missions. This is basically a phenomenon of the late nineteenth and early twentieth centuries, occurring among different untouchable castes. The movements, which may be seen in the light of the increased mobility and politicisation among these castes, have been interpreted in different ways. Some authors emphasise the conscious effort of the community to raise its social and economic status, as compared with other 'untouchable' castes. By others, it has been explained as an act of survival or as organised attempts to break with the oppression of Hindu landlords.

The Coimbatore district was also touched by these events. During little more than five decades, two missions received thousands of converts from the Madhari community. The Church of Sweden Mission worked in the heartland of the highlands, from Tiruppur, Coimbatore and Palgath to Pollachi and Dindigul. Their neighbours, the Wesleyan Methodist Missionary Society, baptised and formed congregations of Madhari Christians further east, from Dharapuram to Karur. These conversions provoked much hostility from the Goundar farmers, but they continued during the period when the preconditions for agriculture were altering.

Not all the changes had consequences for labour relations. Even though the farmers who cultivated in medium-sized or large farms had become deeply involved in profitable production for the market, the labour market does not seem to have changed to the same extent. Throughout the first half of the twentieth century, a substantial proportion of farm labourers still worked under permanent arrangements, tied to the farms. The most visible change that had an immediate effect on the Madhari labourers came after a large-scale, water-power project began to provide the farms with electricity. In the late 1940s and early 1950s, coinciding with a severe drought, a large number of villages were connected to the electricity-supply lines. When the Government gave support to electrification of the villages, and small and efficient pumps could replace the *kavalai*, the advantage of taking on permanent farm labourers began to disappear. This was not just a change of technical equipment. Also the numerous draught animals became superfluous, as well as the need to have leather-workers employed at the farms.

The major research question concerns the relationship between the Goundar farmers and the Madhari labourers working on their lands. The discussion will detail how this relationship was connected with and responded to changes in the preconditions for survival and to the opening up of new opportunities.

In the present study, I am concerned with the development of the social relations between agricultural labourers, who were completely dependent on working for others, i.e. the landless labourers, and farmers who were wealthy enough to employ those labourers; the study therefore has an emphasis on labour relations. However, labour relations alone do not express or explain the social relations between the two. In the villages, people lived near each other and came to interact in all spheres of life, and it is therefore hardly fruitful to isolate labour relations from other social relations. The relations between farmers and labourers depended not only on labour contracts, but also on codes of behaviour and sets of rules explained by local social hierarchies.

In spite of the social gap between the two communities, they both upheld important functions in village rites and ceremonies. Labour relations were constituted not only by contracts, but also by labour related to the social hierarchies of the village and region; they were therefore to a large extent also based on informal laws regulating the distribution of the village produce. Therefore, in the villages of the highlands, the relationship between a farmer and his labourers did not have the same characteristics as that between an employer and an employee at the workplace. The relationship between the Goundar farmers and the Madhari labourers included such different aspects of life as toiling in the fields, growing crops and carrying messages about death, aspects that were made concrete in local customary law.

The aim of the present study is to make clear the major characteristics of the relationship between the Goundar and Madhari communities, on the one hand, with regard to the division of labour and the control over and distribution of the resources of agricultural production and, on the other, with regard to local power relations. Thereafter, I shall analyse how this relationship changed during a period of fundamental economic change and growing politicisation among the lowest sections of south Indian society. The dynamic I have observed in this relationship points to a situation in which the economic logic of agriculture interacted with the social and political logic of the farming Goundar community's ambition to uphold local power relations. Thereby, the Goundar–Madhari relationship was sometimes altered as a consequence of the increasing influence of industrialisation and of the change-over to cash-crop production for export. At the same time, the Goundars' striving to preserve their political dominance and local control hampered their policy as farmers to keep to the plain economic rationality of farming. As a consequence of the particular construction and the history of the Goundar–Madhari relationship, mobilisation among the Madhari came to have a different form than that of the more mobile Scheduled Castes organising along caste or class lines in south India.

In nearness and distance, social codes kept the two apart. The older Madhari of today face those rules with a certain sense of humour, reversing values. In Arulpuram, they explained: 'We touched the seeds throughout the harvest. But when we had packed the sacks, it all became untouchable to us!' When an old woman showed how water was poured down her throat by the Goundar, as she was not allowed to touch any vessel when she was thirsty and asked for some water, the younger men teased her and asked why she did not demand to have water poured into her hands. But she laughed and replied, 'Why should I? They served me like a queen. I let them do it so that I could rest myself and just open my mouth!'[4]

## AN OUTLINE OF THE PRESENT STUDY

In the chapters that follow, the discussion will start from the early decades of the twentieth century. In Chapter 2, an attempt is made to reconstruct the relationship between the Goundar and the Madhari in the rural Coimbatore district. This reconstruction will be based on material from the first three decades of the twentieth century. As will also be shown in Chapter 3, there is no reason to believe that agricultural labour relations changed to any substantial degree during this period, but there was a constant need for a large and permanent labour force. The subsequent chapters lay emphasis on the process of industrialisation and how it affected this rural relationship, though, in some different respects. While Chapter 3 discusses the period until approximately 1950, Chapter 4 starts from the great drought that struck in 1946-53. The results of the study show that the real change in agricultural labour relations that eventually came about was most accentuated during the six drought-years, when a large number of the landless labourers left the villages to find the means of survival elsewhere, while the farmers had adopt on a new strategy to achieve a profitable production.

From the 1930s, the Madhari community began to organise. The immediate outlook of the movement was religious, in the sense that the Madhari asked to be baptised and wished to follow the teaching of the Christian Church. However, this situation led the mission workers to enter the villages to a greater extent than they had previously done. Social hierarchies and local power relations appeared threatened by the Madhari conversions, and during the 1940s local conflicts were numerous in the villages. In Chapter 5, the presence of mission workers in the area and their significance for the Goundar–Madhari relationship are discussed.

## SOCIAL RELATIONS DURING ECONOMIC CHANGE

During the period studied, agriculture in the Coimbatore district went through changes that not only altered the scale of farming, but also transformed and redirected it towards an increasingly capitalised market. In this transition of the economy, social relations among rural-based groups changed. How social relations relate to fundamental economic transitions is an important research problem. Questions about how social relationships responded or adjusted to changing conditions may be matched by questions about how the process in a region may have been influenced or limited by existing relationships. When the question is approached, it is often, on the one hand, to emphasize either the economic changes and to understand the prevailing social relations as consequences of these changes, or, on the other hand, to stress the relations between socially defined groups of people in which cultural continuity cuts through the centuries, strongly influencing human action.

By way of introduction, some of the more commonly represented perspectives and ways of analysing social relations will be discussed with regard to this major research problem. However, the aim is not to make a full exposition of current debates and the views of the researchers participating in them. The aim is limited to discussing how four different researchers deal with the question of the relationship between rural social relations and the economic changes of the late nineteenth and early twentieth centuries. While making very different contributions with regard to theory and the priority of research questions, at the same time they keep agricultural social relations in a major focus. In spite of applying very different theoretical perspectives, they have also been found to refer, sometimes closely, to the major research problems of the present study, and even though not all explicitly address this problem, their results have implications for it. The four researchers are Christopher Baker, David Hardiman, David Mosse and Jan Breman; the first two are historians, while Mosse is an anthropologist and Breman a sociologist. In the subsequent chapters, the findings from the present study will be discussed with regard also to other related research.

In his dissertation on social organisation in the Ramnad district, south India, David Mosse argues for a 'cultural consensus'. Within and according to this consensus, people act. The actors that Mosse pays special attention to are the Harijan castes,[5] his results showing that the Harijans act primarily in order to achieve higher status for their caste. However, even though this cultural consensus shows inertia, it is not to be understood as completely static. Mosse has a strong emphasis on caste strategies and human action. This is further elaborated in later articles. In a study of Pallar strategies for mobility, Mosse outlines how the Pallar caste employed new identities, 'projecting themselves as Christians, Scheduled Castes', and manipulated those identities in order to maximise access to material and political resources and to promote their interests and caste honour.[6]

The cultural consensus Mosse observes disregards boundaries between religions. There is a continuity in which symbols of different religions are ordered according to the same structuring principles. However, this continuity may be submerged when cultural and religious differences are stressed. When social and political mobilisation among Harijans takes place, it is often articulated through the manipulation of the institutions and symbols that define their subordination. In the situation in Ramnad, Mosse finds that Harijans used their membership of the Roman Catholic Church in order to raise their caste status. In this way, Mosse argues, consensus does not imply political conservatism but rather gives room for political action expressed in the manipulation of rituals and symbols in order to challenge high-caste, political dominance. Thereby, the cultural consensus does not imply absence of conflict but rather channels a lot of tension.

Mosse criticises the position held by Dumont, among others, and emphasises the link between (caste) status and (political) power. He argues that religion and purity are not separated from politics and power in the conception of Harijan subordination and dependence. This position also eliminates all possibilities of an autonomous, subaltern culture, according to him.[7]

At the same time, in his examination of Harijan subordination, he finds that 'discourses of development' which problematise poverty and powerlessness are wanting in the cultural context and the cultural construction of power. The results of the class analysis that Kathleen Gough has carried out in Tanjavur district are 'untypical', according to Mosse. The economic and caste homogeneity identified among the landless labourers in Gough's study has no resemblance in Ramnad.[8]

The initial question raised earlier, which is also central for the present study, is not of major importance to Mosse. When he arrives at the issue of how the economic transformations of the late nineteenth century affected caste relations, he takes his point of departure far back in history. A long continuity is described for the basis of dominance in Ramnad. This continuity dates back to the Vijayanagara empire, ruling over major parts of the Tamil land from the fourteenth to the sixteenth century.

In this period, dominance did not derive from ownership of land, but from holding political and military office. To hold such positions implied honour and rights to shares in the produce and control over the system of redistribution. From the mid-nineteenth century, as a result of the introduction of 'dry land cash cropping, among other things', the basis of political dominance began to change. However, the visible consequences for the Harijan castes are dated one hundred years later. After Independence, government primary schools expanded in rural areas, and educated persons among the Pallar Harijan caste were able to get employment as teachers. As they began to receive cash incomes, they were also able to buy land and build up an position independent of the high-caste, village landlords. The reason why such an exceptionally high proportion of Harijans, and in particular Pallars, owned land in the 1970s (more than 50 per cent of the Pallar community in the district) is attributed by Mosse to a caste order which was not founded on territory and land. Thus, land was available also to Harijans.[9]

To Mosse, the logic thereby remains in the long-term continuance of cultural consensus. Conflicts and tension may be high, and human action may lead to very different results. But both conflicts and actions take place within and in accordance with Culture.

David Hardiman, the historian of the Subaltern Studies collective, presented a profound study in his book about tribal or Adivasi assertion in Gujarat, west India.[10] Aiming to write a history that kept the perspective from within the Adivasi group, Hardiman took to a somewhat unconventional method for an historian, as he himself travelled in the region long after the movement took place to trace its origins via interviews. Oral material plays a central part in the study, since there is a great lack of written material on the subject.

In 1922, a movement that was religious in its expression spread throughout the state of Gujarat among the Adivasi group. A goddess, speaking through spirit mediums, commanded the thousands of people gathered around to stop drinking alcoholic beverages and eating meat and fish, to live a simple life, to take baths during the day, and not to have anything to do with the Parsis. Soon the message included not only commands to change the way of life, but also urged the followers to follow the teachings of Mahatma Gandhi. Because of the goddess, the movement came to be known as the 'Devi' movement. Several such similar movements occurred throughout central India during the late nineteenth and early twentieth centuries. However, Hardiman writes that, where these movements have been previously described, they have been understood as a product of either superstitious beliefs or elite mobilisation of tribals.

The writing of history from an elite perspective is also one of the Subaltern historians' main criticisms of both nationalism and Marxism oriented Indian historiography. Hardiman has little regard for what he calls 'secular-minded socialist historians' with 'dogmatic beliefs'. To understand religion as a hegemonic ideology imposed from above, a political resource in the hands of manipulating leaders, is to subscribe to an elitist version of history. However, it is unfortunate that Hardiman relates to this conventional form of Marxism. In a note, he admits that this has nowadays largely been abandoned, but he does not problematise this further in relation to his own argument. In contrast to the vulgar Marxism outlined, Hardiman emphasises that the Adivasi should be treated as subjects in history and that those were conscious movements that started from within the Adivasi group and were carried on by them. Since religions consist to a large extent of assimilated folk-beliefs, religion among the Adivasi was deeply founded within the group and had a massappeal that cannot be understood to have been imposed from above. The Devi was not part of an elite or Brahmin religion, but purely Adivasi.

This position has consequences not only for the writing of history in the perspective of Marxism or historical materialism, but also for cultural explanations, as outlined in the case of Mosse earlier. For Hardiman, the Adivasi assertion was not expressed through a manipulation of the common religious symbols of Gujarati society, but consciousness and mobilisation grew autonomously from within the Adivasi group itself as a reaction to the relation of dominance they were part of and where they held the position of the suppressed. In the arguments of both Mosse and Hardiman, conflict is central. However, in Mosse's text, conflicts take place within an unified cultural context, whereas for Hardiman it is a matter of conflicts between the Adivasi, who mobilise themselves by a politicisation of their own religion and culture, and an oppressive state and its allies.

By giving equal importance to the religious, social and political sides of the movement, Hardiman aims to contribute to the understanding of the religiosity of peasant consciousness and to the discussion about the structures of pre-colonial society and the impact of colonial rule on this society. By such an approach, Hardiman argues, the way in which the peasants (including the Adivasis) have adapted themselves to and fought against the harsh exploitation of colonial rule, as well as how nationalism worked at the village level, can be fruitfully studied.[11]

Hardiman prefers the term 'Adivasi' to 'tribal' and argues that it lacks evolutionist connotations and has a particular historical relevance in India. Adivasi relates to a development in which people who were free, or relatively free, from outside control during the nineteenth century were subjugated and became dependent on traders, moneylenders and landlords. Protected by colonial rule, all three were able to deprive the Adivasi of their land and labour. There were many different Adivasi *jatis* in Gujarat or what other authors might have called many different tribes. Hardiman makes distinctions between these in his text. However, by consistently using the term Adivasi or Adivasi group, he emphasises that common interests superseded community boundaries. There were an Adivasi consciousness and an Adivasi solidarity that had roots in pre-colonial society but that was strengthened under the pressure of British colonial rule and of those who could benefit from this rule. There were economic differences within the Adivasi group; a few of them had been granted privileges by the *Gaikwad* of Baroda in the eighteenth century. Thereby, the wealthy Adivasi contracted poorer Adivasi labourers to work on their lands. But, according to Hardiman, those labour relations bore no resemblance to the exploitative relations upheld by the Parsi landlords towards the Adivasi during the late nineteenth and early twentieth centuries. This links Hardiman's study with Ranajit Guha's work on peasant insurgency in India, in which Guha searches for the peasant consciousness in contrast to colonial rule.[12]

With regard to the initial question, how social relations were adjusted to, were affected by or influenced the fundamental economic changes that took place in the nineteenth and early twentieth centuries, Mosse and Hardiman approach the issue from different points of departure. Mosse recognises the economic transition, as it opened up the possibility in the longer term for Harijans to purchase land and improve their social and economic positions. This change arrived from outside and people responded to it. However, it was a development that took place within a *longue durée* of cultural consensus. When political dominance did not rely on territory, landowning Harijans were not regarded as a threat to the power-holding castes. Thereby, the economic changes provided them with opportunities in which the manipulation of existing cultural symbols could be used to achieve a positive result.

However, paradoxically, when economic change is described as having paved the way for changed economic relations, there is at the same time a great risk that the important influence of fundamental economic transition on social relations will be underestimated by maintaining a perspective of cultural continuance. Mosse explains the strategy which the Harijans used to improve their situation as double-edged; with earnings in cash, they invested in land and achieved a certain economic independence; at the same time, through the Roman Catholic Church, they were able to raise their caste status and gain political influence. However, these new economic opportunities of earning cash wages are not so much problematised; they just appear. Thereby, growing capitalism is reduced to the introduction of new crops and turning land into a marketable commodity, and the possibilities of Harijans gaining greater access to land is explained by a long-lasting logic of caste-based, political power relations, in which the holders of power, so to speak, do not realise the rising importance of possessing land for gaining political influence.[13]

Mosse argues against M.N. Srinivas' definition of 'dominant caste', the concept Srinivas developed in his study of a Mysore village in 1955. Of Srinivas' three factors (numerical strength, economic and political power, dominance and political rank), the second is immediately related to this discussion.[14] Mosse observes that in Ramnad, the district he studies, economic and political power did not belong to one and the same caste, but to two different and influential castes. Economic power, defined by Mosse as control over production, was separate from political power, defined as control over the redistribution of the produce. Mosse argues that, in the pre-colonial period, the political rights (or power) were superior to economic rights. When the dividing line between interest groups in the village was based on caste status, economic power was thereby only one aspect of the foundation of this status. However, Mosse argues that the old basis for political power was eroded during British colonial rule by legislation, the introduction of cash crops and other 'idiosyncratic' factors.

Mosse's primary aims in his 1986 study are firstly to discuss the nature of social and religious institutions. Secondly, he analyses the strategies employed by untouchable communities to achieve higher status, and, finally, he explores how Christianity has become 'embedded' in the indigenous social and religious order. In the major part of his work, he discusses ideologies of caste, caste status, and Christian and Hindu religious life. The emphasis on cultural continuity is strong. However, when he arrives at the impact of new laws under colonialism and the orientation of the economy towards the world market and as he observes the basis of political power weaken and the lowest sections of society gain limited, economic and eventually political influence, the 'cultural consensus' suddenly appears to become restricted to the sphere of strategies for mobilisation and to the logic of caste-based status. According to his study, in the twentieth century, gaining economic wealth could establish an independent basis for political dominance. If the results are read from a viewpoint in which the introduction of capitalism is an integrated part of the basic preconditions for the analytical discussion, the introduction of 'cash-cropping, among other things' obviously made a great difference to social relations.

More than that, by the changes during the last century, as also described by Mosse, the cultural code—Culture itself—can be assumed to have changed. If the argument is made in terms of Culture, it can thereby be understood as a constantly changing process and does not risk being treated as an a-historical phenomenon.

When Hardiman approaches this complex of problems, he sees the fundamental economic changes in the light of the enforced, capitalist, colonial power that makes exploitation of the Adivasi possible. At the same time, this enforced dominance was a major precondition for the emergence of the particular historical situation in which Adivasi consciousness grew. In pre-colonial times, the Adivasi had access to the forest and were under no, or only limited, outside pressure. The arrival of 'capitalist colonialism' changed this for the worse. The Adivasi lost access to the forest, were heavily taxed as smallholders, got indebted to moneylenders and eventually became dependent labourers paid on the level of mere survival by the Parsi landlords. In an effort to free themselves from this oppression, the Devi movement grew.

As will be discussed also in the case of Breman's study in Gujarat, such a deep divide between landowners and agricultural labourers has no resemblance in the highlands of Tamilnad. The Goundar and Madhari communities were no doubt on opposite ends of the socio-economic scale, but they did not live in completely different, almost autonomous cultures. In spite of their different gods and shrines, the Madhari, like the Goundar community, were integrated as recognised members of the village and the available evidence indicates that they had been so since before the colonial era. Their subordination as well as mobilisation cannot be understood without being related to Goundar dominance. This does not mean to deny the Madhari their capacity to act as conscious subjects in history. Like the Adivasi in Hardiman's case, the Madhari also mobilised, but their mobilisation did not grow autonomously. The decision to organise was their own—that is not the question—and also they mobilised *against* dominant exercise of power and *for* more or less well-defined aims. The Madhari had an identity of their own, but this identity was a complex one and can hardly be understood as detached from the ideology of power and social relations of the village.

The claim to a subaltern autonomy is the target of one of the main criticisms of this research position.[15] However, most of the researchers advocating a Subaltern Studies perspective do not argue for a total and isolated autonomy of subaltern groups. The existence of a duality is argued for both in the formation of an autonomous identity without influence from the oppressor's culture and in the formation of an identity in relation to oppression as a negative identity. However, to carry out a study, keeping this duality in mind, may become quite problematic when one leaves the more theoretical level and moves into empirical data. To keep the dividing-line clear between what is an autonomous and what is a dependent (or negative) identity is not always easy. Hardiman seems to have a stronger emphasis on the second form of identity, that which is formed from being oppressed. In the Gujarat case, an awareness of being an oppressed Adivasi and 'a spirit of resistance' is found to have linked different tribal communities together in a political project sharing a collective identity.

In speaking of a common subaltern identity that transgressed community-lines, whether autonomous or not, this does not resemble the situation of the 'untouchable' castes in the Coimbatore region. In Gujarat, several tribal communities achieved a common goal. However, in the Tamilnad highlands, members of the two major untouchable castes, the Madhari and the Paraiyar, mobilised for conversion but never joined forces. If the enmity was not shown in open antagonism, they still did not join in one and the same political or social project. As will be further discussed, the two communities mobilised in quite different ways. Both made their decisions on community-basis, but while the Paraiyar had a stronger assertion of being 'Adi Dravida' (Original Dravidian) and had a much wider range for their mobility, the Madhari mobilisation was not only separated from the Paraiyar, but was also divided by kinship. In their case, kinship lines provided obstacles to a common Madhari mobilisation. If the subaltern category is limited and applied to only the Madhari community, arguing that they were in fact more oppressed than the Paraiyar in the region, it still does not make sense. Not all sub-groups within the larger Madhari community mobilised against the Goundar exercise of power, and mobilisation in the community strictly followed kinship lines. Most of their interaction outside the home village was limited to family relations. To support the argument by saying that a certain subgroup of Madhari in a certain village developed a subaltern identity in the local context would be to reduce the concept to simply a matter of description. In the case of the Paraiyar, it would be more appropriate to argue along Hardiman's lines. However, in the Madhari case it becomes more problematic. The question of mobilisation will be discussed further in Chapters 5 and 6.

Two researchers who have a perspective different from those of Mosse and Hardiman are Christopher Baker and Jan Breman. While Breman's study focuses on Gujarat, and is concerned with one of the tribes or Adivasi *jatis* in Hardiman's terminology, who worked as bonded labourers, Baker comes geographically closest to the subject of the present study. In Baker's volume on the south Indian, rural economy for the period 1880-1955, he divides the geographical region into three different zones. One of these zones comprises the entire highland area, Kongunad. In a thorough and well-documented discussion, he brings the economic and social history to the fore. Breman has a more limited region for his research in the Surat district in south Gujarat, but the period covered is about a century, combining sociological and historical methods. He too focuses on the relationship between economic and social factors. However, while Baker tends to lean more towards the questions of the transforming economy, Breman explicitly studies the impact of the transformation of rural labour relations. Both deal with questions that are at the heart of the present study.

When Baker as historian discusses the economy of the Tamilnad region during the later era of British rule, he observes a specifically colonial economy, building on the previous empires in south India and to some extent structured by pre-colonial legacies.[16] This economy had certain characteristics that were different from those of industrialising European countries. Baker argues that, in Tamilnad, the driving force behind investments and development in agriculture lay within the colonial state, and not among the cultivators of the soil. For the state, there were good incentives to act. Sufficient demand, revenue assessments and food supply all relied on a well-functioning, agricultural economy. However, comparatively strong incentives to work as an entrepreneurial class were not found among the cultivators. Baker argues that while as the Government strove to meet the needs of the colonial power by supporting the growth of commercial producuion and trade, they did not want to see an Indian capitalist class grow to threaten the power of the state. As the consequences of the depression in the 1930s became evident, this double-edged policy of the state became self-destructive to the colonial economy. After Independence, rural control shifted from the zamindar landlords and ryotwari village officers to the market oriented rural elite of farmers and traders that were able to exercise control via the elective bodies of the *panchayati raj.*

Having the rural economy in the main focus, labour relations are the forms of social relations that Baker discusses. The cultivators employing labourers are described as having acted according to the demands raised by the conditions of agricultural production. In his division of three regions, the economic logic applied by the farmers, together with previously existing forms of labour, decided what forms of labour came to exist in each of the regions. In the plains, the farmers maintained an economic hold on the tenants and labourers, by keeping them in debt. The valley mirasdar landlords practised a hard form of indenture, by which the labourers were in fact tied to the land. Baker writes that, when the material and financial needs of the labourers were met by the landlords, those transfers represented a debt and substantiated the labourer's dependence. Thus, labour relations in the valleys were marked by 'dependence'. However, apart from an initial comment on the pre-colonial period, when labourers are said to have been kept outside the village and outside Hindu society as untouchables, Baker does not problematise what constituted the 'dependence' in the valleys as such. Interestingly, he observes that, when the valley landlords strove to change their use of labour in the 1940s, by shifting from keeping labourers under bonds to hiring casual labour according to the immediate needs of the estates, the Government settled the labour disputes that arose by enforcing protection of the rights of the permanent labourers. In consequence, the Government thereby acted to preserve the existing forms of permanent labour, while the landlords acted more in accordance with supply and demand on the labour market.[17]

Both in the plains and in the highlands, labour relations are described as fundamentally an economic arrangement. In the highlands, in Kongunad, Baker finds that the cultivators were more commercially rational in their use of labour and acted as capitalists or semi-capitalists. They invested heavily in agricultural improvements. As the demand for labour scaled up, the farmers attracted extra wage labour by 'modified wage payments'. Labourers are said to have worked as a form of extended family labour, though, not under 'traditional' forms of clientage.[18]

In the present study I have found reasons to question this position. As the authors of the colonial documents generally did, Baker also seems to have overlooked the role of the leather-working community in agriculture. As he relied heavily on Government archival material, the Madhari must have become invisible to him. There were many poor Goundar, owning only a few acres of land, who worked on a casual basis for other Goundars. However, in order to manage the cultivation of the medium and large holdings, particularly when cultivating the more profitable cash crops, the leather-working community formed the basis of the hired labour force. The rapid industrial expansion and the extended commercialisation of agriculture are important features of the history of the highlands, and the farmers acted with a large degree of economic rationality, according to their self-interest. However, the results of the present study show that this did not result in an immediate break of existing relations between different members of the village, or with the particular labour relations at work. These were rather adjusted and applied to the particular situation of the highland farms. Taboos, as well as ascribed roles in production and in the local social hierarchy, appear to have provided the farmers with a set of conditions for labour employment that they extended, but did not transcend. More in coherence with the situation in the plains and valleys, the Kongunad farmers made use of labourers tied to the farms by economic and extra-economic means. A fundamental change in this situation appeared only at the very end and after the period that Baker studies, which ends by the early 1950s. This will be elaborated further in Chapters 2 and 4.

This research position can be formulated in more general terms as a focus on relations that were neither purely feudal nor entirely capitalist and thereby touches upon some of the core questions in the 1970s and 1980s mode of production debate. One group of participants in this debate has argued for the existence of 'semi-feudal' relations of production. As Amit Bhaduri explained, such relations 'have more in common with classical feudalism of the master–serf type than with industrial capitalism'.[19] In his own study of west Bengal in 1970, he concluded that the landowners, who derived their wealth from property rights in land and from usury, chose not to adopt new technologies in agriculture, as this would have undermined their political and economic position. The land they held was leased to sharecroppers on a yearly basis. However, the tenant's share of the harvest was not large enough to maintain his family throughout the year, and he became indebted and thereby also tied to the landowner. As technological improvements increased productivity and output, and thereby also the size of the tenant's share, such a development would serve to free the tenants from their bonds and reduce or even eliminate the landowner's political and economic control of the tenant. Therefore, the landowners abstained from investing in improved techniques. Bhaduri concludes that semi-feudal relations of production acted to restrain a development towards a shift to capitalist relations of production.[20] In the subsequent chapters, the analysis will touch on some of the main concerns of the mode of production debate. However, that debate is not the key question of the present study. The primary aim and leading theme of the work remain to bring out and analyse the core relationship in agriculture between landowners and labourers in the highlands of south India.[21]

In south Gujarat, in west India, the dominant landowners are to be found in the Patidar community, while the resident, landless labourers for the most part belong to the Halpati community. When the sociologist Jan Breman discusses how relations between landowners and landless labourers were altered by the transition of the rural economy into market-oriented production and commercialisation of the agriculture, like Christopher Baker, he emphasises the relations of production.[22] The relationship between the landowning Patidar and the landless Halpatis is discussed in terms of labour relations, and as this relationship carried bonds and a certain amount of patronage, those relations included also duties and rights that transcended the immediate relations within the agricultural production.

Breman's study is primarily concerned with a much later period of history, a period that Breman himself has been able to follow by continuous visits to the region from the early 1960s to the beginning of the 1980s. However, the findings from this recent period are related to the results of historical research that covers most of the twentieth century.

The 'earlier' relationship between the landowning and dominant caste of the Patidar and the landless Halpatis shows much similarity when the situation in the Coimbatore district is examined. The Patidar community, which was able to achieve a higher social and economic position in the late nineteenth century, has been dominant among the farmers in the region, in terms both of economy and influence. The region is referred to as 'Patidar land'.

The Halpati community is in most respects the opposite of the Patidar. While the Patidar gained from the growing production of cotton for commercial purposes and were able to expand their landholdings, the tribal Halpatis became indebted, lost the little land that they had and ended up as landless labourers employed by the Patidar. During most of the twentieth century, they have worked as agricultural labourers, having the Patidar as their chief employers. In spite of being numerically dominant, they have been deprived of wealth and influence and have worked within a system of tied labour.

The dominant form of permanent labour employment in agriculture was the *hali* system. In many respects, this has the same characteristics as the *pannai* system of the Tamil land. The *hali* labourer was tied to the landlord by a debt, too large to repay even in a lifetime. The wife and children were included in the agreement, and wages in cash and in kind were set to meet the basic necessities of life, which meant survival. Having a patron's responsibility, the Patidar acted as 'protector' of the *hali* in relation to the outside world. However, Breman states that this patronage was based on exploitation and coercion, not reciprocity.

Even though they shared the same fate of working under severe restrictions, the Halpatis in Gujarat and the Madhari in Tamilnad differ in important respects. The present study shows a closer relationship between the landowning Goundar and the Madhari than has been described by Breman as the relationship between the Patidar and the Halpatis. Taking the extreme difference of influence and wealth and the taboos existing between the Goundar and Madhari communities into consideration, the relationship between them also included services as messengers in Goundar family matters and an ascribed role in religious ceremonies. It is true that the hierarchical difference between them was manifest in a very distinct way. Economic and political power and influence were extremely uneven, and physical segregation was confirmed by behaviour, religious ceremonies and the different living quarters. However, though they were segregated, both were still members of the same village and interacted in many fields of life and not only in labour. When the Goundar dominance was questioned in any of these fields, they possessed means of enforcing their authority. The Madhari dependence on the Goundar for their survival was obvious. However, also the Goundar community was dependent on the Madhari for carrying out the tasks prescribed to them. Since the Madhari could not easily be replaced by members of another community, however uneven, the dependence was mutual. This was not merely a practical need of the Goundar. Different tasks and specific positions, such as those in religious ceremonies, reflected existing social and political power relations. I argue that also such interaction may have influenced labour relations. When the *pannai* system was abandoned, as it became more of a strain than an asset in promoting the economies of the farms, such considerations may have served to lengthen the duration of the system.

The Halpatis in Breman's study are explained as having had no business in the main village, except in the farmhouses. Their history is described as that of a tribal community that had previously possessed land and a certain degree of freedom only one hundred years back and not, as in the case of the Madhari, that of resident labourers in the villages, having relationships with the dominant landowners long before the economy was turned towards the external market for cash-crop products. This situation in Gujarat was changed for the worse. The Halpatis lost land and eventually became attached to the Patidar. This may explain the distance, in all matters but production, between the two, as described by Breman.[23]

However, it may be discussed whether Breman's point of departure makes the issue of relationships deriving from outside production of minor importance for the subject matter. His major research interest revolves around the relationship between the dominant landowners (the Patidar), the local landless (the Halpatis) and the migrant labourers working seasonally and competing with the Halpatis for available work. The three parties lack a common past, as the Halpatis arrive in the relationship as a proletarianised tribal group and the day labourers as migrants. They meet within the realms of production. Breman argues that 'class oppositions are articulated along caste lines'.

This is not a conclusion that will be disputed here. The point is whether, in such a perspective, one may disregard or avoid a discussion about existing social and political relations that are not explained by production itself, as in the case of the Goundar–Madhari relationship, in which both parties have a long past in common. Such relationships, expressed and regulated in customary law, may have roots in a previous or pre-capitalist society but have over time become remodelled or emphasised in a different way as a result of recent changes in the rural production and economy. They may not derive from production but can be explained by the social hierarchy or in terms of dominance. Still, they may influence existing labour relations.

In the caste–class debate, Breman emphasises that agrarian relations can only be understood by the complementarity of caste and class. He specifies this broad starting-point by the structuring principles of the region studied, and by regarding historical change. The major question to Breman in this connection is how rurally based collectives organised themselves with regard to caste and class. The regional level of the analysis is thereby emphasized. This may be where the problems outlined earlier get lost. By regarding caste or *jati* as one of the organising principles, the Patidar of south Gujarat will be expected to have had regionally common principles for relating to the Halpatis and for taking them on as labourers, irrespective of any further relationships between those communities in the different villages. Such 'further relationships' may not have existed in the Gujarat case. Production may have been the only 'sphere' within which the three parties met. The results of the study are not disputed. However, in the case of the Coimbatore highlands, this is only part of the story.

Therefore, the perspective or the research questions have been formulated to give equal importance to relations of production and relations of social power, the one not determining the other, but the possibility of a mutual influence having been allowed.

## COMMENTS ON THE MATERIAL

In the present work, *the geographical region* studied is limited to the highland plateau. As has been described, this was a region with a particularly rapid industrialisation, as compared with most other regions in south India. The landowners had been able to shift from subsistence cultivation to cash-crop production in only a few decades, and cotton had been found to be particularly profitable. At the same time, an important part of the labour force remained in the villages as agricultural labourers throughout this change. This makes the region particularly interesting for the study of how rural relationships between landowners and landless labourers developed during this period. However, the study moves between a geographical and a social space. In the more general themes, the results can be generalised for the entire highlands where farming is carried out. But in order to consider the consequences of climate and soil for the conditions of agriculture, special emphasis has been laid on the central part of the region.[24]

Although the term 'region' is a problematised concept in itself, in the following text it refers only to a geographical unit in the most general sense of the word. The highlands are fairly flat and are surrounded by mountains on all sides but one. Thereby they have a, very distinct, geographically defined boundary. The Coimbatore district comprises the major part of this region. However, as was mentioned by way of introduction, its boundaries corresponded much better to the geographically and, during periods, politically defined, old Kongu land (Kongu Nadu). Within this highland region, in a broad zone stretching from Avanashi and Sulur downwards and south-east to Dharapuram, most of the land is situated in the rain shadow of the western mountains. This makes the central flat land particularly dry and a substantial part of the cultivation is dependent on irrigation. As it has only a very few rivers and streams, wells were, and still are, of crucial importance. Most of the soil is red and sandy, but there are also sections of black, heavy soil that give the best conditions for cotton. This part of the highlands was also severely damaged by a 6-7 year-long drought between 1946 and 1953. The whole district was affected and rains were very scarce. But within this dry zone, areas can be found that hardly received a drop of rain during the whole period of drought. This situation motivates a closer look at how the social relations developed in this geographical area. Goundar and Madhari lived and worked in all parts of the district. However, the preconditions in the Palladam area provide an interesting basis for a discussion on the transformation of social relations, as they were to a large extent put under strain by the severe drought.

Added to this, there is another phenomenon that may not be so conspicuous, but is still characteristic of the dry zone. This central part of the highlands stretching to Dharapuram was one of the more important areas where large-scale, community-based conversions took place among the Paraiyar and Madhari communities. Many conversions also took place further south-west, around Pollachi, but Palladam was the most marked area.

In analysing community- or kinship-based mobilisation for conversion, we enter into what would be better understood as the social space. People living in the central part of the highlands had relatives outside it, and many of the agricultural labourers migrated seasonally to work in the hills. Consequently, studies of social relations cannot really be restricted to minor, geographically defined regions. Social relations stretch beyond such regions. This explains why the study moves between the smaller and the larger geographical unit, between the dry, central zone and, in particular, the Palladam taluk and the Coimbatore district.

*The material* that forms the basis of the present work has been collected from a variety of sources. On one occasion, when I approached a senior researcher to discuss the topic of the study, he smiled doubtfully and said: 'You are trying to write the history of the invisible.' A lack of material emanating from members of the lowest sections of society has occasionally been given as a reason why historical studies about (previously) untouchable castes cannot be trusted or even carried out at all. Documents written by members of these castes are extremely rare. Not only are diaries and letters lacking—that is generally the case also with the higher castes—but the material collected from Government files and mission reports more often than not carries an upper-caste understanding of society, sometimes mixed with a Euro-centred explanation of how society ought to be organised or how people ought to live and behave. As regards the Government reports, the intermediary informants of the Government officials came mostly from the high castes. The European missionaries, who as a rule wrote down their own observations, often held on to a Brahmanical version of Hinduism, even though the people they worked among practised a religion and interpreted society in a way sometimes far from the classical Hindu scriptures.

Ranajit Guha, the historian in the Subaltern Studies collective, solves the problem in a somewhat drastic way as he searches for the 'subaltern' or 'peasant mentality' in peasant insurgency.[25] He assumes a complete antagonism between the British Government and the peasants, as the latter were understood to revolt against the oppressive, 'superordinate' rule and the former was doing all in its power to crush the uprisings. The texts immediately reveal the elite mentality of the Government. By reversing their values, the mentality of the 'subaltern' or the revolting peasant comes out, according to Guha. This method is further discussed in Chapter 5.

However, by creating an image of absent persons from historical documents, one risks producing an image as stereotyped as that in the minds of some of the British officials, who never sought first-hand information from untouchable-caste members themselves. This is particularly so, as it will reflect only the information that the officials considered it important to know. Much information will be lacking.

In the progress of the present study, the idea of the complete absence of 'untouchable voices' turned out to be wrong. In going through colonial, state and mission archives, the Madhari community appears in the texts. As previously mentioned, in the Government files they are nearly always recorded by the caste name for Tamil-speaking leather-workers. Knowing this, it has been possible to gather some information. Turning to the mission documents, the availability of material is much improved. The converting leather-workers-cum-agricultural-labourers are not only known as Madhari but are also known by their kinship or subcaste affiliation. Villages are mentioned and individual persons can be identified by name. The socio-economic situations of the villages are discussed, sometimes at length.

I agree with Guha that bias is a problem, both in Government and in mission archival material. In addition to this, there is the problem of the misunderstandings of the informants that slip into the texts. But all the different types of material emanating from European or authors with European associations should not be understood to have the same bias. They were rather very different. Apart from the different ideas and aims brought from Europe, it is necessary to regard the different relations that the authors of particular documents had with the people observed. Also within a mission, the different missionaries were differently related to villagers and to people of different caste and class affiliations. Different ideological standpoints and attitudes towards 'the outcastes' become obvious when going through the mission archives. To tackle those problems are not, of course, unique to Indian history. They are part of source criticism.

For the present study, the value of the mission archives should be mentioned. Compared with other archival material, these archives provide first-hand information from numerous villages that has not been found in any other written material. The benefit of consulting the mission archives was well formulated by J.D.Y. Peel when he discussed how he came to use the Church Missionary Society's Yoruba Mission Archive for his research into relations between traditional religion and society in four West African states.[26] He found the documents kept in the archive to be rich in details giving subsequent information over longer periods of time. Reports and letters not only related church events, but it was possible to find information about the lives of congregation members also outside the narrower church domains. Information about the geographical region, as well as a discussion about regional politics, was reported to England, together with notes on the earlier history of the place. However, the most remarkable thing to Peel was to find a wealth of material written by Yoruba church employees. Yoruba clergy, catechists and teachers accounted for more than 57 per cent of the incoming papers before 1880. The advantage of this material lies both in the reduced risk of misunderstandings and in the fact that they were among the first literate Yoruba and were thereby important in the process of Yoruba self-definition.[27]

These comments may account also for the filed documents of the

Church of Sweden Mission and the Wesleyan Methodist Missionary Society. There may not be such an overwhelming number of documents written by Indians in the archives. Peel remarks that the number of Yoruba authors was exceptional and was caused by the recruitment of Christian ex-slaves of Yoruba origin in Sierra Leone. However, in the CSM material, the most lengthy and most interesting descriptions of local situations were given by Indian mission workers. This will be further dealt with in the following chapters.

To make it possible to come to terms with misconceptions in the written information, to find more comprehensive information, and to find a source in which the rural population are not referred to as third persons but speak for themselves, oral material has been collected. Throughout the period studied, communication between people was both written and oral. However, while British administrators, mission workers and business entrepreneurs to a large extent communicated by written documents, local society was basically oral. Agreements and deeds were to a large extent oral and if they were written down it cannot be taken for granted that all essential parts had been included in the document. To a large extent, it was the spoken word that mattered. Thus, oral and written communication lived side by side.

For the historian, the complementarity of oral and written material has to be taken into consideration. Both the reading of a historical document and its author's knowledge of the situation may be marked by misunderstandings. Moreover, whether misunderstood or not, the texts in the documents were structured according to the logic of the observer and of the aims of his mission. Detailed information, that made a great difference in the local context, may not have been important enough for the outside observer to be noticed or written down. In the present study, several explanations of single terms that have been given in interviews have led me to conclude that terms, for example, for payment or for particular parts of customary law have a very local range for their usage. A term used in the rural part of Coimbatore district may have a completely different meaning when used in another part of Tamilnad. Secondly, in written documents, one may come across many single events without any clear connections. The author may hint at ongoing conflicts in an area but found no reason at the time to dwell on the subject. In interviews, those pieces of information can be traced, complemented further and provided with the explanations of the informants. It thereby becomes possible to derive more information from the written documents that previously remained hidden from the reader for lack of knowledge.

Finally, not only the Madhari community are spoken of as third persons. Throughout most of the period researched, the majority of the members of the Goundar community were illiterate. Interviews compensate also for their absence as authors of documents and commentators on history.[28]

Just like all other kinds of material underlying historical research, interviews also carry problems. Specific of this type of material is the distance in time. Most types of material (also written material) that depict an event observed are based on memory. Over a longer period of time, memory may generalise series of events into a story that carries a certain meaning to the informant. Where or when something happened may still be important but may just as well have lost its significance. The event remembered may even have been a series of similar events that took place in different villages over a period of a year's time but has over time been consolidated into one single event in the memory of the informant. To him or her, something important happened that was worth remembering. What is related may be a type of event rather than a particular event in itself. Such information is still important, as it may cast a different light on the reading of documents. But to derive reliable historical evidence from such information may be problematic.

More reliable in detail are all those things that seem plain and ordinary to the informant. For whom did they work before the drought? Was the payment given enough for two or three meals a day? Did everyone stitch leather bags for the wells or was this a task for only a few among them? What tasks did they carry out as a *pannaiyal* (permanent farm labourer)?

A well-known problem to anthropologists is the fact that the researcher's own presence may alter the situation observed. With a foreign visitor living in the village, the village people may behave differently from what they would have done, had the researcher not been there. This situation requires a certain awareness and sensitivity from the observer.

The same problem may follow interviews made over a shorter period of time, while not living in the village, but visiting only in the afternoons and evenings, when people are home from work. It is also necessary to bear in mind that oral material is created both by the informant and by the interviewer. The material is in itself the result of mutual interaction, in which both parties contribute and influence each other.

The difference between living in a village and making observations at all hours of the day, as compared with making visits but living outside the village, is well described by Michael Moffatt. In his study of two Harijan hamlets in Tamil Nadu, the two different methods were applied. The reason was not that Moffatt explicitly wanted to test and compare the two methods, but rather that his first experience of 100% participatory observation provided too few results and was too hard to endure for more than three months. Moffatt concludes that the first method is the best way to conduct anthropological research. However, his initial intention to live under the same circumstances as those of the Harijan in order to identify with them proved to have limited success. After three months, he was well accepted by the Harijan, but as an odd outsider living among them. In order to save time and to cope with the conditions (not least mentally), the second village was visited from outside in the company of an interpreter and Moffatt was firmly identified as the westerner he obviously was. While the first village gave an experience of the tenor of Harijan social life, the second proved more instrumental for ethnographic research.[29]

To come to terms with some of the more evident problems by short visits, as compared with longer stays, villages were visited more than once, and questions were followed up after people had had a chance to 'think things over'. Interview situations may also be felt to be rather formal conversations by the villagers, in which many things are never said for fear of being impolite to the visitor or because the information is not believed to be important enough to be mentioned. Many such obstacles can be minimised by spending the evening in a place, eating together or walking round the village. The interview will not be the entire gain from the visit, but several voices will be heard and not only the leading voice of the community.

However, when interviews do not constitute the entire material but are rather a minor part and other types of material form the bulk of the evidence for the research, this may not be such an overwhelming problem. There will be many possibilities of checking and comparing information from interviews with that from written documents. At the same time, it may be worth while to remember that, also when reading documents, the presence of the researcher matters. The text will, of course, not alter on the paper, but it has to pass through the mind and the preconceived ideas of the reader. In that sense, the text does not come out unaltered, even from the reading of written historical material.

Oral material is an important source of evidence for the historian.

It is essentially different from written material, but most of the problems attached to it are problems that oral material has in common with written documents. As with all other historical material, it has to be treated with careful criticism.

A few further remarks need to be made about method and terminology before passing on to the following chapters. In the subsequent text, where nothing else is indicated, all translations from Swedish into English are mine. The translations from Tamil into English have been made by Ranjini, who acted as my interpreter throughout the village interviews.

Ranjini has for many years carried out social work in Scheduled Caste villages within and outside the Coimbatore district, in particular among women. Her long experience was important during the village field-study, as it facilitated qualitative interviews. During the interviews, certain key questions were asked in every village. These were questions about the history of the village, forms of survival, (in the case of Madhari informants) relations with the Goundar and Paraiyar communities and with other Madhari sub-groups, and (in the case of Goundar informants) relations with the Madhari, Paraiyar and other castes in the village. There were also questions about the drought, the electricity, the mission, and mobilisation within their own community in the village. However, if a certain question led to a lengthy reply full of details, the initial set of questions was not treated as a kind of rigid questionnaire. A certain freedom in the conversation, without passing over any question, was allowed, in order to give the informants the opportunity to relate a variety of events remembered. A formal interview took up to two hours and was made with one or two elderly persons, often in the company of a group of villagers listening and occasionally making comments.

Finally, as has been shown earlier, many different terms are used for the lowest castes in Indian society. In terms of purity, they were regarded as 'untouchable' and socially segregated in many physical ways. Some terms have derived from a particular political situation, like the Gandhian term 'Harijan', which aimed to upgrade the untouchables as a fifth *varna* and as pure as any 'child of god'. 'Scheduled Caste' and 'Scheduled Tribe' were terms of the British administration, officially introduced in the 1930s. To be listed in one of those categories implied access to certain benefits in a system of quotas. The present-day, common term 'Dalit' emphasises the oppressed position of this group of people. The relationship between 'tribe' and 'Adivasi' has been discussed earlier.

There is no term for this large group of people, who belonged to the lowest socio-economic strata in India which is not political in any sense. In the present work, the names of the different communities are used as far as possible. When that is not the case or when it is of importance for the discussion to use other terms, the terminology will follow that of the material and the historical period studied. This means that *untouchable* will primarily be used before the 1930s and afterwards when the material so indicates. The other term used is *Scheduled Caste*. This may seem to be a contradiction, since, according to the Indian Constitution, Christians are excluded from that category. However, the distinction between Hindu and Christian Scheduled Caste members in the Coimbatore district was almost non-existent in daily life during the period studied, the term therefore indicating that the socio-economic situation that they had in common was more apparent than the religious divide between them.

## NOTES

1 IOR, District Officers' Collection, Downing Collection, diary 10.12.37. The Tamil words are transcribed. In the diary they are in Tamil script. See further the 'Glossary' where Tamil words are transcribed and explained.

2 ICS—Indian Civil Service. IOR, District Officers' Collection, Downing Collection, diary 6.11.37.

3 Consequently the name Tamilnad refers to the Tamil-speaking region of south India. It does not denote political boundaries, and can therefore be used also for the period before the creation of the State of Tamil Nadu.

4 Arulpuram 26.1.1995, interview.

5 That is, 'child of God', a Gandhian term for 'untouchable' castes and a term preferred by Mosse.

6 Mosse 1986; Mosse 1994, in particular p. 100. In support of his argument, Mosse refers to Appadurai 1981, Appadurai and Breckenridge 1976, Bayly 1989, Dirks 1987 and Stein 1980.

7 The interrelationship between religion and politics in Tamil society is further elaborated by Pamela Price (1996). According to her, the cultural *longue durée* of political conceptions and values, such as 'kingship' and 'honour', is carried through history over several centuries to the present day. Changes did take place during this period, but only within certain limits. Honour and status are therefore considered independent variables

in political action. Cf. Price 1996, pp. 1-8, for an introduction to the argument, and Mosse 1994, p. 68.

8 Mosse 1986, p. 8; Mosse 1994, pp. 67-8, 98-100; Gough 1981 and 1989.
9 Mosse 1986, pp. 89, 107, 513-14.
10 Hardiman 1995 (1987).
11 Hardiman 1995 (1987), pp. 1-17.
12 Hardiman 1995 (1987), pp. 11-16, 83, 123, 127-8; Guha 1994 (1983).
13 Mosse 1986, pp. 107, 330, 354.
14 Mosse 1986, pp. 110-15, referring to Srinivas 1955, p. 55.
15 For an analysis of the Subaltern Studies position and a critical discussion, see O'Hanlon 1988, Prakash 1990, and O'Hanlon and Washbrook 1992.
16 Baker 1984.
17 Baker 1984, pp. 10, 156, 172-3, 522-33.
18 Baker 1984, p. 209.
19 Bhaduri 1973, p. 120.
20 Bhaduri 1973, pp. 135-6.
21 See Thorner (1982) for an overview of the mode of production debate. Criticism of the main arguments in the debate has, among others, been published by M.M.S. Pandian (1990).
22 Breman 1985.
23 Breman 1985, pp. xx, 88-95, 115-19, 122-3, 127-32.
24 See the Maps for more details.
25 Guha 1994 (1983).
26 Peel 1996.
27 Peel's experience of the mission archives stands in stark contrast to Kooiman's pessimistic description of the documents in the London Missionary Society and Church Missionary Society archives. According to Kooiman, they are heavily biased and the information is limited to internal concerns of the missions. His criticism was first presented in an article in 1983, and thereafter repeated in 1989. Peel 1996, pp. 74-8; Kooiman 1983, pp. 121-2; Kooiman 1989, pp. 4-7.
28 The debate about the use of oral sources in history has been carried on since the 1970s, Paul Thompson's work *The Voice of the Past* being one of the major contributions. I will not go further into that debate but limit myself to making clear how I have come to use oral material in the present study. Cf. Thompson 1988 (1978).
29 Moffatt 1979, pp. xiii-xliii.

CHAPTER 2

# Power and Dependence: A Reconstruction of Social Relations

In the study of relationships between people, there is no natural beginning, no period in time 'when it all began'. If we study the farmers and labourers in rural Kongunad in the early decades of the present century, we find that people were deeply involved in webs of interaction relating both to contracts and to informal rules linking them to earlier history. The new circumstances that had been building up during the late nineteenth century had established the forms of labour relations that were now in operation. During the coming half-century, the preconditions and means of survival would change rapidly. But before going into how the societal processes of the twentieth century affected agrarian relations, the prevailing relationship between the major landowners and their agricultural labourers will be discussed. An attempt to reconstruct the relationship will be made for the first three decades of the twentieth century.

In the central part of the highlands, the Palladam taluk, the Goundar and Madhari communities were generally represented among a handful of castes. The landowners who controlled the major part of the land were either Goundar or Naicker; the agricultural labourers were generally of the Madhari or Paraiyar castes. However, many Goundar, who owned only one or two acres of land, supplemented their income by casual agricultural work. There were also members of other castes who owned or leased land or worked as labourers on the lands of others. But they were much fewer than the members of the earlier-mentioned communities. This study focuses on only two of these castes, the Goundar and the Madhari: the former, because they were not only the major landowners, but also in terms of dominance the most influential persons in the region, and the latter, because they had skills that were essential to the farmers. No farmer could do without them.[1] This will be further discussed later.

The Goundar and the Madhari interacted in many areas. As already mentioned, they did not only meet as employer and employee in the material production. Though they played very different roles and participated to different extents, their relationship involved also the local rituals and social obligations, all of which expressed the social hierarchy of the village These different spheres did not exist autonomously, but there was a mutual interaction and influence. Labour not only related to agriculture or the breeding of cattle, but was also embedded in rituals and social life. Occupations were understood in terms of social status.

There is still a necessary, analytical distinction to be made. In a changing society, economic shifts can be rapid, and labour relations have consequently to be adjusted to new circumstances. But during such a change, values and norms for social interaction that have their original logic in earlier economies may prevail and take on new meanings and functions in the local society under transformation.

To enable us to consider this, the relationship is analytically deconstructed and discussed with regard to relations developing from production and relations developing from the local social hierarchy in the villages. This is strictly an analytical distinction. Empirically, the division was not so clear-cut and should not be understood as a reflection of how people perceived how they related to one another. The necessity of the analytical separation of relations of production from relations of social power arises from the situation in which agriculture became increasingly involved in and influenced by the urban-based, industrial expansion and the capitalist economy. It may be assumed that altered or new labour relations developed from this situation, while the local power structures lived on intact. This might just as well have created a changed frame for local power relations. It can also be discussed whether norms and values that were explained by the local power structures may have limited the options available to different groups of people that opened up within the expanding industrial enterprise. The analytical distinction allows questions such as these to be further discussed.

When the subject of social hierarchy is taken up for discussion, it should not be understood as being identical with caste or as it is locally expressed in the *jati.* Caste was a dividing line between groups of people. But caste relations had many, different, local expressions and were not always a boundary between social divisions. Members of a certain caste in a village may have carried out duties to the village community that members of the same caste of the next village were not made to do. Local circumstances can explain such differences. Caste is therefore only to a certain extent related to occupation. But the deviation from this relation is too noticeable to allow of the conclusion that caste and occupation corresponded. Such a general statement would rather obscure the more detailed discussion of the local social structure.[2]

In a more general sense, agrarian labour relations were related to caste in the region. Members of high castes generally held a dominant position in the economy as well as in social life. The agricultural labourers were basically found among the untouchable castes. At the same time, the dominant farming community was more homogeneous socially than economically, while the agricultural labourers were divided by caste but lived under more similar, economic conditions.

A more adequate way to proceed in this discussion is to think in terms of social power relations. In this way, the transformation of the relationship between the major landowners and their agricultural labourers in Kongunad, even though it was *one* relationship, will be related, on the one hand, to the material production and reproduction, expressed in economic power relations, and, on the other hand, to the production and reproduction of social power relations.

## THE CONTESTED TERM 'SLAVERY'

'Slavery' was the most common description given by the missionaries to the working conditions among the Madhari. Ever since the missionaries had their first contact with them in the 1930s and until the late 1950s, when systematically organised, development work among Madhari groups was beginning to be established, they were understood as living close to slavery or even as being the slaves of the landowning Goundar community. When the missionaries approached these agricultural labourers, it was always with indignation that they reported to the Mission Board about the shocking 'slave conditions' and the obstructive 'slave mentality' of the people of this group.[3] But it is unlikely that slavery, in the sense that people were bought and sold with the soil or were completely without personal rights, actually existed in this highland area at the turn of the century. The Madhari worked under certain ties to the farming Goundar community. But these ties were hardly equivalent to chattel slavery. At the same time, it is misleading to think that the conditions under which the Madhari worked throughout the twentieth century were stable and immutable in a society that was undergoing several major changes.

During the whole period, a substantial part of the agricultural labour force was employed on casual terms. Daily or weekly agreements appear to have been the most common method of taking on casual labourers. These labourers were an extra resource of manpower for the landowner, and a British administrator, observing them in 1819, regretted their situation and treatment.[4] The prevalent term for a worker on daily wages was coolie or *atta* coolie. The coolie was a hired worker, a man or woman whose income depended solely on the daily demand for labour. It was often understood in a wide sense, and referred to all kinds of non-skilled labour taking on odd jobs. The term 'coolie' was not limited to only agricultural labour. But when 'slavery' is mentioned in the reports of the missionaries who worked in the region, it does not refer to casual labour, but to labour under bonds.

Slavery is itself a contested term in the debate about the labour relations prevalent in south India. The focus of this debate is generally not on the twentieth century, but on the early colonial period. Some authors have stated that the level of slavery has been underestimated, particularly as a result of placing too much reliance on badly informed, nineteenth-century, British officials. Dharma Kumar is self-critical when she introduces the reprint of *Land and Caste in South India* in 1992. She thinks that her study of 1965 was 'typical of its time' in trusting the official records. At the same time, she took a stand in her study against the position held by Surendra Patel among others,[5] that there was only a small number of landless agricultural labourers before the arrival of the British. Where slavery existed, it prevailed in a very mild form. It was argued that this class of labourers expanded only after the arrival of the colonial power as a result of proletarianisation.[6]

Kumar has continued her critique of this position. On the assumption that there was a firm relationship between caste and occupational status, particularly in the wet-cultivation areas, she uses population statistics to support her point. She finds that the class of agricultural labourers and slaves was as substantial in 1800 as it was by the end of the century. A problem which arises while going through the British records is that the administrators used terms to describe the labour conditions that were more familiar to themselves, such as 'agricultural serf' or 'allodial slave of the soil', than the terms they were faced with in India. Yet Kumar's own position sometimes becomes obscure, when 'serfdom', 'slavery' and 'bondage' are used interchangeably, particularly in her earlier text. In her 1992 study, she has chosen to rely on local caste names in order to avoid the ambiguity of the more universal terms and their use in British records. But also in this study Kumar remains within the discourse of 'slavery', and of slaves *versus* free men.[7]

Benedicte Hjejle also believes that it is relevant to speak of 'slavery' before the arrival of the British colonial power. She argues that slavery in south India managed to survive, disguised under a different name, the introduction of the Slavery Abolition Act of 1843 and the Penal Code of 1861. She spares no deprecatory judgements about the quality of the 1843 Act, condemning it for lacking any idea of the extent and nature of Indian slavery.[8]

Nancy Gardner Cassels contests this position. She finds that Government officials spent much time studying Indian religious and social institutions in order to respect them. Even though they might sometimes have ended up with wrong assumptions, they were not merely interested in getting access to and exploiting Indian labour on the British estates, thus remaining cynically ignorant of the existing forms of bondage. Gardner Cassels stresses as a matter of fact that the Act made it impossible to invoke the law to support the institution of slavery. The subsequent practice of tying labourers by debt bondage would not change the fact that the judiciary strove to establish social justice in the criminal law. But Gardner Cassels observes that the most obvious obstacle to the enforcement of this law lay among the labourers themselves. Being illiterate and indebted to the landowners, there were many difficulties to be tackled before the labourers' grievances could be turned into judicial action against their masters. They lacked both means and courage and, if they learned at all about their new rights, their present poverty would rather make them sell their labour than challenge those who fed them.[9]

From the outset, Hjejle establishes a correlation between the existence of Mirasi estates and agricultural bondage. In areas where the mirasidars held large estates and could enforce their rights to labour, slavery prevailed. Consequently, Hjejle observes that, slaves did not to the same extent work the lands in the mainly dry-cultivation areas or in areas under Moslem rule.[10] But, maybe as a result of the strong emphasis in her argument on the importance of Mirasi rights for the existence of slavery, Hjejle makes no distinction between the labour conditions in different Mirasi-dominated areas in her conclusions. A different picture emerges when she relates the reports of the Collectors of Chinglepet, Trichy and Tanjore. In these reports, the different levels of personal rights of the labourers become visible. In all three districts, most of the 'slaves' were reported to work in wet-land cultivation. But the lack of personal rights, as described by the Collectors of the two latter districts, does not correspond to the situation as described by the Collector of Chingleput. Here, too, the 'villains' were always sold together with the land and were held as village property. They worked in rotation for the mirasidars. At the same time, they held their house sites and backyards free of rent. Occasionally, they were given land, together with implements and seed, and paid a fee to the mirasidars by giving them a share of the produce from this land. Obviously, there were differences between the labour conditions also in the areas where Mirasi rights predominated.[11]

Kathleen Gough's earlier study of the Tanjore region, seen from the viewpoint of two villages, also deals with the term 'slave'. The main emphasis of her study is on the 1950s, when she carried out her fieldwork. However, though the primary material was collected in the years of 1951-3, she has made an attempt to reconstruct the social structure, as it was expressed during the different periods of history from the Cholas up to 1951. Going from 'a complex form' of the Asiatic mode of production to the arrival of the colonial power on the subcontinent, she comes to the conclusion that agricultural labour was to a large extent done by slaves. As Tanjore is incorporated as 'a colonial segment' in the world capitalist system, the social structure changes. At the time of the introduction of the Abolition Act, the former slaves became semi-proletarian, meaning that they produced commodities for the bourgeoisie but were still not regular wage labourers. Finally, in the Imperialist stage, a class of proletarians had developed in which the non-agricultural, wage workers were found. The agricultural labourers working for the bourgeoisie or the petty bourgeoisie, reimbursed in other forms, are categorised as semi-proletarian.[12]

In making this reconstruction, Gough suggests a hypothetical account of Tanjore from pre-history to 1951 in the light of historical materialist theory. The purpose of her argument is not to discover hitherto hidden, primary evidence of the prevailing labour relations in Tanjore history. (In speaking of the slaves in the early colonial period, she refers to Hjejle.) On going through earlier research, Gough rather suggests a way of systematising history according to major theory.[13]

Later studies have questioned the position that refers the condition of the agricultural labourers to the general theme of slavery. David Washbrook states that no class of *adimai* (*adi* = foot, generally translated: 'slavery'), with the exception of those labouring in the Kaveri delta and Malabar, were treated as chattel slaves in the decades around 1800. He also objects to the generalising of findings from a limited area to a larger geographical region. The conditions for production varied much between regions, which affected also the labour relations. According to Washbrook, the eighteenth- and early nineteenth-century, agricultural labour relations have to be understood in the context of the whole economic system.

For balancing the instabilities in the economy caused by an unreliable climate, imperfect markets and war, Washbrook has found that the most important mechanism was the 'advance'. He argues that it worked in all spheres of the economy as an advanced share of the costs of production and was generally to the advantage of the producer or labourer. He finds that the levels of advances were apparently high. More than 20 per cent of the expected value of the crop could be demanded by the cultivators, and advances exceeding 50 per cent of the final value occurred in the cloth trade. The advances given to labourers could be just as favourable. To a landowner, the land itself was of very little value unless there were labourers to work on it. To be able to keep up a system of coercive control over the labourers that allowed for sales of labourers together with the land, labourers must have been available in abundance. According to Washbrook, this situation existed in only a small number of delta tracts and on the west coast. The general situation during the second half of the eighteenth century was rather one of labour scarcity. The rising demands for labour during the wars created a situation for the Pariah (Paraiyar) labourers in which they could gain property and demand rights. The landowners had to compete for labourers by offering them shares in the social product.[14]

Washbrook does not argue for the existence of a mild form of slavery, against the position held by Hjejle, nor for the absence of a large class of agricultural labourers, as Patel did in the early 1950s. He would rather not use the term 'slavery' at all but focus on the economic system and on the logic of the labour market, where the need for agricultural labourers was great.

In his argument about the causes of the degradation of the Paraiyar labourers, Washbrook departs from the function of the 'impersonal' market, together with the effects of colonial policy. He argues that the policy and the actions taken by the British East India Company had consequences also for the labourers, among others. After the Company had established control, the demand for labourers as soldiers or within the service sector diminished. The goal of the Company was to increase valuable (agricultural) production and profit. In order to activate private capital in agriculture, Mirasi and Zemin rights were restored in land and labour. Washbrook argues that the British policy of restoring 'ancient Hindu order' in fact implied a more coercive control over labour than they had previously experienced. Their rights and their shares in the social product were affected when the Company increased taxation. As a result of the reduced demand for their labour and of the enforcement of new laws, the Paraiyar were directed to agriculture, and their options in choosing between different trades became limited. As already mentioned, slavery was prohibited by law in 1843, but the keeping of labourers resident on account of indebtedness was fully accepted by the British Government. As the advance system made most labourers technically indebted, the court considered labourers who left the farms as 'runaways', and issued notices of constraint. Thus, in spite of the abolition of slavery, the law operated to direct labourers into agriculture and under the firm control of the landowners. Washbrook argues that, as the wages for those labourers were to be determined by the laws of supply and demand, while the courts did not protect the customary rights formerly held by the labourers, they ended up with a decreasing real share of the social produce and more dependent than before and, eventually, their social status was reduced to a sub-human level.[15]

So, while Hjejle, Kumar and Gough more or less concentrate on the agricultural labourers who resided in the delta regions and on the mirasidars' estates, understanding their position as 'slavery' and assuming that this was the rule in a larger region or within the agricultural economy, Washbrook turns the argument the other way round. He emphasises that agricultural labourers, as a rule, had personal rights according to customary law and were able to expand them during the late eighteenth century but that those rights lost part of their power as the Company established its rule. Agricultural labourers completely without rights were the exceptional cases, and not the rule in the early colonial period.

The differences between the authors may also be seen in their points of departure. Hjejle sets out to trace the slaves of south India whom she believes to have been neglected in previous research. Kumar wants to disclose the forms of agrarian servitude and labour. Gough, though she focuses on the period after 1951, makes an attempt to reconstruct the social structure of the Tanjore region, lying at the heart of the Kaveri delta and the mirasidar lands. Washbrook has a different point of departure. He takes account of the colonial power and its capacity to enforce the law and gives preference to the economic logic. From there, he goes on to discover the social consequences of these actions.

All four authors conclude that the ties that kept the labourers under the control of the landowners were constituted by resources that had been advanced, and that had to be repaid by the labourer before he could regain his mobility. But the authors disagree on the reasons why such ties came into practice.

Washbrook argues for a system of advance payments from expected shares in the outcome of the harvest. From a situation in which the advance had been to the advantage of the labourer by the end of the eighteenth century, the practice had probably become 'oppressive' a century later. The advance was still there but had become a tool to control and coerce labour.[16]

In contrast, Gough and Hjejle rather see a new form of bondage emerging as the result of the Abolition Act. The period until the Penal Code was passed was, according to them, important to the owners of big estates. As the agricultural labourers were 'freed', they were also accessible to the labour contractors of the tea and coffee estates. Hjejle estimates the total net immigration of Indian labourers, most of them coming from the Madras Presidency, between the years 1843-1903 as 1,451,319.[17] To meet this competition, the agricultural labour force was re-organised, and labourers became tied to the landowners by debt.[18]

This was convenient to the landlords, says Gough. While the abolition of slavery facilitated the export of indentured labour and it became possible for agents to kidnap them to the foreign estates, the landlords could keep a sufficient number of labourers by this new form of bondage without having to carry the burden of 'a growing slave population'.[19] Hjejle presents a slightly different view by pointing to a report by the Collector of Trichinopoly in 1846, only three years after the Abolition Act. He estimated that about 3,000 of the Pallar 'slave-caste' had left for Ceylon, which had caused 'considerable inconvenience to the slave proprietors'. It was indeed a loss of labour, but it had also given the remaining Pallars an opportunity to demand higher wages.[20] The scarcity of labour, witnessed by the tea- and coffee-planters, is reflected in the crude methods employed to secure labourers for the estates. At the estates, the labourers became as dependent and indebted to the labour contractors as they had been to the village landlords. This will be further discussed later.[21]

By the late nineteenth century, the difference between advance payments and borrowed money may have become insignificant in practice. After being advanced resources in cash or in kind, the labourer found himself 'in debt' by the end of the year. The fact that the labourer could be kept under the landowner's control and was not allowed to move elsewhere in order to earn the money he owed the farmer indicates the existence of informal law at work.[22]

This form of labour was used under different names in different regions. *Pannaiyal* and *padiyal* are the most common terms during the second half of the nineteenth century. Literally, the *pannaiyal* were the farm labourers (*pannai* meaning farm, and *al* meaning labourer) or 'permanent farm servants', as they were frequently called by the British officials. *Padiyal* were labourers paid by a *padi* or a measure of grain. But the information revealed in the British documents would rather indicate regional differences explained by ecological conditions and forms of production than by a general understanding of two distinctly different forms of labour contracts valid for the whole Tamil land.[23]

According to the authors discussed earlier, caste played a significant role in labour relations. Kumar states that the caste system was the main reason for the durability of serfdom. Indebtedness, though important, is ranked second.[24] Washbrook also pays attention to caste. In his study, the Paraiyar are in the main focus. But his reason for focusing on this caste only is entirely different from Kumar's. Washbrook argues that all classes protected their skills and negotiated their price, and the agricultural labourers did so too. However, as Washbrook does not bring in the Pallar, Chakkiliyar, Madhari or other untouchable labouring castes but lays all his emphasis on the Paraiyar, it is apparent that he believes that caste divisions mattered. He writes of 'the Golden Age of the Pariah', not the golden age of the agricultural labourers. As a distinct caste, the Paraiyar had 'power' both to put up organised labour protests and to carry the myth of a fearsome and wild origin.[25]

The debate about agricultural labour conditions and slavery in the Tamil land, discussed earlier, has mainly focused on the early colonial era. In the subsequent pages, I shall limit the geographical scope and move further on in time, to concentrate on the labour and social relations from 1900 to the 1930s, in the Coimbatore district.

Researchers have sometimes understood the Coimbatore district as being different from the lower lands of Tamilnad. In the typology suggested by Christopher Baker, he goes far in pointing to the specificity of the region by treating it as a special case, different from the valley and the plain regions in Tamilnad. This distinction is based on differences due to its geographical location and climate, as well as to its specific history as a border area between influential kingdoms, used for trade and warfare. These conditions set up the framework for the specific economy that came to develop in the region.[26] The question then remains whether the relationship between the landowners and their labourers, as it was expressed in the lowlands and the wet-cultivation regions, was relevant also to the basically dry, Coimbatore district cultivating food and cash crops.

The following is an attempt to reconstruct the position of the major farming caste, the Goundar, in relation to the agricultural-cum-leather-working caste, the Madhari, within the social structure in the central parts of the Coimbatore district.

## BONDAGE IN THE COIMBATORE DISTRICT

By the turn of the twentieth century, agricultural production was undergoing a fundamental change, to which the existing labour relations had to adjust. There were constraints on economic expansion in the Kongunad highlands. One of the obstacles the larger farmers had to overcome was the risk of a shortage of labour. Before the introduction of cash crops, and particularly the rapid expansion of cotton cultivation in the late nineteenth century, the labour supply had been a minor problem. Cattle-breeding and the cultivation of dry-land crops did not require large numbers of permanently available labourers. Therefore, the agriculturists in the highlands in the early nineteenth century were not as dependent on having a considerable number of accessible labourers, constantly looking after the irrigation, as were their descendants by the end of the century or their contemporary counterparts in the wet-cultivation areas. Adding to the changes in the production was the migration of labour from the villages to the estates.

Broadly speaking, labourers could be hired on either permanent or casual terms. To employ *pannaiyal* seems to have provided the farmers with a high degree of flexibility. The earlier-related results reveal a combination of formal and economic ties, expressed in one-year agreements, functioning together with informal, customary rules for division of labour and the sharing of village resources. In principle, this provided a system in which labourers could be taken on and kept for long periods, as well as dismissed by the end of a contractual year, according to the current demand for labour. Documents that will be discussed further down show that *pannaiyal* was the form of permanent labour employed in the highlands.

It can be assumed that the farmer's decision depended upon the size of his farm and the crops grown, as well as on whether one particular crop predominated over others. A substantial farm would allow for more labourers to be taken on, while a farmer with only a few acres would employ only a single free hand during peak periods in agriculture. The cropping pattern may also have set framework for labour demands. Some crops were labour-intensive, while others needed very little attention, except during harvest. Cultivating one single crop over a large part of the land could give the advantages of large-scale production, but at the same time could result in an increased competition for hired labour during the seasons with a heavy work load. A mixed cropping pattern could level out the demand for labour on the farm, since the peak seasons would fall in different times of the year. At the same time, this might necessitate a permanent labour force.

But, as assumed, the economic logic worked together with the social logic, and the prevailing social structures may have had a major impact in deciding the terms of the labour contracts that were 'available' to the farmers in the local region.

To reconstruct the Goundar–Madhari relationship, as it was expressed in the Coimbatore district during the early decades of the twentieth century (from approximately 1900 to 1930), it is again necessary to return to the situation on the arrival of the British, this time in Kongunad. This is due to the fact that parts of the relationship have roots before the arrival of the British, while other parts will be explained by the transformation of the agricultural economy that was initiated by the British. This retrospect may not explain the relationship as it appeared around 1900. During a full century, historical events and processes are most likely to change the substance of social relations and labour institutions and the way that people perceive them, even though they are still carrying the old names. But this will shed some light on the question of why certain groups of people have come to relate closely to each other in a situation in which this does not appear to have been immediately necessary.

Hjejle, who stresses the close relationship between the Mirasi estates and the existence of slavery, argues that, in the absence of numerous Mirasi estates, slavery never existed in the Coimbatore area.[27] Even though Mirasi land did exist—with small numbers and large holdings—the Mysore rulers made no effort to respect the Mirasi rights. On the contrary, it happened that land was given to former tenants.[28] At the same time, the Collector of Coimbatore, in his report to the Madras Board of Revenue in 1819, asserted that 'the slaves are on the whole better treated by their masters than the common class of free labourers'.[29] But what was 'a slave' in the Coimbatore district in the early nineteenth century, and who were the labourers that the Collector observed?

When Francis Buchanan travelled on a Government mission through the recently conquered highlands in 1801, he made notes on agricultural practices under Mysore rule. In three different places—Bhavani-Kudal in the north-east, Dharapuram in the south-east and in Pollachi in the south—he made notes about labourers whom he recorded as 'Puddial' (i.e. *padiyal*). These labourers were advanced a sum of money at the beginning of the year; they were also given a place to live or paid house-rent. Their monthly wages were paid in *padis* of grain, while annually they were given grain and cash payments in combination. If they were still unable to repay the advance by the end of the year, the landowner would not allow them to leave, and they had to stay in his service. Buchanan made a distinction between the *padiyal* and the sharecroppers. The landowners were reported to have preferred the former, while the labourers tried to become sharecroppers.[30]

It is difficult to judge whether this form of labour actually was called *padiyal* in the highlands and was, because of the expanded cultivation on farms (*pannai*) over the century, changed to be called *pannai-al* (farm labourer) or whether Buchanan observed a form of labour that was familiar to him from previous observations in other districts and gave the same name to it in his report. But his observations indicate that labour employed on permanent and contract-like terms in a system of advances paid to the labourer was not introduced during the British era but had roots in the region before the arrival of the colonial power.[31]

However limited their options, these labourers were not slaves. To use the term 'contract' may seem inappropriate in a situation in which agricultural relations cannot be described as capitalist. However, the use of this term indicates that the labourer was an economic actor. The options available to him may only have been to enter into a *pannaiyal* agreement or to go hungry. However, nothing indicates a situation in which members of certain castes were by birth and caste affiliation obliged to become attached to a farmer as *pannaiyal.*

Official documents from the early colonial period show that cattle were the back-bone of the economy. The Board of Revenue categorised in 1816 those who owned cattle and land in three groups. The wealthiest were the cattle-breeders, who owned hundreds of animals. This was a limited group, who also owned and tilled land but based their wealth on cattle. Secondly, there was a group of cultivators, who owned cattle, not in hundreds like the former, but rather in tens and twenties. These cultivators could produce a modest surplus from the sale of grain as well as cattle. Finally, the Board distinguished a third group producing at the best for subsistence.[32]

The importance of cattle for the economy is also revealed by Kumar. Referring to Thomas Munroe, she relates that there was not a man in north-east Kongunad at the time when the Ceded Districts were settled who was worth £ 500 'and, if cattle were excluded, nine-tenths of them would not have £ 5'. Munroe may be suspected of exaggerating an economy in tatters due to exploitation under the Mysore rule. That may be so. But, interestingly, the statement discloses an economy in which the possession of cattle implied economic strength.[33]

The British presence in south India was focused much on revenue and revenue collection, which is also reflected in official records. Already on the arrival of the British, when the highlands were ceded and Captain Alexander Read was assigned the task of securing administrative control and settling the area, the main task for him was to organise the collection of revenue. After having surveyed the land, Read began to settle it in the form of small farms with landholders who were individually responsible for their holdings and answered directly to the Collector. The peasants or 'ryots' were to pay an annual fee in return for a title to the land, a *patta.*[34] A situation in which revenue collection was a major goal may have consequences for the reading of official records. As land was the major source of taxation, there is a risk that other trades, important to the local economy, was given less attention in the official documentation. To give an example, growing prosperity was often measured by the amount of increased assessments for individual holdings.[35]

In writing the Manual of the Coimbatore district in the 1880s, Nicholson realised the difficulties of getting a correct picture of the number of cattle held in the district. The British administration had paid much attention to land and land revenue, while the taxation of cattle and sheep had ceased. Therefore, Nicholson found, the old figures were simply repeated with some variation, and the numbers of cattle were regularly understated. As the figures were prepared during the hot season, most of the cattle were not to be found in the villages, since they were grazing in the woods or in the mountains. Having said this, Nicholson made an attempt to get more accurate figures by estimating the number of cattle based on the existing number of ploughs, and by calculating the need of hides for the 81,000 water-lifts in the district, as well as for the basket-boats, shoes and the export trade. He also estimated the annual death rate of cattle. His results showed that in the 1880s 900,000 horned cattle were held in the district, not counting the calves. This was to be compared with 501,055, the figure given as the total number of cattle of all ages in the Government registers.[36]

Looking at the bottom end of the agrarian structure, Buchanan's reports and those of the Collector of Coimbatore provide some information. The Collector had observed a better treatment of labourers under bonds than of the 'free' labourers. In Pollachi, eighteen years earlier, Buchanan found that the bond labourers in their turn were striving to become tenants. The latter statement is not very surprising, but the former gives an interesting indication. Working attached to a farm or a farmer and economically controlled by the advance was to be preferred. To have been 'free' to choose whom to work for might also have implied a 'freedom' from security of livelihood.

## Informal Rights and Formal Bonds

When the Coimbatore district entered the twentieth century, the industrial processing of textiles had begun to grow in the urban centres. Its raw material, cotton, expanded over the fields, and groundnuts became a most profitable crop in parts of the region. The industrialisation and its consequences for rural social and labour relations in the highlands will be further discussed in Chapter 3. What follows later is an attempt to establish the general features of these relations in the early decades of the twentieth century. In particular, the relationship between the major landowners and the agricultural labourers they depended upon will be discussed.

Christopher Baker discusses the labour relations prevailing in the highlands in his comprehensive work on the Tamilnad rural economy.[37] After having observed the relative labour scarcity around the turn of the century, Baker relates from Nicholson's Manual of the Coimbatore district of 1887 that growing labour scarcity was caused by the better possibilities of setting up holdings. Referring to the Royal Commission on Labour in India of 1931, Baker asserts that labourers were better off and had a higher local status in Kongunad than in other parts of the Presidency. These labourers were *pannaiyal*, permanent farm servants, and were employed 'more like an extension of family labour', according to Baker. In contrast, the *pannaiyal* of the plain and valley regions were not extended family labour. The labour relations prevalent in those areas were rather a result of old forms of labour under extra-economic coercion in a new shape. Baker's position is that the permanent farm labourers of the highlands differ in this respect. In the highlands, the labourers were lodged in the farmers' houses and took their meals together with the cultivator and his family. Their pay 'was not unlike' a family share of the results and reached a high level, as compared with the rest of the Presidency during the depression of the 1930s.[38]

Baker's optimistic description of the highlands would have been probable if the farming population of Kongunad had consisted of only Goundars, poorer Goundars working for the wealthier families in their community and, as a result of the progressive settlement of cultivators as *patta*-holders (entitled to land) under the ryotwari system, also able to set up their own farms on a few acres of land.[39]

In the 1880s, Nicholson observed that low-quality land was obtained by labourers and small farmers, and he complained about the negligent way in which it was cultivated. The fact that labourers got hold of land may have led to a shortage of labour for the wealthy Goundars, just as Baker assumes. But, from Nicholson's descriptions, one is led to think that at least some of the land purchased could hardly have maintained a family.

The famine in the 1870s had taken many of the labourers' lives and was felt by the landowners in the form of increased labour costs, according to Nicholson's statements. However, he noted that the number of labourers was now increasing as a result of small farmers and tenants losing land, and he found the labourers' situation to be 'very precarious'. He also observed the labour force growing as more children were born to labourers. Taken together, these different statements by Nicholson make it somewhat difficult to conclude that labour scarcity was caused by labourers purchasing land.[40]

The more important reason for labour scarcity around the turn of the century is rather to be found in the expansion of agriculture itself as it was being drawn into a capitalist economy, an expansion that required more capital input, more land or more efficient land use and more labour. The consequences of the famine put a further strain on labour resources. This transformation happened concurrently with an increased labour migration, in which agricultural labourers took up work on the estates in India and abroad. From the late nineteenth century, the planters in the Nilgiris came to focus their recruitment campaigns on the Coimbatore district. In this situation the agricultural labourers available, who were mostly among the landless population and indeed consisted of poor Goundars but most likely to a larger extent of untouchable Madhari and Paraiyar, were not sufficient. The untouchable, landless, Madhari community are mostly absent in Nicholson's Manual. When he speaks of the problems of the lower classes, he generally means small farmers, tenants and poor Goundars, not untouchable, landless labourers. It may also be observed that the Re-settlement Registers of the Coimbatore district of 1912 almost completely lacks Madhari or Paraiyar landholders in its records.[41]

In support of the statement that the permanent farm servants of the highlands worked as extended family labour, Baker refers to P. Gopalaratnam's survey of 1931. He relies on N. Ganesamurthi (1935) to show the high proportion of permanent farm servants to cultivators.[42] Both studies are detailed in description but limited to small areas in the vicinity north to north-west of Tiruppur. Ganesamurthi's study covers Perumanallur *kasbah* (revenue unit[43]), consisting of five villages; Gopalaratnam restricts his study to one village, Madathupalayam. Both describe a situation in which commercial crops have succeeded food crops on the cultivated lands. The improved variety of Cambodia cotton is grown, being absolutely dominant in Perumanallur. In Madathupalayam, Gopalaratnam relates that Cambodia was introduced by 'a big dealer in cotton' from Tiruppur around 1915 and that it came to replace wheat completely. In these tracts, Cambodia could not be cultivated without irrigation. Consequently, the number of wells had increased in Perumanallur over the previous decade, and also in Madathupalayam the number of wells was high. To draw the water out of the wells, the farmers used leather bags and therefore had to rely on leather-workers. The centrality of the leather-working Madhari community in agriculture, which can be seen in both Ganesamurthi's and Gopalaratnam's studies, made them indispensable to the Goundar farmers. As will be argued, the results lead to the conclusion that the Madhari were the *pannaiyal* tilling the lands of the Goundar and constituting the major part of the landless, agricultural labour force.[44]

The vital role of the leather-workers in the Coimbatore district is also better explained when the importance of cattle and cattle-breeding in the rural economy is brought to the fore. But in the light of the structure of the social hierarchy and the customary rules for social intercourse, it is not likely that the Madhari were ever let into the houses of the Goundar and even less likely that they shared their meals.

To look for information about the past in old stories and tales that are told in our times is a method sometimes used when no other types of source exist. Baker never makes use of this kind of source, while Brenda Beck, as an anthropologist, frequently refers to tales and epics, sometimes considering them for what they reveal about how people today explain their history, sometimes using them as a historical source.[45]

Stories are interpreted as indicative of historical events that, in the story, may take a personalised form. Beck traces close relationships between castes in Kongunad several hundred years back, with the arrival of the right-hand castes in the region.[46] There are many tales known to elder Goundars which explains the history of their community. Some of these tales indicate closer relations in the past between them and other castes. One such story, well known in the dry region, tells about a Goundar man being shaved by the Barber. But something happens outside of the house, and the Barber rushes out to see it and leaves the poor Goundar in a precarious situation with half his chin shaved. The Barber does not return for a long time, and the Goundar feels more and more uncomfortable. Finally, he calls for his eldest son, and even though this is inappropriate for a Goundar, the son shaves his father. From that day, the eldest son of a Goundar was expected to become a barber.[47] All the informants laugh at this ridiculous story, after having told it. No Goundar would ever think of 'lowering himself' to become a barber, even though barbers have an important role to fulfil in Goundar ceremonies.

Using old tales as a historical source is not unproblematic. There is a great risk that the tale has changed its shape, its actors and its points several times according to the situations in which it has been told. The importance of such stories may be lie in their explaining how a community or society *wants* to explain its history or origin at a certain time, while there is a risk that the historical evidence in a tale as a single source will be limited.

But in spite of their limitations as historical sources, these long-lived stories can give an indication of the questions that can be put to older historical material. But no such stories as may reveal a closer relationship between Goundar and Madhari have been found, either among local informants or among the older missionaries who have worked for many years in the region.[48] It is really most difficult to accept that Madharis shared the Goundars' meals in their houses only one generation before a time when they were not even allowed to enter their houses, come close to their food or touch their water.

Returning to Baker's argument, describing the *pannaiyal* as extended family labour, it is more likely that his description relates to other, poorer Goundars working as agricultural labourers for their wealthier relatives. The Madhari, the majority of the agricultural labourers under *pannaiyal*, seem to remain hidden to him in the sources he consults.

In the available studies revealing information about labour conditions, the information indicates a high proportion of *pannaiyal* in relation to casual labourers. In Cox's Gazetteer of 1933, there is an estimate of 'farm servants' that comes close to one-third of the agricultural labour force.[49]

In relating this, it has to be observed that all the evidence indicates that only male individuals were registered as *pannaiyal*. Their wives and adult children, who would be giving priority to serving the same farmer as a result of the head of the household being the *pannaiyal*, would be regarded as casual labourers in the records. A substantial proportion of the casual labourers were in this way involved in the *pannai* system, while working and being remunerated as casual labourers.[50] Therefore, there is no real point in trying to measure the exact number of people involved in the *pannai* system as employed labourers, in contrast to those working as casual labourers. When, together with the male members of the households, the female members, who were not formally taken on as *pannaiyal* but worked on daily or weekly agreements, at the same time were informally included in the *pannai* system, it is important to note that the figure in Cox (1933) is far too low to show the range of the *pannai* system in the agricultural, landless labour force in the early 1930s. Baker notes the dramatic increase of permanent farm servants (*pannaiyal*) to landowners from the late eighteenth century to the 1930s, and states that no nineteenth-century report indicates such a high ratio as that of the 1930s. His observation is further confirmed by the results in the present study. The reasons for increasing numbers of permanent labourers will be further elaborated in Chapter 3.[51]

Older Goundar informants are careful to emphasise the legality of the *pannaiyal* arrangement. They stress that this was not a form of slavery, but a contractual settlement between an employer and his employee.[52] However, the Madhari informants do not recall such an individual agreement. When the question was pushed further, they would agree that only the male head of a family was the actual *pannaiyal*. But, as an informal part of the deal, the family members were expected to work on a casual basis for the same Goundar family.[53]

The socio-economic village studies by Ganesamurthi and Gopalaratnam relate this situation in different ways. However, both describe a situation in which the Madhari worked 'attached to' or 'joined' the farms. In Perumanallur *kasbah*, Ganesamurthi observed that they were advanced 10 rupees when they joined, money that had to be repaid before the labourer was allowed to leave. He also found most of the casual labourers to be women. This is an observation that supports the conclusion that only men were taken on as *pannaiyal*, while their wives and children worked on daily or weekly arrangements.[54]

Gopalaratnam gives a more summary description of the division of labour in the village, sometimes as notes of mere observations. Gopalaratnam writes:

> The chucklers are the dependants of the Gounders and individual families get attached to each holding. The men serve the cultivator throughout the year while their women occasionally render help in odd works on the farm. . . . The *chuckli* is the *mamool* distributor of water when the mhote is working and does sundry other pieces of work including the stitching and mending of leather buckets, ropes, etc., for which alone he is paid extra.[55]

With regard to the question of whether the *pannaiyal* agreement was a settlement between individuals or involved the whole of the labourer's family, it is interesting to note that Gopalaratnam had obviously got the impression that a family became attached to a holding.

However, also Ganesamurthi reveals some unfamiliarity with the villages that he studies and he makes some unfortunate generalisations in his report. In Perumanallur there was a somewhat unusually large community of Goundar as compared to the rest of the village population. Out of 333 families, 205 are recorded as Goundar. Of the remaining families, not more than at the most 35 of them can be assumed to have worked in agriculture; 18 of these were Madhari (recorded as 'Chukkiliar'). In a summary about agricultural labourers Ganesamurthi records that 'Goundars, Madharis or Chukkiliars' worked as permanent labourers attached to the farms, stitching leather items and helping in agricultural operations. In a subsequent paragraph, only the Madhari are mentioned as having become tied by an advance of money. However, it is entirely wrong to assert that the Goundar were working with leather, and this summary way of writing about agricultural labourers may easily lead into wrong conclusions. This situation will be further discussed later.[56]

## THE PANNAIYAL: AN ACKNOWLEDGED MEMBER OF THE VILLAGE

As previously observed, not every farmer in Kongunad held *pannaiyal.* With too little land, it was neither profitable nor necessary. At harvest, casual labourers could be employed, and for the rest of the year family labour was sufficient. For a farmer cultivating only a few acres, the income from this land had to be supplemented by labour on the lands of the wealthier landowners. According to farmers in Semmipalayam village recalling the 1930s and early 1940s, the owners of large holdings would employ more than 20 *pannaiyal*, and the *Ur*-Goundar of Mandiripalayam recalls that 10 acres was the general limit at which a *pannaiyal* was employed.[57]

Mandiripalayam and Semmipalayam are situated in the middle of the dry belt just south and west of Palladam town. As in the other villages located in the area between Tiruppur in the north and half way from Palladam to Pollachi further south, the agricultural land is mainly red soil with pockets of black loam. Until the mid-twentieth century, different varieties of cotton were cropped on both rain-fed and well-irrigated lands. The garden cultivation provided coconuts, vegetables, chillies and millet, and the dry sorghum varieties were the predominant food crops. In this area, the division of land was uneven and the land concentration high. A selection of twenty-five *kasbahs*, situated in Palladam taluk, shows that 61.7 per cent of all *patta*-holders cultivated less than 10 acres each, or 22.8 per cent of all *patta* land in 1912. On the upper half of the scale, 38.3 per cent of the holders cultivated 77.2 per cent of the land. In some of the *kasbahs*, the registers reveal *patta*-owners listed for over 500 acres of land. But as such influential landowners were most likely to hold land in more than one *kasbah*, this only gives an indication of the wealth controlled by a small number of landowners in the central part of the highlands.[58]

Considering the statement by the *Ur*-Goundar of Mandiripalayam, that 10 acres was the minimum amount of land for employing *pannaiyal*, the above figures may provide an indication of the scale of employment of permanent labourers. The figures show an uneven distribution of land among the *patta*-holders. More than one-third had the economic capacity to employ permanently attached labourers. And as those owners controlled 77.2 per cent of the land, it is reasonable to assume that as a rule they employed several *pannaiyals*. This means that three-quarters of all *patta* land were most probably worked by a combination of *pannaiyal* and casual labourers. The upper half of the remaining landowners could most likely work their lands with their own labour, with additional coolie workers during harvest, while the rest would have had to supplement their income by working elsewhere as agricultural labourers.

The Goundar predominance among the landowners is also revealed in the Re-Survey and Re-Settlement Registers of 1912. This estimate is based on the total amount of land in each *kasbah*, including not only cultivated land, but also roads, lakes, temple and village sites. In an area of eighteen *kasbahs*, having Palladam as its nucleus, members of the Goundar community were registered for 55 per cent of the total land. One of those *kasbahs*, Anuppapathi, was an exception, being completely dominated by members of the Nayakkan (Naicker) community. If this *kasbah* is removed from the calculation, the Goundar land ownership amounted to 57 per cent of all land. Land registered as roads, streams, etc., may be estimated to have amounted to 15 per cent, which leaves 28 per cent of the total land to members of other castes and various kinds of common ground. But the division of land between castes varied in the different *kasbahs*. In seven of the selected *kasbahs*, Goundars were registered for 64-88 per cent of all land, which means that in these *kasbahs* only a handful of acres, enough to erect a house upon, was owned by members of the other castes.[59]

Thus, by the turn of the century the *pannaiyal* played an important role in the rural economy in the Coimbatore district. Within the *pannai* system the labourers had access to resources by rights to shares of the produce. Before British rule was established, as suggested by David Washbrook, this might have been to their advantage. The reports about 'slaves' could have been a misconception or a misuse of words by the officials; this may also have been a mere use of rhetoric in a political situation. But just as the government officials did in the nineteenth century, also the missionaries in the early twentieth century consistently spoke of 'slavery' and described the exploited labourers as being weighed down by debts. Assuming that the system of advances had now become oppressive, there are reasons to believe that this economic coercion ought to have operated within a social structure in which the right to a share in the village resources still existed, even though economically weakened.

When Swedish missionaries took up work in the rural areas of Coimbatore district in the 1920s, they met with the relatives of the Paraiyar who had converted to Christianity in the Dharapuram area. These people had seen their kin benefit from conversion, and now asked the nearest missionaries for baptism. And, as had happened in Dharapuram, a decade later, groups of Madhari came with the same request.[60] Generally, when reporting the situation of the agricultural labourers to the Mission Board, the missionaries did not distinguish the different forms of employment or contracts that the labourers worked under from each other. Even if they knew about the differences, it is unlikely that such information was of importance in the congregational work, and the Swedish addressee in Uppsala was not likely to value these facts.[61] In describing labour relations, 'slavery' was the term commonly used. The Madhari labourers were described as working in slavery or almost as slaves.[62] It is therefore not surprising that only once in the entire material of annual reports from the Coimbatore district mission stations during the years from 1919 to 1970 is the name of what is called 'a customary contract' between labourers and landlords given in its Tamil form.[63]

In 1956 the Rev. Tage Holmberg writes: 'However, the problems confronting the Mathari Christians, living half way to slavery as they do, with drum-beating at Hindu festivals and many other dubious things regarded as part of their ordinary duties, as per "*urimai*" (customary contract between them and the landlords)—those problems are by no means solved as yet.'[64]

What Holmberg observed was obviously not a mere labour contract. Labour appears to have been a part of *urimai*, with Madhari living 'half way to slavery' in a contract with the landlords. But the contract is understood as 'customary' and included drum-beating at Hindu festivals and 'other dubious things'. According to Holmberg, these were 'duties' related to caste, as this is a description of the Madhari. What was so 'dubious' remains hidden, but, obviously, drum-beating at Hindu festivals and other duties that were common and customary to the Madhari appear problematic to Holmberg, considering that they were Christians.

Therefore, this is not an expression of *pannaiyal*, which was an agreement including only labour. *Urimai* rather indicates a relationship having both economic and social aspects, which points to a history before the further expansion of *pannaiyal*.

Linguistically, *urimai* denotes a very close relationship. Among the different meanings of the word are 'ownership, that which is owned, claim for right of possession, liberty, slave, dependant, acquisition, duty, and the services of a bondservant'. But it also denotes other intimate relations, such as 'wife, privilege of intimacy, and love'.[65] When the older Madhari of today explain the *urimai* that they experienced, it is not primarily understood as duties and services under bonds. *Urimai* is by all informants defined as the labourers' right to a share of the produce. At harvest, every labourer had a share. Even if the Goundar landowner was not present when the harvest was to be divided, no one could question the right of the labourer to take his share. When cattle died, both Madhari and Paraiyar had rights to the meat. If the buffalo or ox died in the area where the Madhari lived or worked, it belonged to them, and vice versa. If it died anywhere else, the meat was to be divided between them. But it was always the Madharis who handled the hides on the Goundars' account. This was the *urimai*, the right and liberty, of the labourers. To have the right to claim *urimai* gave a kind of security to the Madhari. But rights were only one side of the coin. As Holmberg wrote, *urimai* also carried duties—or the right of the Goundars to certain services of the Madhari. In this way, *urimai* reinforced the hierarchical social structure of the village, where certain rights that were held by one particular caste were at the same time denied to the other.[66]

This bears a resemblance to the results presented in Brenda Beck's study of the Coimbatore highlands. The piece of evidence brought out in Holmberg's report reveals information on what may have been the Madhari's part of customary services and rights in local society. Beck attempts to reconstruct a schedule of the 'traditional economic ties' in Kongunad society as a whole. On the basis of information from a Pandaram priest in Palaiyakottai, a town in the dry-belt region, Beck sets up a table of the 'rights, duties and remuneration' for every caste in relation to certain, titled, Goundar families. These families are at the top of the socio-economic structure. The Madhari are at the bottom end. The table gives a somewhat ideal-type impression. The titled families are seen as examples of 'the average landed family "writ large"'. According to Beck, the information derived from the interview gives an indication of a system of land rights more widely practised in the past.[67]

Whether the particulars given were practised in Palaiyakottai to their full extent or not, they uncover the principles of a complex system of interrelated mutual relationships. They also reveal agrarian relations that linked the Goundar, as farmers, to the Madhari, as leather-workers and field labourers.

The distinction between 'right-hand' and 'left-hand' castes is important in the study. It was only the right-hand castes that were involved in agriculture and had a close attachment to the land. Other castes, also high up on the social scale, such as Naicker and Chettiyar, are categorised as left-hand castes and excluded from the system of local rights and services due to the Goundar family. Basically, the members of those castes engaged in trades other than agriculture and generally had Telugu as their mother tongue in common. The Goundar community, who is a right-hand caste, was the most prominent farming community. Within the left-hand division, the Madhari are the exception, holding the occupations of agricultural labour and leather work. Recorded as a service to the titled family without remuneration, the Madhari were obliged to send one man from every household for field work whenever so required by the Goundar. On those working days, the Madhari man could expect a meal at noon, and whenever cattle died in the village, the Madhari had the right to the meat.[68] The description of the Goundar's relationship to the castes involved in agriculture comes very close to the meaning of *urimai*, as discussed earlier.

Information from a survey by S.V. Duraiswami in 1934 indicates that not only agricultural castes held shares in the produce of the village. The survey is at the same time an account written on behalf of the farmers and tenants who could not make ends meet, facing falling prices of agricultural products and large debts. To prove this, Duraiswami calculates the income and expenditure for five cultivators from Avanashi and Andiyur: two tenants, two landowners and one landowner who was also a leaseholder. Among the expenses, the formulation 'chukkler [i. e. Madhari leather-worker], carpenter and other mamools' is found.[69]

*Mamool* means 'established custom'. As explained by the Rev. E. Jacob, a native of Nallakalipalayam, south of Tiruppur, *mamool* is a share different from the annual share in the harvest. It was given in the form of vegetables, grain and cotton throughout the year to the agricultural labourers, when they needed it, and to the carpenter, washerman and barber, and to members of all other castes that served the Goundar as remuneration in kind for the work they performed. Most of these did not cultivate land of their own but had rights to a share of the village produce controlled by the Goundar.[70]

The existence of a system of services and distribution of resources in which the whole village community was involved questions one of Beck's conclusions from her interview with the Pandaram priest. Rather than a system of 'land rights' surviving from the past, this points to a wider social system, a system in which the members of local society were hierarchically ranked, interrelated and granted security for their livelihood by the exchange of goods (shares of the proceeds from cultivation and cattle-breeding) and services (as related to caste).

Beck states that the relationships between castes in her table have roots in earlier history and claims validity for this system for 'several hundred years at least'. But to base such an assumption on an interview in 1966 may seem somewhat risky. Even if the Pandaram priest may have been assigned the task of memorising and relating the local history, the influence of a full century in which the economy was greatly and increasingly dependent on the cultivation of land may have affected the role of the Goundar community in his story. There may be a risk of overrating the importance of the Goundars as farmers and of this system as a system of *land* rights, as suggested by Beck.[71]

The attachment of the (left-hand) Madhari to the (right-hand) Goundar community may also be more fruitfully understood in the light of the earlier, cattle-based economy of Kongunad. More than being understood as a purely agrarian relationship, the Goundar–Madhari attachment ought to be seen as the result of an earlier relationship between owners of large herds of cattle and labourers who pastured the cattle and took care of dead animals, hides and meat. As already mentioned, on the arrival of the British in Kongunad, wealth was based to a large extent on cattle. The transformation of this economy into settled small farmers, still having their herds but more and more cultivating dry-land crops and in increasing amounts also cash-crops, may accordingly be assumed to have altered and adjusted labour relations to the new economic realities. During the nineteenth century, the Madhari became more involved in agriculture. Their skills in leather-work were crucial to farmers who depended on well irrigation in cultivating the soil. The Madhari would still be the leather-working caste but were increasingly identified also with the cultivation of crops.[72]

Cattle do appear in Beck's table, but in a subordinate way. The titled family's head man is said to have had the rights to the Goundar's bull calves born during the year, and the Madhari had the right to dead cattle and leather-work. But in relating the information in the table to Beck's assumption that local folklore would suggest that these rights and obligations had existed for hundreds of years, the importance of cattle for the Goundar economy is underestimated.[73]

It should also be remembered that the Pattagar of Palaiyakottai, the town of the Pandaram priest, was one of the most influential cattle-breeders of Kongunad, raising the Kangayam breed, which was the jewel in the crown of the Kongunad cattle breeds. Nicholson stated that this most influential of all the Pattagars kept herds of from 500 to 1,000 head and large numbers of cows and bulls for breeding only. The Pattagar carried out experimental breeding not only with Indian cattle, but also with European. In 1933, Cox, in a volume which was to accompany the Manual that was basically the same as Nicholson's in 1887, up-dated these figures. The Pattagar of Palaiyakottai, 'the best and largest breeder', accounted for about 2,000 head of stock, according to Cox. Three hundred of those were sold annually for breeding. These, the best of the cattle, never reached the ordinary markets, either in 1887 or in 1933, but were purchased by dealers from such distant places as Tiruchirapalli and Ceylon.[74]

## Advances and Remuneration

Two major ways of safeguarding their livelihood were available to the Madhari. The information indicating the existence of *urimai*, the rights and duties regulating the sharing of village resources, suggests a kind of system for security and survival. This system was probably caste-based with a local range. Remuneration in such a system would mean being granted a share of the produce. At the same time, a pre-paid share, such as the advance given to the *pannaiyal*, served to restrict the mobility of labourers. However, a widespread understanding of labour under bonds, both by contemporary observers throughout the century and in current literature, is that it was the lending of money that had these effects.

The missionaries nowhere reveal that they were aware of a difference between the advance payments and the lending of money. David Bexell, a Swedish missionary, was deeply upset when he reported on the conditions of the agricultural labourers in the Coimbatore district. The heaviest burden enslaving them was their debt. He writes:

> The wretched debtor without considering the consequences in fact sells himself, with his family and yet unborn generation, as slaves to the landowner, who rubs his hands with delight at this profitable bargain. Every attempt of uplifting these village people will be in vain as long as they are in the clutches of these unscrupulous masters. The debt grows continually by an enormous interest being added to the initial loan.[75]

Bexell first arrived in the district in 1889, assigned to Coimbatore. After many years in the lowlands, he returned as an old man, and work was taken up in the rural areas in the 1920s. Previously, the congregation consisted of members of urban-based, high castes. But, as the rural work increased, large groups from a completely different and lower, socio-economic stratum of society began to turn to the mission for conversion and baptism. In the 1920s, the new congregation members were primarily found among the Paraiyar community; in the early 1930s, Madhari groups began to approach the mission.[76]

Bexell rhetorically describes a situation of slavery, the labourer 'sells himself, with his family and yet unborn generation', but remarks that the ties were constructed by borrowed money. 'A debt' and 'debt-bondage' are the general descriptions recurring in the mission reports.

Bexell obviously also believed that the 'uplift' of the poor was impossible as long as the labourers were dependent on the farmers. Attempts had been made to distribute land among the Paraiyar to eradicate the effects of debt-labour. But it had not turned out well. Bexell blames corrupt agents and 'the slavery bond nature' among 'the untouchables' for this.[77] Another attempt to undermine the aims of bondage by debt was made when 'a bank', or rather a fund, was initiated to provide loans on favourable conditions, and to pay debts to the landowner on behalf of the labourers, thus making the labourer indebted to the mission instead of to the landowner. But these new loans were of a different kind, as they were both free of interest and labour was not a part of the conditions. These loans had become purely financial debts.[78]

The missionary Ernst Heuman[79] described how the Government made efforts to initiate cooperatives among the labourers, so that they could by their labour become owners of the pieces of land on which their houses were built. This would prevent the landowner from using the threat of eviction as a means of coercing the labourers. But the landowners, who were also the employers, immediately offered a loan to the workers. If they accepted the landowners' offer, their payment was reduced. And when the Government official arrived, presenting 10 rupees to the worker, the gift was turned down out of fear of the landlord on whom they had become dependent.[80]

The crucial role of indebtedness, as related to labour, is discussed by several authors with regard to different periods in history. As discussed earlier, the logic presented is generally the same. The settlement was arranged in such a way that the borrower was unable to repay the debt, and the lender could secure labour services for as long as he needed. To extract profit from interest, was not the issue; the idea was to ensure a supply of labour.[81]

Bexell's firm assertion that 'the debt' grew by an 'enormous interest being added to the initial loan' complicates the picture. In principle, such interest would not have made any difference to a lending farmer. A larger debt would not have made the *pannaiyal* more dependent than a small one. According to the logic presented earlier, as long as he was in debt, he would also have been dependent.

Hypothetically, in a situation in which the lender wanted to bring a piece of land under his control, a high unpayable interest rate would gain this end. Eventually, when an indebted landowner ended up in arrears, his land would be taken over by the lender. But if the aim was to restrict the mobility of labourers, a medium-level interest rate combined with restrictions to stay in the area and work for the lending farmer as long as the debt was outstanding, would work better. It had to be possible to make interest payments regularly to secure man-power over a certain period of time, but the level of interest should not be set so low that it enabled the borrower to save and repay the loan as a whole. However, in a patriarchal situation, where customary law restricted labour mobility and secured hierarchical power relations, keeping interest on a loan would, on the whole, be unnecessary. In such a situation, the labourers who were 'part of the system' would also be available to the landowners. Their needs, including loans to meet larger expenses, would be met within the customary laws of society.

However, if the amount that the labourer owed the farmer was not borrowed money at all, but advance payments of future remuneration, the question of interest payments is not an issue. The labourer would simply have to work until he had caught up with his wages. According to this logic, it is possible that Bexell confused the initial payments to the *pannaiyal* with their future loans or with loans given to casual labourers. Bexell may very well have correctly observed borrowed money and heavy interest payments. His mistake would rather have been to draw the conclusion that it was these loans that tied labourers to a certain farm.

A system of advance payments to *pannaiyal* agrees best with the information in the more detailed documents from the Coimbatore district. Ganesamurthi, whose work was referred to earlier, reported 'advanced' money in Perumanallur in 1935.[82] Also interviewed informants residing in the villages, whether Madhari or Goundar, make a distinction between borrowed money and advances of future remuneration. The latter could be both in cash and in kind. The initial money or grain given to the *pannaiyal* was an advance that had to be adjusted to the labourer's share in the coming harvest. The same condition applies to additional advances given throughout the year. If the whole share had been advanced, the *pannaiyal* could still borrow necessities, in cash or in kind, at any time of the year. But the different sources of information diverge as to whether these loans carried interest or not, and there may not have been a general rule. However, there is no substantial evidence that the advance carried interest equal to the conditions of a loan. They were plain advances of future pay. On the other hand, they may have served as a means to make the *pannaiyal*, as it were, indebted to the landowner. When the year came to an end and the labourer realised that he and his family could not live on what remained of his share, the initial advance would have to be carried on into the next year, as a debt.[83] There does not seem to be any reason to think that the landowners expected the *pannaiyal* to repay the initial advance. It was rather a way of securing controlled labour for the lender—the borrower at the same time exchanging freedom for security.

Goundar informants would rather emphasise the formal side of the advances and explain that no landowner would easily trust an indebted labourer who wanted to leave the village, promising to return with the money. Therefore, it was only 'natural' to forbid the labourer to leave while owing money.[84]

To seek information about payment for agricultural labour leads one to a variety of sources. Going through the different types of material available gives a picture of structured and detailed forms of remuneration for different kinds of work. But it seems that not only the task performed decided the payment, but also that the particular form of labour relation, as well as the occupations decided by caste affiliation in the village, had an impact on the forms of remuneration.

Of the observers who were 'outsiders' to local society, the missionaries working in the villages provide the empirically most detailed information. Though not systematically collected, but rather in support of descriptions of the situation of the untouchables, the reports are generally based on day-to-day observations in the villages. However, there is a difference between the information given in the documents of the Methodist Missionary Society (MMS) and of the Church of Sweden Mission (CSM), the former working in the south-east of the highlands and in parts of the southern hill areas and the latter in the centre, west and south. The MMS missionaries appear to have approached people very systematically, going from one Madhari or Paraiyar sub-caste to the other, submitting reports to the home board on 'the growing harvest' and the ability of the converts to endure suffering and persecution. But they rarely made comments about the social or economic situation of the people. The CSM missionaries were, on the other hand, rather overwhelmed by the rush of converts and found difficulties in organising the work. In the reports, these missionaries deplored the situation of the poor and expressed anxiety about the difficulties these people faced. They were perceived by the missionaries as powerless and exploited labourers—and the missionaries wrote at length about their situation.

G. Stephen, an Indian pastor working in the Coimbatore district from the 1930s onwards, writes:

> They [the Madharis] are practically the slaves of the gowndas, and work in their fields from sunrise to sunset. When they receive their hard-earned daily

wage, it is called 'alms'. Their dependence on the Gowndas makes them very afraid of them; their uttermost poverty makes them do anything to earn a few paisa or receive a meal.[85]

E. Jacob recalls the practice of using the word 'alms' for wages from his youth. This was not a formal name for any particular remuneration, but a way of expressing 'the benevolence of the rich towards the poor'.[86] This practice obviously upset Stephen.

Other information about remuneration in the central parts of the highlands has been collected by interviews with elderly informants or with persons who themselves had reasons for collecting such information. However, they provide additional explanations to the discussion earlier and will therefore be discussed in this connection.

A.M.R. Durai, who gained his information while working as a social worker, often mediating between Goundar and Madhari in conflicts, describes different forms of payment:

At harvest, the Goundar would leave rice on the threshing ground for the Madharis, plus something apart from this, like ten bags of food grains. They also received food when they came for work. It was limited, but sufficient. There was no starvation. During Devali and Pongal and other festivals they would receive dresses and so on. The Goundars fulfilled their requirements.[87]

The annual pay for agricultural labour was, as discussed earlier, in shares of the harvest. This was their right or within the *urimai,* as long as they fulfilled their part in the division of labour within the village. This was the 10 bags of food grains, in Durai's example.[88] As indicated in the village studies earlier referred to, a share in the village resources was a *mamool,* a customary share. But not only agricultural labourers could count on a *mamool* share. As was discussed earlier, oral evidence, together with contemporary surveys, indicates that members of various trades performing services to the farming Goundar community received *mamool.* This form of remuneration was paid throughout the year and was recorded as a cost for the owners of land in Duraiswami's calculations.[89]

As part of the deal, the agricultural labourers received a meal during the working day, irrespective of whether they worked as *pannaiyal* or as casual labourers. But grain left on the threshing ground was only a little extra after harvest, and it appears that practices were very different between villages and individual farmers as to whether the labourers could take such a bonus for granted. As related by Jacob, the privilege of collecting the superfluous grain could cause conflicts among the labourers.[90] The gifts of clothes at festivals, related by Durai, was something expected from the *pannaiyar* in his relation to his *pannaiyal.*

The payment called *devasam* has also to be mentioned in this context. It does not appear in its Tamil form in any of the material consulted until 1967, when it was found in the notes made by one of Staffan Lindberg's field assistants with reference to a conversation with Nachimuttu Goundar in Veerapandi, south of Tiruppur. When asked how the Madhari labourers were treated, the Goundar man replied: '... sometimes they will be given some devasam (in kind) as salary instead of money.'[91]

In the central dry region, the persons interviewed in 1995 relate *devasam* to payment in kind for the *pannaiyal's* labour. Without exception, the Madhari informants immediately refer to child labour, when the child was mortgaged for one year for an amount of money forwarded to the parents and sometimes for nothing, except for the food provided during the working day. Unless the parents were able to settle the advance by the end of the year, the sum would be deducted from the monthly pay or the child would have to stay for another year. As a rule, children pastured the Goundar's cattle, cleaned and looked after the animals, and slept in the cattle shed during the night to prevent theft. The *devasam* was given as simple food grains, measured as half a bag to a full bag of *ragi, cholam* or *cumbu.* In Uppilipalayam the child was given two meals a day of porridge, chillies and butter milk.[92]

This kind of child labour prevailed in the area during the whole period and outlived *pannaiyal* as the dominant form of tied labour by decades.[93] This may also be the reason why *devasam* is today immediately associated with child labour. This was also the case when Lindberg did his field research in 1967. In his notes, he generally referred to 'child pannaiyam'. This is in itself a contradictory term, as children were never employed as *pannaiyal.* But the misunderstanding can be explained by the fact that children were almost the only bonded labourers in 1967.[94]

But Nachimuttu Goundar did not speak of child labour, but of payment to Madhari labourers in general. Sometimes Madhari labourers were given *devasam.* Jacob, who left the district in 1963 for higher studies, when *pannaiyal* still worked for the farmers, ascertains that *devasam* was the payment in grain given to the *pannaiyal.* No one but they would receive this kind of pay. Eighty-year-old

Duraisamy of Uppilipalayam was himself tied to a Goundar in his youth. When he relates that 'I worked as pannaiyam and got *devasam: cholam, cumbu*', his experiences correspond to those of Jacob.[95] Duraisamy was young at the time. His task was to take care of the horses for the local *kanakuppillai*, the accountant having responsibility for the land registers in a number of villages and in this case a Goundar man.[96]

Payment in kind was not only given in grain. Liquor or a voucher for the local pub would occasionally replace grain or money. Liquor was sometimes also provided at weddings and funerals by the Goundars, as part of their deal with a *pannaiyal* or with the Madhari community in the village.[97] The missionaries tried their best to persuade people to abstain from alcoholic beverages, as they believed that they turned people into drunkards and made wages disappear into the liquor shop. But their efforts met with little success. In 1938, a missionary reports that 'the outcastes' had stopped drinking in only one of the villages where the mission worked. The labourers were reported to fear that, if they refused to accept payment in any particular form, they would cause a conflict with their employers.[98]

An addition to the Madhari's income, irrespective of whether he was a *pannaiyal* or a casual labourer, was the meat from dead animals. No one else but Madhari, and occasionally also Paraiyar, would eat the meat from animals which had died of natural causes. Corpses were considered unclean and impure by the higher castes, and it was the task of the Madhari to take care of them. The habit of eating carcasses would bring them many disparaging judgements and added to their low status, but it gave them a possibility of supplementing their food with meat.

Different local practices in relation to dead animals appear to have been upheld. Most of the evidence reveals a situation in which the meat was given free but in which the hides belonged to the farmer. In such situations, the Madhari either bought the hides and sold the produce or was paid to produce leather items from the hides for the Goundar. However, evidence has also been found that the Madhari had sometimes to pay for the dead animal. It may then be assumed that the hide belonged to them. This was not a regular payment for labour. It was a right that they guarded, and sometimes they ended up in conflicts with the Paraiyar over dead cattle.[99]

There was apparently a variety of sources for the income of a Madhari man, as an individual labourer and as a member of the

Madhari community. Most of the documents that give indications of the forms of payment state that the Madharis' needs were met on a low but sufficient level.[100] Therefore, as long as the Goundars needed the Madharis *as a group*, even the casual labourers achieved a certain amount of security.

## Exit from the Rural Economy

As argued earlier, the presence of the Madhari was of crucial importance to the Goundar farmers. But the Madharis were not the only agricultural labourers. Next to them in numbers were the Paraiyar, and these two castes constituted the bulk of the Scheduled Caste population in the district.[101] The contact between these two groups was limited to participation in the same religious ceremonies or working side by side in the fields. Apart from that, they avoided each other, sometimes regarding each other with mutual contempt.[102] In the dry region, they were able to move out of the village to a much greater degree than the Madhari. As a rule, they went to the hill estates for up to 10 months a year, only to return to their home villages during the spring.[103] The Rev. Anders Andrén remarked in 1955, after a visit to Manelaroo estate, that 'It sometimes seems as if the best people in our villages have migrated to the estates'.[104] And while the Madhari were described as backward and were said to create extreme difficulties in the work of social uplift, information was given on how the Paraiyars were getting organised and becoming members of the Scheduled Caste Federation.[105]

Labour on the estates was organised in a system of pre-employment advances. This was, according to Barbara Evans, almost universal in the Tamil districts from where the majority of the estate workers in the Nilgiri hills migrated in the early twentieth century. In their home villages, agricultural workers, often indebted, were approached by labour contractors or *maistris* offering an advance on future wages on condition that the borrower became employed. The *maistri* would argue that the estate wages were much higher than the coolie wages in the villages and that the advance would make them free from debts in their home village.[106]

Once on the estate, the worker would start to repay his or her advance by labour. However, sick-leave days and additional advances from the wages would further reduce the pay by the end of the season, and the labourer might find himself ending up with a deficit. In that case, he would have to sign on for another year. If the worker was able to finish the year without owing money to the *maistri*, the labour contractor would argue for the benefit of taking a new advance before leaving for the home village. Occasionally, the *maistris* even refused to accept repayment, so as to not lose their hold over the workers. According to Evans, once one entered into the labour relations of the estates and planters, there was no exit from them.[107] In this way, the *maistri* system reflected the *pannai* system, and Evans' survey shows, by comparing the agricultural labour relations in Malabar on the west coast with those of the Tamil districts, basically Coimbatore, that the *maistri* system effectively adapted and adjusted itself to the prevailing agrarian labour relations through non-market mechanisms, to gain the maximal use of the labour force in a situation of labour scarcity.[108]

In exceptional cases, also individual Madhari took up work on the estates. One-hundred-and-two-year-old Abraham of Mandiripalayam, who was an estate worker in his youth, remembers how the *maistri* gathered people and handed out money 'from a sack' as an advance on the salary for the coming year. The fact that labour was better paid on the estates made the *maistri's* offer attractive. But even if the space in the labourers' row of houses was free of charge, the living costs easily exceeded the wage.

The *maistri* was dependent on being able to bring a certain number of labourers to the estate during a season. Abraham remembers that the *maistri* received a commission equivalent to 50 paisa per labourer, which was taken from the labourers' salaries. But no sources indicate that the Madharis left for the estates other than in exceptional cases, and only the casual labourer could consider leaving the village as a possibility.[109]

In Dharapuram, in the eastern part of the dry belt, the Kongu sub-caste of the Paraiyar community had approached the Methodist mission about conversion. When the Madharis followed their example, the missionaries were appalled by the poverty prevalent among these people. In reporting on this in 1935, W.A. Sandford related as a matter of fact that the Madharis could not abolish their poverty by going to the estates, as the Kongu Paraiyar did. Sandford's conclusion was that they lacked the courage and capacity.[110]

In the Methodist mission's files, approximately 6,000 Christian Paraiyar were reported to live in the Anamalai hills; half of this group were reported to belong to other churches than the Methodist mission in their home villages. As the missions had divided the area between themselves, so as not to intrude on each other's congregations, the majority of these Paraiyar most probably belonged to the Lutheran mission and church[111] and consequently lived in the central parts of the highlands. They were most probably the Paraiyar who had converted as a result of the presence and work of the Church of Sweden Mission.[112]

At the time when the Paraiyar were in their home villages, the Methodist missionaries realised that they had become politically conscious while working at the estates. W.J. Noble and Duncan Leith[113] observed on a secretarial visit to the Anamalai hills that the option of going to the estates had 'helped to free some of them from serfdom and debt, and has brought prosperity into some of the villages of the plains'. If courage was what the Madhari lacked, as Sandford believed, this was something that the Paraiyar could obviously gain while working on the tea estates. It was above all the women who became active in the villages. Six years earlier, a missionary expressed worries about the consequences of women attaining political awareness. The Self-Respect Movement and the Congress Party were agitating in the major villages, and pictures of Gandhi and of a woman who was jailed for participating in the Civil Disobedience Campaign had been found on the walls of houses where Christian women lived. Also the girls at Woriur High School had shown an interest in politics, but the missionary hoped that this interest and energy would be redirected away from politics and channelled into service.[114]

But the Methodist documents do not speak only in terms of character when discussing the reasons why some labourers converted *en masse*, while others abstained. The Methodist mission worked in two large areas in India. The southern area stretched from Dharapuram to Tanjore and the eastern coast. This was not a uniform area, and the missionaries faced great problems in the eastern section in the 1920s. Unlike Dharapuram, where Paraiyars were converting *en masse* and the work was prospering, the missionaries were not able to reach the Paraiyar in the eastern section. The progress was understood to be caused by the fact that the Paraiyar in the west were less dependent on the landlords and on work in their home villages, as were the Paraiyar in the east. In the Tanjore region, the Paraiyar were reported to have worked under bonds as *pannaiyal* for the local landowners and were much less mobile.[115]

The comparison that the Methodist missionaries made between Paraiyar under bonds and Paraiyars working for most of the year on the estates can be related to the situation of the Paraiyar and the Madhari in the highlands. It would suggest that the reason why the Madharis stayed in the villages rather than found employment on the estates was related to the working conditions and the labour relations. Working as *pannaiyal* tied the labourer to a landowner and identified him with the village and its farms—its *pannais.* In the highlands, this situation was combined with the specific geographical conditions forcing landowners to rely on well irrigation and therefore on leather-workers. What at first sight may appear as a difference between castes, in which one of the castes is not only described in terms of poverty, but is also ascribed moral and psychological qualities, is rather the result of the different forms of labour employment which had been adjusted to the requirements of the agricultural production.

However, there is a major difference between the Paraiyar of the Tanjore area and the Madhari of the highlands. In the Tanjore district the Paraiyars were not indifferent to change. A revolt among the *pannaiyal* was organised in the mid-1930s.[116] It was a political mobilisation, supported by the Communist Party and the Provincial Agricultural Labour Federation in order to secure the rights of the *pannaiyal.* To obtain a more intensive, commercial form of agriculture, in a situation with an increasing labour supply and a declining market as a result of the depression, the farmers had made attempts to rationalise the use of labour. This led to the bringing in of casual labourers, which made the *pannaiyal* lose their bargaining position when they tried to negotiate a good deal for their share in the harvest outcome. As the conflict escalated, the Government of Madras intervened, and an agreement was made in 1944. According to this, daily wages would be increased, the labourers would be guaranteed their share of the harvest, import of labour was banned and the mirasidars were prohibited from dispensing with or evicting their tied labourers. This agreement was not kept, and the mobilisation of *pannaiyal* spread further north. In the 1950s, the conflict abated. A Pannaiyal Protection Act was passed and land-ceiling legislation prepared. The mirasidars were to be resident, again employing *pannaiyal* and some casual labour.[117]

This conscious organisation among the bonded labourers, in order to achieve certain aims among those, as outlined earlier, could not be seen among the Madhari *pannaiyal.* A statement by the Panchayat President of Semmipalayam is rather significant as regards the position of the Madhari in the central part of the highlands. Sivasubramaniyan

Goundar related that the Madhari were always employed as *pannaiyal.* The Goundar farmers always asked them first when something needed to be done on the farm. While the Paraiyars became educated and preferred to work for the British on the estates, on the railways or as their domestic servants, avoiding much of the dirty work on the farms, the Goundars in the village related how they could trust the Madhari labourers with the agricultural work, knowing that they would carry it out to their liking.[118] Sivasubramaniyan Goundar explains: 'We kept them low.' According to him, the Madhari themselves remained attached to the Goundars in the village' and would never leave them. While relating this, his tongue slipped, and he immediately corrected himself, saying: 'They were just like slaves to the Goundars. Not exactly slaves! So much affinity, so much preferences the Goundars are giving them.'[119]

### Affirming the Social Distance

A visible sign of the social divisions of the village was their separation in space. Roads and streets separated not only blocks of houses, but also members of the different castes. According on their rank and closeness in the social hierarchy, the members of these castes did or did not mingle. In this way, the social structure was embodied in the physical structure, the physical space and distance to a great extent reflecting the social space and distance. On the outskirts of the main village or at a distance of up to a kilometre away as a hamlet on its own, the Madhari settlement was situated. This was sometimes referred to as the *cheri* or the *valavu.* In the land registers of the Re-Survey and Re-Settlement of 1912, there is a portion of land marked as 'Chukklers' village-site' in several of the villages.[120]

Prior to 1940, the Madhari community of Mandiripalayam lived near the entrance of the village but separated from the other villagers. Their houses were huts or a simple construction covered by worn-out leather bags used for lifting the water out of the wells. This spot was at a lower level than the rest of the village area, a stream ran through it and it was constantly damp. During the monsoons, the spot was flooded, and the Madhari dwellings were usually washed away. In the 1940s, when the CSM took up work in the village, discussions between the mission workers, a wealthy Goundar, and Morris, the Collector of Coimbatore, resulted in a new settlement half a kilometre away from the main village on higher land.[121]

This social distance was strictly kept between the Madharis and the Goundars. The Madharis would generally not enter the Goundar street. A *pannaiyal* could come to the Goundar's house, but he would not be permitted to enter it and no Goundar would think of going into the Madhari settlement. The Goundars would not even allow the Madharis to touch them without considering this as an insult. This was much the same situation as that between the castes of different status in other parts of Tamilnad. The striking difference in the highlands appeared in the field, where the Goundars without hesitation worked behind the plough side by side with their Madhari labourers. Performing such work would have been impossible without now and then touching each other.[122] But there is an expression among the Madhari that says that 'in the night time there is no caste'. When Durai asked the Madhari people around Arulpuram, south of Tiruppur, whom he worked among, why they used to marry their daughters at such an early age, he was told that in this way they were trying to protect them from being violated by the Goundar men.[123]

The distance between social groups was also manifested in daily life. Clothing may serve as an example. A Madhari man, like members of other Scheduled Castes, was not allowed to wear cloth below the knees and above the chest. Women could not wear a sari blouse. When a man met somebody of a higher caste in the village, he was supposed to fold his *dhoti* to the waist, remove the towel from his head and put it under his arm, while crossing his arms over his chest and bowing his head. Even though Madhari men were the cobblers and the only ones who stitched sandals, they did not use footwear themselves.[124]

Most older Madhari informants related incidents in which they had been punished for violating these rules. Eighty-year-old Samuel of Palam remembered from his childhood in the 1920s a very cold day when his uncle and a friend were freezing, and his uncle, though hesitatingly, put on a shirt. Some Goundar men saw this, ran up to them and started beating and scolding the two men. Not until the father of Samuel's uncle came running and tore off the shirt did the beating stop. And after having given them a severe warning, the Goundar men left.[125]

In this way, it was not possible to move in daily life without affirming a position in the local social hierarchy. It could be argued that the rules of dressing and behaviour were a form of physical control of the lowest social divisions. At the same time as they were denied a certain behaviour, the forms they had to adjust to affirmed a low position. It followed logically that people who acted like that and held such occupations had to be kept at a distance and be kept down.

In the whole of Tamilnad, the playing of drums was associated with the Paraiyar caste and a certain drum, the *parai*, gave them their name.[126] These drums were used for various reasons. They were a means of proclaiming an official message, as well as an important part of the temple processions. Drums were also used to announce the news of a death or a wedding.

But this general rule does not seem to have applied to Kongunad. In this region both Paraiyar and Madhari played the drums on important occasions, and the tasks assigned to the two castes appear to have differed between villages. In various missionary documents, from the CSM and the MMS alike, members of the Madhari community are reported to have played drums in religious ceremonies.[127] But it was only the Madhari who made the drums, as this was work with leather. As stated by Holmberg, this was a part of the *urimai* and, as such, was a service expected from the Madhari by local society.[128]

When those among the Madhari who had converted to Christianity refused to play the drums, this caused grave conflicts and attracted punishments from the higher castes, particularly from the Goundars.[129] But Johannes Sandegren[130] was not completely against the playing and dancing in front of the Hindu idols by the Christian Madharis. Naturally, he wanted these 'habits' to be abolished, particularly since part of the payment was in liquor. But to force the Madharis to abstain from participating would mean that the mission caused them to fail to secure an income. As they lived on very limited margins, this would cause starvation, according to Sandegren.[131]

In spite of different local practices, generally a Paraiyar man beat the larger drum, the *tandal*, to assemble people and give messages. This man was the *tandalkkaran*, who had this duty as a profession. A smaller tambourine, the *parai*, on the other hand, carried the message of a Goundar death and was played by Paraiyars in front of the house of the dead person. Old Selvam, a Paraiyar woman, relates how the men played continuously day and night until the body was cremated, while the Paraiyar women sang, praising the virtues of the dead, and wept.[132]

However, only a very few Paraiyar lived in Mandiripalayam. Here, the Madhari had three main duties of drum-beating: by the temple, at a Goundar wedding and at a Goundar death. On every occasion, they remained outside the temple and houses. But the Madhari informants declare that this was explained by the fact that the Paraiyar were too few. As discussed earlier, many members of the Paraiyar community in the district migrated to the estates for the greater part of the year. But in villages where the Paraiyar were strong enough to guard this right, the rule was that they beat the drums at the Goundars' houses.[133] This shows that caste and customary occupation did not go strictly hand in hand and that caste on the principled or regional level was not the definite dividing line for customary duties. The local situation and needs appear to have had priority over such principles.

To deal with death and unclean tasks was the duty of the Madhari. These duties were generally paid for, and therefore, in spite of the low status identified with them, were considered as a legitimate right to be guarded. The duty of removing dead animals and the right to the meat have been described earlier. Even if eating this meat was unthinkable for any member of the higher castes, it led to a celebration in the Madhari settlement.[134] But there was another obligation which is described only in the Lindberg material of 1967 and by the interviewed informants. No missionary document mentions the obligation of carrying death messages for the Goundar families to their relatives. It was still practised in 1995, even after telephones had been installed in many of the Goundars' homes. But it is unlikely that such a customary duty first appeared late in the twentieth century, in a time of expanding communication networks. It is more probable that the carrying of death messages had deep roots and it deserves to be mentioned in this context, in spite of the lack of sources dating from the early part of the century.

In the Lindberg material, informants describe how the Madhari men were recognised as soon as they came in sight of the village. With sticks in their hands for protection against the dogs, they approached one village after the other, and the sight of the men and their sticks left no uncertainty. They were coming with the news of a death in the Goundar community. In each village, they received two or three measures of *ragi* or *cholam* for their labour or two to three rupees each. The journey might have taken a few days and was an interruption in their regular work. Jacob, who at the time worked as an assistant to Staffan Lindberg, wrote in his diary that this made the men breathe 'the air of relief'.[135]

The call from the Goundar family to carry the news of death to their relatives was immediately obeyed.[136] When interviewed in 1996,

Jacob recalls that the *pannaiyal* of the family was the one entrusted to go with the message. He would know the Goundar family members, and they would recall him as the *pannaiyal* of their relative.[137] In Vavipalayam, an interview given in 1967 was twice interrupted when the interviewed person had to go with a death message. It was Israel, a sixty-year-old Madhari man, who abruptly left Jacob while answering questions. As shown in the Lindberg Census, Israel worked as an agricultural coolie, just like everyone else in the village. According to Lindberg's records, no *pannaiyal* worked in Vavipalayam. Assuming that the records are correct, Israel might have been asked to go as having been a former *pannaiyal* or because he was the headman of the Madhari village.[138]

But also here there are indications of different local practices. Jacob, who grew up in Karunagarapuri, witnessed this practice in the nearby village of Kondampatti. There the death messages were carried by the Paraiyar community.[139]

## MUTUAL, UNEVEN DEPENDENCE

To survive in the highlands, whether on the most basic level or as farmers asserting a powerful position in society, meant adjusting to some of the preconditions given and making use of the advantages possessed. For the majority of farming Goundars, family labour was sufficient, with some addition of casual labour during most of the year. For those who had only a small amount of land, income would be supplemented by labouring on other farmers' lands. But the availability of water was necessary for all who cultivated irrigated crops. Without a well, a farmer in the dry zone could grow only dry-land crops. But, in this region, approximately three-quarters of the land were owned by farmers possessing more than 10 acres and consequently capable of maintaining the expensive well irrigation. This made it possible for them to run their farms at a high level of efficiency by making investments in oxen and the *kavalai* equipment. But, more than that, they were also dependent on labourers to provide the *kavalai* with suitable leather bags. To ensure themselves a constant labour supply, they employed *pannaiyal* in numbers related to the size and the needs of the farm. This gave the leather-working Madhari a crucial role in agriculture and an advantage in relation to other agricultural labourers. But their central role was probably established much earlier than at the time of the agricultural expansion in the nineteenth century. As skilled leather-workers, they were likely to have been essential to the cattle-breeding, Goundar economy before the arrival of the British in Kongunad.

Also the Goundars had an advantage in agriculture as cultivators in relation to other cultivators. Even though there were other landowning castes in the central part of the district, they were generally outnumbered by the Goundars, or members of the Goundar community would own most of the land in the village. The Goundar community was also politically the most influential in rural Kongunad. Compared with one another, the Goundar and the Madhari were at the opposite ends of the scale. The Madhari were in no way able to match the Goundars' economic and social superiority, but both parties had key roles of their own in the agriculture of dry, central Kongunad.

These conclusions make Baker's position problematic. His statements, that the *pannaiyal* of Kongunad had different labour relations to the landowners than those of the *pannaiyal* of the wet-cultivation valley zones, and that the Kongunad *pannaiyal* worked and lived as extended family labour, is contradicted by the information given about the Madhari *pannaiyal.* All the sources that speak of the social position of the Madhari in Kongunad describe a people of low status, despised and disregarded, a stigmatised group. At the same time, as discussed earlier, everything points to this group being a major part of the agricultural labour force and the bulk of the labourers being under bonds as *pannaiyal* in the dry area.[140]

Reading Gopalaratnam's and Ganesamurthi's studies in this perspective confirms the importance of the Madhari in agriculture and at the same time shows their distance to the Goundar and the rest of the population in the main village.

Baker's description of the labour relations in Kongunad covers a development over a period of 80 years. On the basis of material from 1887 to 1947, he makes an analysis of the relations from the mid-nineteenth century to the 1930s. He relates that relations were good, even intimate, and that payment could be compared to a family share reaching a high level, compared with the rest of the Presidency, during the depression of the 1930s. But this intimate relationship has no similarities with the Goundar–Madhari relationship, as revealed in the material discussed earlier. Even assuming that this familiar relationship existed in 1850 and thereafter disappeared, it is most unlikely that such a relationship would not have left any traces in later sources of the 1920s or the 1930s or in memories or stories related by Madharis or Goundars in the region.

Around the turn of the century, there was a period when labour scarcity had become a problem in agricultural expansion. This happened concurrently with the earlier change to growing more cotton on the lands and further labour migration to the estates, and somewhat later to the urban industries. It had created a situation in which increasing numbers of labourers were kept under economic or extra-economic ties, often in combination. Most likely, the advances to *pannaiyal* served to secure labour for the lender, and repayment was in reality impossible. In this way, the lender would ensure that the indebted labourer remained in the vicinity as long as he owed money.

Though uneven in status and on different economic levels, the dependence for survival was mutual. Within what earlier has been termed *urimai*, the results imply that the labourer was assured of his share of the harvest and of property that was rightfully his, according to local customary rules. But it was his only as long as he worked for the Goundar landowner. *Urimai* can from this point of view be understood as an expression of the local, economic power relations, as it implied control, or lack of control, over economic resources, and provided forms for regulating and maintaining the power relations between owner and labourer. At the same time, *urimai* also carried social duties or services to the local society that did not relate to the material production. The playing of drums in front of religious processions was one such service expected from the Madhari or Paraiyar. Living within the realm of the *urimai* of local society would therefore mean living as an acknowledged member of that society and having security of livelihood. The complexity that can be revealed within the *urimai* relationship, carrying both social, economic and religious rights and duties, indicates a history before the further expansion of *pannaiyal* contracts in the late nineteenth century. It is not necessarily explained by an agricultural economy, but would also be logical in an economy based on cattle.

To work the land by *pannaiyal* meant keeping a labourer attached to the farm, identified with the *pannai* and always available. His geographical mobility was controlled, and he was not allowed to leave the village without permission. Although he was to that extent completely dependent on decisions at the landowner's discretion, the *pannaiyal* had rights and would not be rejected if he demanded those rights as long as he had kept his part of the agreement. Formally, the agreement was between individuals, between the farm labourer and the farm owner. But the *pannaiyal's* family members would give priority to work for the same landowner, and the money owed by the *pannaiyal* was at his death taken over by his son and ensured the transfer of bondage from father to son.

Within the village and between all castes, social divisions were manifest at a distance. Moving in daily life—expressing oneself, dressing and eating—was not possible without confirming one's social position in the local hierarchy. The lower the caste, the more restrictions in space. To keep the social distance was a very visible and concrete matter. An inappropriate touch by an untouchable was an insult and a shame to a member of the higher caste. The houses, and to some extent also the streets, of the high castes were protected from intrusion. Behaviour and speech marked subordination or superiority by manners and grammar when addressing a person considered lower or higher than oneself. A remarkable exception from the rule of distance appeared in the field work, in which Goundar and Madhari carried out part of the work side by side.

Participation in the religious ceremonies of the village expressed social rank. Each caste, understood as local *jati*, had specific tasks and obligations. The general rule of the highlands seems to have been that separate services for local society were assigned to particular castes; Madharis and Paraiyar held in general certain different obligations and rights. But, as in the case of Mandiripalayam, the principal caste-lines were crossed. The Goundars of Mandiripalayam did not go to the nearest village to ask the Paraiyar living there to beat the drums at the death of a family member. As very few Paraiyar lived in the village, the right to play the drums had instead passed to the Madhari. In this way, customary obligations had a relation to caste in the most local sense. But, generalising for a larger region, it is more appropriate to speak of obligations related to social hierarchical divisions expressing social power relations. This is not intended to reduce the understanding of religious life and rites to mere reflections of the social structure. The religious life and culture, myths and meanings, were an essential part of life in the village. That is not questioned here. But ceremonies, rites and behaviour were not part of an autonomous arena, existing, with its own logic, separately from the social and economic divisions in the village. It was rather integrated into the complex, socio-economic relations of the villagers, and here the focus is on those relations.

When they are described in this way, the agrarian relations of the Kongunad dry zone may appear to have been closed, immobile and unchangeable. All the parties were controlled and interdependent, going into a clinch in which no one dared to move, fearing to lose whatever positions they held. But the Paraiyar contradict this view. They came and went in the villages, as they generally worked for most of the year on the estates in the mountains. Though this labour could make them dependent on labour contractors, it provided them with opportunities to organise, earn more money and improve their economic situation in the home villages. The Paraiyar had in this way found an exit through which they could escape from their confinement in the socio-economic structure of the local area. They could turn down agricultural labour in their home villages, as they had alternatives, and consequently they were not regarded as only agricultural labourers, but also as having other occupations. The socio-economic structures of the villages were not unchangeable; there were apparently options for mobility. But the Paraiyar were at the same time not indispensable for agriculture. Indeed, they were needed as casual labourers during the harvest, when the work load increased. But throughout the year it was not they, but the Madhari whom the landowning Goundar depended on. The Madhari labourers were in this way an essential part of the system and found security for themselves within it. But this total dependence on one caste as the most important among the labour force was a vulnerable relationship. Further into the twentieth century, as we shall see in the following chapters, industrialisation and its consequences for agriculture, the severe drought, and kinship-based mobilisation among the labourers had great effects on the Goundar–Madhari relationship. The ability to uphold their domination over the labourers was the strength, as well as the Achilles' heel, of the Goundar. Any mobility among the Madhari would mean a threat to the Goundars' control over the labourers.

## NOTES

1 According to the Census of 1921, the last to give population statistics for both Goundar (one of the major Vellalar communities) and Madhari (Chakkiliyar), the Vellalar community numbered 694,906 persons and the Chakkiliyar 206,162. Of the total population in the Coimbatore district, the Chakkiliyar community constituted 9.3 per cent, and the Vellalar 31.3 per cent. Using population statistics involves problems and the information has to be treated carefully. In this connection it may be

noted that the Goundar community accounted for the major portion of, but not the entire, Vellalar community. Census of India 1921, Vol. XIII, Madras II, Tables II and XIII.

2 Over a longer period, Ludden observes how service occupations (washermen, barbers, shepherds, etc.) in Tiruneveli have been open to socially downwardly-mobile castes. Ludden 1989 (1985), p. 64.

3 CSMA, MBa 1931:224, p. 14; CSMA, MDc 2.6.1945, to the Mission Director from Knutsson; CSMA, MBa 1949:489, 1948, p. 2; CSMA, FaR, A IV:4, Jothipuram 1956, p. 3.

4 From a quotation from a report by the Collector of Coimbatore. Gardner Cassels 1988, p. 73.

5 Patel 1952, pp. 32 and 63.

6 Kumar 1992:1, pp. 186-8.

7 Kumar 1992:1, pp. 41-3; Kumar 1992:2, pp. 80-1, 88, 104.

8 Hjejle 1967, pp. 97-8.

9 Gardner Cassels 1988, pp. 61-3, 85.

10 Hjejle 1967, pp. 86-7.

11 Hjejle 1967, pp. 79 and 83.

12 Gough's theoretical position may seem somewhat square-shaped. However, this may be explained by the situation in which the argument was presented. The mode of production debate was still heated. It had passed through different themes, and Gough's argument was a contribution to an ongoing discussion about how to characterise the existing mode of production in colonial India. Gough argued against the existence of a specific colonial mode of production. See further Thorner 1982, 11 Dec., p. 1999.

13 Gough 1978, pp. 26-7; Gough 1981, pp. 105-37.

14 Washbrook 1993, pp. 74-6.

15 Washbrook 1993, pp. 82-5.

16 Washbrook 1993, pp. 74-5.

17 Hjejle 1967, p. 103, Table 1.

18 Gough 1978, p. 35; Hjejle 1967, pp. 100, 102-6.

19 According to Gough, the conditions of untouchable labourers under debt bondage changed only a little from those of *adimai* throughout British rule. Gough 1978, pp. 35, 42.

20 Gough 1978, p. 106.

21 Evans 1990, pp. 49-50.

22 Haruka Yanagisawa argues for the practice of using advances in order to tie labourers into servitude in the Tiruchirapalli district during the nineteenth century. Thus, the mirasidar landowners aimed at securing labourers at wages below market rates. The Acts of 1843 and 1861 had very limited effects to strengthen the position of the labourers, argues Yanagisawa. It was rather the Act of 1861 in combination with increasing opportunities to migrate to foreign estates that worked to improve their

economic position. Yanagisawa 1996, pp. 36-9, 201-2.

23 Hjejle 1967, pp. 100-1; Kumar 1992:1, pp. 41-3, 75.

24 Kumar 1992:1, p. 75.

25 Washbrook 1993, pp. 77-8.

26 Baker 1984, pp. 93-7. Dharma Kumar notes that within the Coimbatore region there were exceptionally few 'slaves'. See, for example, Kumar 1992:1, p. 43.

27 Baker 1984, pp. 57, 325; Hjejle 1967, p. 86, relying on Buchanan, 1807; Kumar 1992:1, p. 19. Kumar also points to the fact that the Coimbatore district had fewer but very large Mirasi holdings than the rest of the Tamil land. Kumar, 1992:1, pp. 19-20.

28 According to Washbrook, labourers could gain from conflicts that broke out between rulers, merchants and labour controllers (landlords, 'head' artisans, etc.). For example, the land that belonged to the privileged Nayars and Nambudiris was taken by Tipu Sultan, the Emperor of Mysore, and given to the 'slaves' and labourers of Nayars and Nambudiris, in order to break the landlords' dominance. Washbrook 1993, p. 81; Hjejle 1967, pp. 78-9.

29 Gardner Cassels 1988, p. 73, quoting A. D. Campbell, who paraphrased the Collectors' answers, in Board of Revenue Proceedings, 25.11.1819, *Parliamentary Papers* 1828, XXIV (125), op. cit., p. 899.

30 The sharecropper, called 'Pungal' (*pangan*, one who shares), was advanced cattle, implements, seed, money or grain, and a house by the wealthy landowner. He cultivated the land and earned a share of the harvest. Buchanan 1807, pp. 217, 315, 320. The highlands, including the areas that eventually came to be the Salem and Coimbatore districts, were gradually conquered by the British between 1792 and 1799. Wadhawa 1973, Vol. 1, pp. 496-7.

31 David Washbrook discusses the system of advance payments in different trades as a share of the costs of production to producers and workers in late eighteenth-century south India. Washbrook 1993, pp. 74-5.

32 Mukherjee 1962, p. 45, referring to the Board's Consultations, Vol. 707, p. 1816.

33 Munroe was assigned as assistant to Alexander Read and answered for the settlement of the northern section of the Ceded Districts in the 1790s. Also Christopher Baker discusses the cattle-breeding in Kongunad. He prefers to see cattle-raising in the late nineteenth century as complementary to intensive cultivation but, at the same time, shows the importance of cattle and how cattle were exported through local markets as far as the valley regions in eastern Tamilnad. Likewise, when grazing-lands were taxed under the ryotwari system, the *patta* land increased by 50 per cent between 1855 and 1875 in Dharapuram taluk in the south-east of Kongunad. Kumar 1992:1, p. 21, calculations based on G. R. Gleig, *The Life of Sir Thomas Munroe*; Baker 1984, p. 203.

34 What Read invented, and later abandoned, was adopted by Thomas

Munroe and implemented on a large scale in the Madras Presidency after Munroe became the Governor of Madras. IOR, Baramahal Records, 10.8.1794, § 1; Bayly 1990 (1988), p. 89; Mukherjee 1962, p. 16 and Chapter 12; Spear 1992 (1958), p. 637.

35 Kumar 1992:1, p. 20.

36 The number of cattle held may be compared with the size of the population in Coimbatore district. According to the 1881 Census, the population of the district amounted to 1,657,690 persons. The estimate of the number of wells may have been too high. In Cox 1933, the figure for 1897 is 65,461 wells. Cox 1933, p. 171. Nicholson, 1887, pp. 54-5, 243, n. 46; Census of India 1881, Part I, Table II.

37 Baker 1984, p. 209.

38 Baker 1984, pp. 209-10.

39 For an explanation of the ryotwari land-revenue system, see Ludden 1989 (1985), p. 104.

40 Nicholson, 1887, pp. 166, 179-80, 270.

41 Yanagisawa has compiled data about the extent of land assigned to the Adi Dravida. In this connection, Adi Dravida refers to all untouchable castes. On the basis of statistics from the Public Works and Labour Department 1931, he estimates the Adi Dravida-share of the total number of *pattas* held in the Coimbatore district to 0.4 per cent. Yanagisawa 1996, p. 216; DRCC, Re-survey and Re-settlement Registers 1912, Palladam taluk; Evans 1990, p. 48.

The re-settlement of land was the basis for revenue collections, which it was decided in 1855 should be conducted in all districts every thirty years. However, the system was heavily criticised and was abandoned in 1937. The general figures for the division of land might not have changed dramatically over that period of time. However, for the individual tax-payer, the revenue collection might have turned out extremely unjust. The 1912 Re-survey and Re-settlement was the second and last carried out in the Coimbatore district. As with all land records, the details of the Re-survey of 1912 have to be regarded with some caution, though there is no reason not to rely on the general figures. Kumar 1984 (1982), pp. 229-30; Report of the Land Revenue Enquiry Committee 1937, p. 12.

42 Baker 1984, pp. 209-10, referring to Gopalaratnam 1931, p. 523, and Ganesamurthi 1935, p. 277.

43 *Kasbah* is the geographical administrative unit next to *taluk*. A certain number of *kasbahs* make one *taluk*, and a certain number of *taluks* constitutes one district.

44 The predominant water-lifting technique was the *kavalai*, in which two bullocks pulled water out of the well and let it discharge into the irrigation canals. Gopalaratnam 1931, pp. 523-4; Ganesamurthi 1935, pp. 271-2, 277; Thurston 1909, Vol. 2, p. 5.

45 Brenda Beck has written extensively about Tamil culture, and in particular

about the Kongunad region. She traces the arrival of the Goundar community in the highlands to the Chola period between the tenth and the twelfth centuries. In a contribution to *Perspectives on a Regional Culture*, entitled 'Centres and Boundaries of a Regional Caste System—A Study of Coimbatore and Neighbouring Districts', Beck presents a study of the Goundar caste. Beck 1972, pp. 39 and 42; Beck 1979, pp. 54-92, see particularly p. 86.

46 Beck 1972, see particularly pp. 31-40.

47 Mandiripalayam 2.2.1995, interview.

48 When asked 'Why are you Madhari?' and 'Who are the Madhari?', the Madhari women of Mandiripalayam related a tale of their past. In the tale, the Madhari were said to have been the guards of a princess, the daughter of Tirumalai Nayak, at the ceremony when she reached puberty. The way the ceremony was described reflected closely the ceremonies practised among the Madhari when their daughters reached puberty. See Ulrici Collection, (1) The Pioneer Church, (3) [untitled document]; Mandiripalayam 31.1.1995, interview. See also Chapter 5.

49 The figure given by Cox is 28 per cent. Cox 1933, p. 148.

50 Ganesamurthi 1935, p. 277; Cox 1933, p. 148.

51 Baker 1984, pp. 209-10.

52 Semmipalayam 1.2.1995, interviews, Narayana Goundar and Sivasubramaniyan Goundar.

53 Mandiripalayam 31.1.1995, interview, Abraham.

54 Ganesamurthi 1935, pp. 270-1, 277. See also Cederlöf 1997 (forthcoming).

55 Chuckler, chuckli = Chakkiliyar or Madhari, *mbote* = water-lift. Gopalaratnam 1931, p. 523.

56 Ganesamurthi 1935, p. 277

57 Semmipalayam 1.2.1995, interview; Mandiripalayam 2.2.1995, interview. Both Narayana Goundar and Ramasamy Goundar are referring to the time before Independence and the great drought. The limit of 10 acres for employing a *pannaiyal* has been given in several interviews. See, for example, Arulpuram 29.1.1995, interview. The *Ur*-Goundar was a village elder and leader.

58 In Thongattipalayam one *patta* holder is registered for 517.6 acres, while in Appanayakanpatti a holder is registered for 531.68 acres. The total acreage of *patta* land in the selected area was 84,319.88, of which 65,111.71 acres were cultivated by farmers holding more than 10 acres each.

DRCC, Re-survey and Re-settlement Registers, Palladam taluk, 1912, a selection of the following *kasbahs*: Vadugapalayam, Kasbah Ayyampalayam, Pongalur, Thongattipalayam, South Avanashipalayam, Vadamalaipalayam, Kamanaickampalayam Krishnapuram, Kettanur, Elavanthi, Velarasikallipalyam, Palladam, Naranapuram, Madapur, Sembipalayam, Ichipatti, Kodangiripalayam, Peruvayi, Karadibavi,

Mallekavundanpalayam, Velampalayam, Anuppapathi, Puliyampatti, Jalakkarisal, Appanayakanpatti and Kangayampalayam.

59 DRCC, Re-survey and Re-settlement Registers, Palladam taluk, 1912, a selection of the following *kasbahs*: Vadugapalayam, Kasbah Ayyampalayam, Pongalur, Kettanur, Elavanthi, Velarasikallipalyam, Palladam, Naranapuram, Madapur, Sembipalayam, Ichipatti, Kodangiripalayam, Peruvayi, Karadibavi, Mallekavundanpalayam, Velamplayam, Anuppapathi, and Puliyampatti.

60 The first Madhari conversions are reported in 1931. CSMA, MBa 1932:146, p. 3.

61 Once the India secretary replied to a contribution from a missionary to the Church of Sweden Mission year-book that the article was too detailed for an ordinary reader to grasp and referred in particular to the names of castes mentioned. The article was thereafter revised. CSMA, Paul Sandegren Collection, Vol. 1, 1920-70, no date (most likely in the 1960s), Anders Andrén to Paul Sandegren.

62 The general position of the Swedish missionaries was well summed up by Sigfrid Estborn in *Our Village Christians* (1959), where the Madhari were described as dependants and slaves of the Goundar and it was said that they lacked the urge for mobility. Estborn 1959, p. 37.

63 The annual reports for the years of 1944 and 1954 are not available in the CSM archives. The original manuscripts for all annual reports of 1949, except 'CSM in India', were mislaid and never found during the year in which they were written.

64 CSMA, FaR, A IV:4, Jothipuram 1956.

65 Tamil Lexicon, p. 442.

66 See, for example, Arulpuram 26.1.1995, interview. About eating the flesh of cattle that had died of natural causes, see also Thurston 1909, Vol. 6, pp. 116-17.

67 Beck 1972, pp. 42-9, Table 1.2, pp. 44-7. Interview given in 1966.

68 There is an ongoing discussion about whether right- and left-hand castes also indicated social status, left equal to low and bad, right equal to high and good. Beck's Table 1.2 would suggest that this is either a late interpretation or that it does not apply to the south Indian situation. Beck 1972, p. 47. See also Niels Brimnes (1995), who discusses the many severe conflicts between right- and left-hand divisions of castes, and the gradual disappearance of these conflicts between the seventeenth and nineteenth centuries.

69 Duraiswami 1934, pp. 137-43.

70 Jacob 1996, interview.

71 See Beck 1972, p. 49, on land rights.

72 The skills of leather-workers were not replaceable. Abraham of Mandiripalayam, 102 years old, describes how hides were prepared: 'The new skin of a buffalo is put in lime-water for 34 days. If it is properly

soaked, it will be very thick after the 34th day. All the small things fall off, and it can be scraped by a tanning knife and become very soft and flexible. It will then be soaked in water and again scraped. *Aavarai* [a local plant] will be crushed and a lot of water added, so that it becomes a juice in which the leather will be soaked for another 8 days. Oil (*kadukka*) and wheat flour is then added to the skin. Thereafter, it is ready for making *pari* or *seruppu*.' Mandiripalayam 31.1.1995, interview.

In a historical account of the Kongu country from the earliest times to the arrival of the British, M. Arokiaswamy emphasises the need of 'leather-workmanship' in agriculture. He dates the arrival of the Madhari community in the region to the Vijayanagara period, in the fourteenth to sixteenth centuries. Arokiaswamy 1956, pp. 342-3.

73 Beck 1972, p. 42 and n. 62.

74 Nicholson 1887, p. 245, n. 46 (beginning on p. 243), and p. 57; Cox, 1933, p. 164; Royal Commission of Agriculture in India 1927, pp. 548, 561-2.

75 CSMA, MBa 1931:224, p. 14.

76 Tiruppur Baptismal Records.

77 CSMA, MBa 1931:224, p. 14.

78 CSMA, MBa 1941:362, p. 3; CSMA, MBa 1948:508, p. 5.

79 Ernst Heuman, missionary for the Church of Sweden Mission, 1886 (Santal), 1903 (India), Bishop of Tamil Evangelical Lutheran Church, 1921-6. Heuman was the first bishop of the TELC. See also CSMA, MBa 1920:214, p. 6.

80 CSMA, MBa 1921:206, p. 3.

81 Hjejle 1967, p. 100; Kumar 1992:1, p. 75; Athreya, Djurfeldt and Lindberg 1990, pp. 133, 241.

82 Ganesamurthi 1935, pp. 270-1.

83 Semmipalayam 1995, interview, Sivasubramaniyan Goundar; Jacob 1996, interview.

84 See, for example, Mandiripalayam 31.1.1995, interview; Jacob 1996, interview.

85 A report submitted by G. Stephen to Sigrid Hård af Segerstad at her request. Hård af Segerstad 1967, p. 16. This way of denoting wages as charity was not unique to the Coimbatore district. Another term for payment is *siraipanam*. The information comes from Commissioner Gray in a study of the Chingleput district in 1918. This district had several Mirasi estates employing *padiyal*, at the time still known as *adimaiyal*. The 'slave-money' was given together with payment in kind. But this payment did not need to be in cash, also cloth given at festivals could be regarded as *siraipanam*. One of the thirty-two acts of charity according to the *Sastras* was to give food to prisoners, or to give *siraisoru*—prisoner- or slave-rice. This was a moral duty. But the term *siraipanam* has not been found in any of the sources of Kongunad. Hjejle 1967, p. 123.

86 Jacob 1996, interview.

87 Durai 1992, interview.

88 CSMA, FaR, A IV:4, Jothipuram 1956; Arulpuram 1995, interview; Jacob 1996, interview.

89 Jacob 1996, interview; Ganesamurthi 1935, pp. 270-1, 277; Duraiswami 1934, p. 137.

90 In Semmipalayam, west of Palladam, the *pannaiyal's* family members would come for the harvest. At that time, *karudu*, measured as one or two baskets of the crop harvested, was given as wages for full-time work. Semmipalayam 1995, interview, Sivasubramaniyan Goundar. I am grateful to A. Veluppillai, N. Ganesan and S. Amirthalingam for tracing the term *karudu* in the Coimbatore dialect of Tamil.

91 Lindberg Collection, Field Notes, Vol. 1, p. 56, an interview carried out by G. Kasturi in Veerapandi. Linguistically, the term may derive from the Sanskrit word *devasa*, meaning 'daily' or 'belonging to the day'.

92 Mandiripalayam 31.1.1995, interview; Uppilipalayam 29.1.1995, interview; Semmipalayam 1.2.1995, interview; Arulpuram 26.1.1995, interview. One bag was equal to one *marakkal*, or approx. 4-5 kg.

93 Problems of giving regular education to Madhari children were often explained by their long working hours. CSMA, Unsorted documents, 'CSM in India' 1942.

94 Lindberg Collection, Staffan Lindberg Field Diary, Vol. 2, p. 29, Vavipalayam 21.6.1967.

95 Uppilipalayam 29.1.1995, interview; Jacob 1996, interview.

96 Arulpuram 26.1.1995, interview.

97 CSMA, Unsorted documents, 'CSM in India' 1938, p. 20; CSMA, MBa 1941:362, p. 3.

98 CSMA, Unsorted documents, 'CSM in India' 1938, p. 20.

99 Ganesamurthi 1935, p. 275; Arulpuram 29.1.1995, interview; Ulrici 1993, interview.

100 Not only their material needs were provided for. When, for example, the Madharis lacked an animal for an offering ceremony, it could be provided by the Goundars. In Kulathupalayam, celebrations for the goddess Pattatharasi were held when the Madharis could afford it. An old woman in 1967 remembers a festival when she was 18 years old. At the ceremony, a sheep was offered to the goddess and was paid for by a collection in the Madhari village. But when they found that they could not afford a sheep, they were given one by a Goundar. Lindberg Collection, Field Notes, Vol. 2, p. 13.

101 Beck 1972, pp. 58-9, Table 1.3.

102 The missionary Anna Irbe reports that not only caste-people had doubts and hesitated to send their children to a school to which Paraiyars went. The Sakkilis (i.e. Madharis) also had doubts, 'although our Paraias are by far cleaner than the Sakkilis'. A few years later, Irbe reported that

Madhari and Paraiyar children coming from the same village could not stay in the same boarding school, as they regarded each other with mutual contempt. Mixing children of the two castes from different villages, children who did not know each other, was, on the other hand, possible. This unfriendly relationship was confirmed in all interviews given in the area in 1995. CSMA, MBa 1936:198; CSMA, MBa 1938:449.

103 MMS, Report of the Trichinopoly Mass Movement Commission 1935, pp. 38-9.

104 Ulrici 1993, interview; CSMA, MBa 1956:155/56, p. 7. Manelaroo estate was situated in Cochin pastorate, to which congregation members from Palladam and Dharapuram pastorates had migrated.

105 CSMA, MBa 1947:393, pp. 1-2. See also CSMA, MBa 1941:362, p. 37.

106 The terms *maistri* or *kangani* were used interchangeably.

107 Evans 1990, pp. 49-50, 56.

108 Evans 1990, pp. 45, 56.

109 According to the Royal Commission on Labour in India in evidence given by five members of the United Planters' Association of South India, the *maistri* had sub-suppliers, often family members, who brought 15-20 labourers each to the *maistri*. A common number of the total number of labourers brought by the *maistri* to the estate was around 100. All labourers worked under contract, and the agreements between the planters and the *maistris* were oral. Royal Commission on Labour in India 1931, p. 196; Mandiripalayam 31.1.1995, interview; Uppilipalayam 29.1.1995, interview; Semmipalayam 1995, interview, Narayana Goundar.

110 William Arthur Sandford, missionary for the Wesleyan Methodist Missionary Society 1899, 1902 (India). MMS, Report of the Trichinopoly Mass Movement Commission 1935, pp. 38-9.

111 The only estimate in the CSM documents of the number of Lutheran Christians living on the estates was given in 1936, when Johannes Sandegren wrote that between 800-1,000 of them worked on the Valparai hill-estates. CSMA, MBa 1936:146, p. 5. The Tamil Evangelical Lutheran Church was inaugurated in 1919. Diehl 1974, p. 17.

112 MMS, Report of the Trichinopoly Mass Movement Commission 1935, p. 41.

113 W. J. Nobel, missionary for the Wesleyan Methodist Missionary Society 1900 (Ceylon), 1922 (London, Mission Secretary), Duncan G. M. Leith, missionary for the Wesleyan Methodist Missionary Society 1901 (India).

114 MMS, South India Provincial Synod 1931, p. 112; MMS, Report of the Secretarial Visit to Burma, India and Ceylon 1937, p. 91.

115 The Foreign Field 1927, July, p. 235. In the Tanjore region, the untouchable caste population was mainly constituted by two major castes, the Paraiyar and the Pallar. Most of these people worked as agricultural labourers in permanent or casual settlements. The difference of mobility and social standard between Paraiyar in the highlands and

in the lowland valleys was observed also by the Lutheran missionaries. In contrast to the Tanjavur area, the Paraiyar in the highlands were considered 'almost independent'. See also Baker 1984, p. 87; Gough 1989, pp. 239-42, 365-7.

116 In his study on Tamilnad having the Tiruchirapalli district as a major focus, Yanagisawa describes an increasing labour mobility from the 1920s to the 1940s. From initially being expressed by strikes, he concludes that labour resistance was stronger and better organised in the 1940s. Yanagisawa 1996, pp. 104.

117 In his village-based study on economic transition in Tanjavur district, J. Jeyaranjan observes that the Acts aimed to protect the rights of the *pannaiyal* did not include holdings of a smaller size than 6.67 acres. In the case of Iluppakkorai, nearly 80 per cent of the landed households owned less than five acres, and those owning more often did not keep them under one single name. As a result, they were not covered by the Act. Jeyaranjan 1993, p. 77; Baker 1984, pp. 196-9; Gough 1978, p. 44; History of Land Revenue Settlement and Abolition of Intermediary Tenures in Tamil Nadu 1976, p. 225.

118 Semmipalayam 1995, interview, Sivasubramaniyan Goundar; Arulpuram 29.1.1995, interview.

119 Semmipalayam 1995, interview, Sivasubramaniyan Goundar.

120 *Cheri* meaning village, *valavu* meaning house. DRCC, Re-Survey and Re-Settlement Registers, Palladam Taluk, 1912; see, for example, Vadugapalayam and Velarasikallipalayam. In the CSM documents, the segregated settlements for Scheduled Castes are such an evident fact that they are taken for granted and seldom discussed. The *cheris* were simply referred to as the 'outcaste's village'. SKMT 1951:18, p. 236. See also Ganesamurthi 1935, p. 275.

121 The CSM mission workers were the Revs. Bertil Envall and A.S. Muttiah. Mandiripalayam 1995, interviews, Subban James in the Madhari settlement and Ramasamy Goundar, the *Ur*-Goundar.

122 Mandiripalayam 2.2.1995, interview, Ramasamy Goundar; Jacob 1996, interview; Durai 1992, interview; Envall 1995, interview.

123 Durai 1992, interview.

124 Mandiripalayam 31.1.1995, interview, Abraham.

125 Samuel 1992, interview; Mandiripalayam 31.1.1995, interview.

126 Thurston 1909, Vol. VI, pp. 77-8. They are also known as Adi-dravida, the original Dravidians, by the missionaries in the Coimbatore district.

127 Sometimes the drums were exchanged for the blowing of shells, as in the case of the Paraiyar sub-group Sangu, meaning 'conch shell'. However, regionally, other castes carried out the same tasks. Thurston 1909, p. 81; Lillie 1956, p. v.

128 CSMA, FaR, A IV:4, Jothipuram 1956; Jacob 1996, interview.

129 CSMA, MBa 1946:357, p. 1.

130 Johannes Sandegren, missionary for the Church of Sweden Mission 1907, Bishop of the Tamil Evangelical Lutheran Church 1934-56.
131 CSMA, MBa 1936:146. See also Chapter 5.
132 Arulpuram 26.1.1995, interviews, Natarajan Goundar, Rajamanickam and Jeyaraj; Kuppandampalayam 1995, interview, Selvam.
133 Mandiripalayam 31.1.1995, interview, and 2.2.1995, interview.
134 Andrén 1993, interview; Lindberg Collection, Field Notes, p. 55, an interview by G. Kasturi with K. Subramaniyan, a Devangu Chettiar from Veerapandi.
135 Lindberg Collection, E. Jacob Field Diary, Vavipalayam 16.5.1967, Lindberg Collection, Lindberg Field Notes, Vol. 1, pp. 83 and 88, Kupandanpalayam and Veerapandi, in B. Sankaran's handwriting. See also Arulpuram 26.1.1995, interview.
136 Lindberg Collection, E. Jacob Field Diary, Vavipalayam, 16.5.1967 and 18.5.1967.
137 Jacob 1996, interview.
138 Lindberg Collection, Census, p. 15; Lindberg Collection, E. Jacob Field Diary, Vavipalayam 16.5.1967 and 18.5.1967.
139 Jacob 1996, interview.
140 Baker 1984, pp. 209-10.

# CHAPTER 3

# Development and Bondage

The primary processing of cotton developed rapidly during the first few decades of the twentieth century. Factories were erected, and Tiruppur and Coimbatore grew into busy commercial centres. From the villages, agricultural labourers—in particular, the landless labourers—joined the expanding industrial labour force. But these labourers did not come from all sections of the agricultural work force. The results of this study rather indicate that the Madhari were among those who never became integrated into urban industrial enterprises during the earlier part of the period studied. As a rule, they did not leave their home villages to become industrial labourers. Contrary to what might have been expected, the industrialisation of the cotton production in the region did not bring about any immediate reasons why the Madhari should break with the customary bonds of the agrarian labour relations by which they were tied or provide any opportunities to do so.

Coimbatore was one of the earliest districts in the Presidency to be industrialised and the textile sector came to have strong links with the rural economy. Therefore, in studying the transformation of the relationship between farmers and agricultural labourers, it is essential also to examine this relationship in the light of industrialisation.

The following discussion will be divided into two major sections. During the whole period, industrialisation in the district had consequences for the relationship between Goundar and Madhari. But with regard to the development of this rural relationship, the process of industrialisation took an important turn from the mid-1930s to the mid-1940s. The effects until then were fundamentally different from those that began to appear after the depression and the introduction of industrial goods in agriculture. Although the Madhari remained as agricultural labourers throughout the whole period, the labour relations that a large number of them formed a part of underwent important alterations. The informal relationship between the two also came to be changed during this later period. By a very slow process, rights that the Madhari had in local society appear over time to have become more dependent on the *pannaiyal* form of labour than on the Madhari as a community and, as such, also part of the village community as a whole. From the late 1950s onwards, the *pannaiyal* form of labour also appears to have become less frequent on the farms.

As a consequence, in dealing with industrialisation in the district, it is not the process, as such, that will be discussed. Initially, some brief comments need to be made. However, as the major focus here is on how the relationship between the rural agricultural labourers and the major landowners was affected by industrialisation, this chapter is not intended to cover the whole of the industrialisation process. It will take up only whatever in the process may provide explanations of the relationship between the Madhari and the Goundar. The selection of material and the questions taken up derive from this major research problem.

From outside the region, the demand for the products of the district was rising at the turn of the century. Growing opportunities for the farmers to make profits were supported by the Government, and enterprising groups in the district responded by expanding the cultivation of cash-crops and investing money in factories. Cattle were still of great economic significance, but land and its produce had steadily increased in importance over the last fifty years. The major farmers of Kongunad were deeply involved in economic growth. By changing their cropping pattern and investing in industrial processing units, they responded to the rising demands for cotton. Instead of exporting their produce to be refined outside the district, they now built mills, and the basis for the textile industry was developed. Cotton production in itself may be suspected to have acted as an incitement to invest in ginneries, as ginning the cotton would substantially reduce its volume and make its transport to the market cheaper. At the same time, having built a ginnery, the farmer would be further inclined to grow more cotton.

Tiruppur soon became the centre for cotton export, Pollachi was the great cattle- and leather-market in the district, and an increasing number of cotton-ginning and -pressing mills had been established in Coimbatore and Tiruppur. Communications and transport were being improved to reach the tea estates in Anamalai and Nilgiri.[1]

As a consequence of the rural economic expansion and the changed form of production, the results of this study give reasons to conclude that labour became a resource to be guarded. The expansion was based on extended cash-crop cultivation and necessitated the cultivation of more land under irrigation. This could not have been realised unless the farmers were assured of a sufficiently large labour force. Competition for labour made securing permanent labourers for the farms increasingly important. And, as will be argued, side by side with the growing industrial enterprise and the extended commercialisation of agriculture, agricultural labourers remained under extra-economic ties. The form that industrialisation came to take during the years preceding the depression did not present any obstacles to but rather allowed and even necessitated the employment of bonded labourers in agriculture. As was shown in Chapter 2, the numbers of *pannaiyal* increased.

But it was not just any labourers that were required. An agricultural expansion dependent on well irrigation put the leather-workers in a central position. Thus, the initial period of industrialisation, until the 1930s, served to confirm further the position of the Madhari as agricultural labourers, working in close dependence on the farmers.

To keep permanent labourers entailed costs for the farmer throughout the year. Casual labourers may have received higher wages for the particular task that was to be done, but in order to carry the costs of a permanent labourer and to be able to make full use of his capacity, the economy of the farm needed to be of a certain size. One of the physical preconditions for keeping *pannaiyal* was therefore the scale of cultivation. The *pannai* system would not have worked in a situation in which the land was cultivated by numerous, individual, small farmers. Chapter 2 showed that most of the land was managed in the form of large farms in the early twentieth century. This uneven distribution of land was further emphasised by the effects of growing rural indebtedness during the following decades.

The *pannai* system seems also to have been functioning well when the wealthy farmers invested in industrial processing units from the 1920s onwards. The fact that farmers became involved in industrial enterprises does not appear to have resulted in a transfer of *pannaiyal* from agriculture to industrial labour. From the results of this study, there is no reason to think that the transfer of rural surpluses into industrial investments uprooted the *pannaiyal* form of labour.

At times, the legal side of *pannaiyal* has been emphasized, while the informal ties have been overlooked or denied. It has been argued that *pannaiyal* was nothing but a form of indentured labour. The fact that labourers were prevented from leaving the villages was, according to this position, not caused by the labour contract itself, but by the financial ties of indebtedness. The combination of one-year contracts and debts served to keep the labourers available to the farmers. The conclusion follows that labour was controlled by formal rules. But the results of this study that were partly presented in Chapter 2, suggesting that labour was locally controlled and performed within the context of customary law and informal rules, have been further confirmed when research has been done on the period up to the middle of the present century. As a formal settlement, *pannaiyal* was a form of contract labour working on one-year terms. But the debts that kept labourers resident do not appear to have been a form of lending, irrespective of the labour contract. Also for this later period, the results suggest that they were advance payments from the *pannaiyal's* remuneration and therefore a part of the *pannaiyal* agreement. Consequently, it can be argued that contracts and lending were not two separate settlements between the landowner and the labourer that worked concurrently to keep the latter tied to the farm, but that the resources provided to the labourer that came to restrict his mobility were part of the labour contract as advances. Thus, the contract itself had an informal side. This position would explain better why there were casual labourers who were as heavily indebted as the permanent labourers but who were free to leave the village to earn money elsewhere and repay the lender. There is no reason to think that lending, as such, carried restrictions on mobility. Such restrictions only appeared in connection with the *pannaiyal* form of labour. Thereby, the *pannai* system helped the farm economies to withstand the competition for labour that they faced from the industries and the estates.

Also, the Madhari do not appear to have acted as labourers free to choose between the option of being a contract farm labourer or an industrial wage labourer. There are no indications of a striving among Madhari labourers to join the work forces in the factories or on the hill estates. The results would rather suggest that the Madhari realised the benefits of living in local society in a system based on informal rules, benefits that were not matched by incentives outside the farms that would attract them.

The 1930s and 1940s saw important industrial innovations that were introduced into agriculture and came to affect agrarian relations. It was the introduction of electricity and mechanical equipment that interacted with a rationalisation of the market caused by the depression to create new preconditions for both farmers and labourers. In the coming decades, the conditions for the Madhari labourers were changed. On the one hand, they were no longer a necessary and natural part of the agricultural production, indispensable to the farmers as a result of their skills as leather-workers. Industrial goods replaced those skills. The Goundar, on the other hand, strove to make as efficient use of the labour market as possible in a new situation, and the bonds between Goundar and Madhari gradually loosened. The consequences of industrialisation were not the sole cause of this outcome, but were definitely one of the most important.

A result of the investigation worth noting is also the fact that many of the Madhari in the later part of the period, when the majority of them had become labourers for daily wages, expressed a wish to stay under the security and protection of bonds, rather than work as wage labourers in a free, but insecure, labour market.

This may seem as like a futile dream of the good old days, that in reality had been bad. However, after the dramatic fall in the number of *pannaiyal* employed on the farms, there are reasons to think that the meaning of *pannaiyal* changed. It was no longer a '*pannai* system', but the man employed as *pannaiyal* seems to have become the trusted overseer. To achieve such a position was more likely something to hope for a coolie labourer in the late 1960s. This last point will be discussed in Chapter 4.

## GROWING INDUSTRY, GROWING BONDS

The region's economy during the first few decades of the twentieth century was expansive. Manuals, gazetteers and statistics for the Coimbatore district show a growing number of factories, railways, roads, wells and other irrigation works. The economy as a whole was growing, signifying a qualitative change, and was becoming increasingly diversified. Both Goundar farmers and Madhari labourers were drawn into the transformation. But the question to be further examined remains whether their relationship was changed to any extent as a result of the growing commercialisation of agriculture and expanding industry. The general results of the study of the first phase of the consequences of industrialisation for rural relations, which has been summarily discussed above, can be summed up in three major points. The discussion that follows will begin with the agricultural labour relations, particularly those in the *pannai* system. Thereafter it will continue by examining the economic preconditions in terms of land ownership that may be suspected to have had an impact on those relations. Finally, the discussion will move into the possible consequences for existing labour relations of the important and new economic activity of the wealthiest farmers as part of the industrialisation in the district.

1. Through the growth of the textile industry, the need for more permanent labourers developed. As will be argued, the changed cropping pattern, in which more water for irrigation was needed, increased the demand for draught animals and cattle feed, as well as for labourers to supervise irrigation and work in the fields. It follows that, when the growing industries in the towns and on the tea estates in the hills engaged in competition for labour and casual labourers began to leave the villages, the farmers made sure of securing agricultural labourers by tying increasing numbers of them to the farms through the *pannaiyal* form of labour. The fact that the essential, *kavalai* water-lifts were worked with leather bags gives one explanation of why the Madhari community remained important to the farmers and were therefore given priority before agricultural labourers from other castes.
2. One of the preconditions for the employment of *pannaiyal* was the scale of farming. The distribution of land recorded in the land registers of 1912, discussed in Chapter 2, gives support to the assumption that a great number of *pannaiyal* could well be supported. But on account of the inheritance of land, the strain placed on the farmers' economies by the rapidly growing indebtedness from the turn of the century until the thirties and the effects of the 1930s depression and of the Second World War, it may be assumed that the large landholdings were difficult to keep together. However, the results show that neither inheritance nor economic difficulties gave reason for a reduction of the total number of *pannaiyal* in the central parts of the Coimbatore district. Those developments do not seem to have resulted in a trend to lay off *pannaiyal* or to rely on coolies.
3. In previous studies it has been argued that within the district a small number of wealthy farmers were able to make investments in industry in an enterprising way. Such investments began in the 1920s and were carried on during the subsequent decades. It

> has been further argued that, by keeping an involvement both in agriculture and in industry, these factory-cum-landowners came rather successfully through the depression. But not even such involvement of farmers in industry appears to have given them reason to break with the *pannai* system.

Until the late 1930s, and even the 1940s, the results suggest that agriculture in the Coimbatore district, and particularly in its central parts, depended upon a well-functioning *pannai* system. The industrialisation process did not pose a threat to its existence.

## Competition for Labour

It was the rapid growth of the textile industry and the conversion of the cotton produced to make goods for an extended export market that made the difference when the economy of the Coimbatore district expanded. Cotton was an old crop in the region and was suggested as a profitable crop by Alexander Read in the 1790s. But the lack of good communications had throughout the century created a major obstacle to a profitable trade. In 1794, the Board of Revenue in Madras, although encouraging cotton cultivation, found transport over such long distances too great a difficulty to be overcome. It was not until late in the nineteenth century that this problem was beginning to be solved.[2]

Growing cotton was encouraged by the British administration, but the increase was at a slow pace. When the Civil War in America ruined the cotton fields of the American south, the demand for Indian cotton rose and exports increased. But the effects of the war gave the Indian producers only a temporary income. When the war was over, cotton exports declined. However, by the end of the century, the demand for cotton was again rising, this time on the domestic market, and the first mills for ginning and pressing were established. It was during this period that the cotton market was organised in the highlands. This happened concurrently with the introduction of the high-yielding, long-staple, Cambodia cotton and led to a capital inflow.[3] Cotton now became a product to be exported out of the region on a large scale.

The Season and Crop Reports show that increasing amounts of land were put under cotton cultivation in the district, until it claimed 16 per cent of the total cultivated land in 1930-1. Between 1920 and 1930, the food crops *cholam*, *cumbu* and *ragi* declined from 63 per cent to 50 per cent of the total cultivated land. Cultivation of cash-crops showed the opposite trend. Groundnuts, cotton, sugar cane, gingelly and tobacco increased on the cultivated land from 22 to 28 per cent.[4]

The Cambodia variety was greatly in demand, particularly by the large textile mills in Bombay. Its long staples could be spun to a thin, strong thread and be woven into high-quality textiles. This variety also had the advantage of sustaining cultivation on red loam and clay and not only on the intensively irrigated, black soils. Even though irrigation was preferred, the Cambodia crop was also grown when irrigated by surface water, and sometimes even by the more unreliable rains.[5] Introduced in 1900, the Cambodia quickly came to be the most important variety. In 1929-30, it was cropped on 48 per cent of the total area devoted to cotton cultivation in the district, yielding 68 per cent of the cotton produced. Karunganni, an improved local variety, occupied 37.5 per cent of the land where cotton was cultivated, yielding 28 per cent of the harvest.[6]

To develop further and promote agricultural production, the Agricultural College in Saidapet was re-organised and transferred to Coimbatore, where the old model farm dating from 1876 was opened as the Agricultural University in 1909.[7]

The number of primary processing factories in the district rose dramatically over the following decades. In 1888, there were only 2, European-owned, textile mills; in the 1920s there were 5 mills, and Indian owners entered the market, gradually taking over the larger part of the textile industry. Twenty years later, the number of mills had increased to 36. Between the years 1911 and 1941, the number of ginneries grew from 5 to 149.[8] The textile industry as a whole was increasingly favoured by low labour costs. The wages of several of the categories of textile workers were the lowest in the Madras Presidency and, according to Baker, the lowest in India.[9]

Until the depression in the 1930s, the area of land under cotton cultivation increased rapidly. The number of units for the industrial processing of cotton grew simultaneously. These were continuous, though fluctuating trends. By 1930, approximately one-third of the cultivated land in the Coimbatore district was under cotton. The irregular demand for the crop and the climatic shifts over the years, factors that set the limits for the unirrigated cotton crops, can be seen in the annual statistics. Also prices had a governing effect on cultivation. In 1925-6, a little more than 300,000 acres produced cotton, while more than 360,000 acres were under cotton cultivation in 1929-

30. In the Gazetteer of the Coimbatore district, Cox attributes this steep rise to the favourable prices of that year.

The intensively irrigated, garden cultivation practised by the farmers on parts of their lands was well suited to such fluctuations. The farmers grew many different crops, in case there was a fall in prices or declining demand for one or two of them. This was a form of cultivation that could comparatively easily be adjusted to the market. The major trend in the Coimbatore district up to 1930 shows an increase of cash-crop cultivation, while the older, dry, millet crops, that over centuries had been adjusted to the local climatic conditions, decreased. As cultivation of land had become increasingly important, the need for manure had increased as well and cattle was grazed in a system of rotation between the different fields.[10]

In Palladam taluk, this trend is revealed more clearly than in the statistics for the whole of the district. In most parts of the taluk, cotton was non-existent in 1896, which was before the introduction of the Cambodia variety. But already between the years 1896 and 1910, there was a noticeable increase in the cultivation of cotton and tobacco, and to some extent also paddy and horse gram. Over the same period, dry crops, particularly *cholam* and *cumbu*, declined, in some *kasbahs* drastically.[11] The crops that dominated the taluk were significant for the climatic conditions and the agricultural economy. *Cholam*, which was used as food for both humans and for cattle, occupied around 40 per cent of the total area cropped throughout the 1920s, while in the district as a whole the figure was about 25 per cent. The 1920s figures for cotton varied slightly around 30 per cent of the total area under cultivation in Palladam. In the entire Coimbatore district, the figures varied between 15 and 20 per cent. 1929-30 seems to have been a 'peak year', when 83 per cent of the total cultivated land came under either cotton or *cholam* (36 per cent of the former and 47 per cent of the latter).[12]

The change in cropping pattern had immediate consequences for labour requirements. Cotton cultivation was labour-intensive, as compared with the cultivation of the common millet varieties or some of the other cash-crops. This increased demand was accompanied by other effects. The increase of *pannaiyal* in relation to coolie labourers in the early twentieth century, which by 1933 was estimated to amount to one-third of the agricultural labour force, finds its explanation here. Concurrently with the rising demands for agricultural labour, labour demands were scaled up in the capitalist enterprises in the district.[13]

Evans, whose research on tea-estate labour was discussed in Chapter 2, describes the competition for labour between the urban industries and the tea estates. She argues that two separate labour flows developed as a result of different labour-recruitment methods and the pre-existing, socio-economic order of labour. She concludes that the social composition of the industrial labour force originated from a slightly higher social stratum than did the estate labour force. Potential industrial labourers are also reported to have bribed their way into the factories by offering gifts and free services to the workers in them, and labourers already employed in the factories were able to recommend their relatives for vacancies. Poor Goundars would much rather seek industrial employment than labour contracts on the estates, while sheer poverty was an obstacle to the propertyless, untouchable labourers doing the same.

Being nearer to the home villages and under less severe climatic conditions than in the hills, the urban industries could more easily attract labourers than could the estates. The estates in the Nilgiri hills suffered from an insufficient labour supply, and caste preferences found no space to develop in the recruitment of labourers. To make labourers available for estate work, the recruiters linked their efforts directly to the pre-capitalist economies in the villages by giving advances, in order to free the labourers from agrarian debt-bondage and to provide them with the material means to leave their villages for long periods and make the journey to the hills, though this did not free them from extra-economic ties but tied them anew by inheritable debts to the labour contractors. Evans argues that pre-capitalist constraints governing agrarian labour were in this way transmitted by the labour-contractor system to the capitalist sector in the estates.

Wages were not high either in the industries or on the estates. Evans emphasises that the estate economies depended on the rural economy, since one man's wages in the estates could not support a family. The children and the parents had to be maintained in the village, sometimes together with the wife. Therefore, it was essential for the contractors to uphold the ties between the estate and the village in order to secure estate labour. Evans argues that the growth of the capitalist economies of the estates was in this way subsidised by the pre-capitalist economies in the villages.[14]

All the interviewed Madhari and Goundar informants from the Palladam taluk also stated that the labour contractors on the tea estates originated from their own or nearby villages. They were people who were familiar with the villages from whence they recruited labourers and who could easily get information about economic and family conditions.[15]

As was discussed in Chapter 2, there were structural obstacles to the Madhari leaving the farm economies and seeking employment in the factories and, except for individuals among them, they did not go to the estates either. Hypothetically, if the Goundar farmers were to let them go, the Madhari would have to leave the *pannai* system. That would include leaving a system in which resources were available to them, in shares of the harvests and other produce.[16]

This security, embraced by customary law, would be exchanged for the possibility of seeking work in the labour market in competition with members of the higher Paraiyar and Goundar communities, who already had a foothold as labourers in the factories and the estates. In the factories, they would be working for the lowest wages in the Presidency. Even hypothetically, there was little incentive to seek employment outside the farms.

A situation of labour scarcity does not necessarily result in an increase in the numbers of bonded labourers. If they had had the strength to organise among themselves and use the advantage of the high demand for their labour, an equally possible development would have been the labourers making demands for higher wages or other benefits, as did the Pallar after the abolition of slavery, when labour migration out of the Tiruchirapalli district caused labour scarcity.[17] However, as discussed in Chapter 2, nothing indicates that the Madhari still residing on the farms took to such methods.

All the agricultural labourers were by no means employed as *pannaiyal*. It may even be assumed that the increased demand for agricultural labour encouraged labourers from neighbouring districts to migrate into the region and join the casual work force. However, there are no reasonably reliable, migration statistics before 1921 to support such an assumption.[18] Nevertheless, *pannaiyal* was the form of permanent labour that the farmers relied on. It is most probable that increased competition for labour in a situation in which labour demands were scaled up in agriculture led the farmers to take on more labourers on long-term settlements, and therefore the number of *pannaiyal* rose in relation to the casual labourers.[19]

Palladam taluk, which showed such a high increase of the share of cotton in the total cultivated area, was likely to have been one of the regions in the district where labour demand increased rapidly during these initial decades of the twentieth century.

A survey in 1935 of Perumanallur *kasbah*, including five hamlets situated immediately north of Tiruppur, may serve as an example of the relation between *pannaiyal* employment and cotton cultivation, but also of the growing need to secure labour when intensive cotton cultivation increased.

N. Ganesamurthi's survey of Perumanallur shows that in the village large proportions of cotton to the total cultivated area were grown. If compared with the figures in Cox (1933), the result was even greater than for Palladam taluk in total. However, there is a time-lag of two years to be considered between the figures given by Ganesamurthi and by Cox, and the comparison has to be made with some caution. Yet it is interesting to note that, while in the taluk as a whole, cotton amounted to slightly less than 25 per cent, the crop was grown on 28 per cent of the cultivated land in Perumanallur. Of the cotton grown in the village, 99 per cent was irrigated, and the number of wells was reported to have increased because of the intensive cultivation in the area.[20]

Over the first three decades of the century, the Season and Crop Reports show that the amount of land watered by well irrigation in the Coimbatore district as a whole increased by more than 30 per cent, from less than 300,000 acres to more than 400,000 acres. The greater part of this increase took place between 1915 and 1923.[21]

Irrigation and leather work were the trades of the Madhari, in Perumanallur as in the whole of the district. Ganesamurthi noted that they stitched the buckets for the wells, made sandals and helped in agricultural operations. Old animals were also sold for 10 rupees to the Madhari for slaughter. 'Giving help' seems a rather mild way to describe the labour conditions of the Madhari. Ganesamurthi is more precise when he writes that the Madhari in the villages of Perumanallur *kasbah* 'joined the farm'. When joining, they were advanced 10 rupees that had to be returned before they were allowed to leave. During the year, they were paid monthly in *cholam* and *ragi*, and in a customary (*mamool*) fixed share of the harvests. The term *pannaiyal* is not used in the survey, but the description of the labour conditions corresponds well to those of the *pannaiyal* in the district.

The majority of the casual labour force were reported to be female labourers. Most likely, they were the wives and unmarried daughters of the Madhari *pannaiyal*.

Also Goundars were reported to work on a permanent basis. In contrast to the Madhari, they were not advanced money when they took up work but were paid in kind according to 'age and efficiency'. These permanent labourers worked on one-year contracts that were renewable at the time of the Pongal festival celebrated immediately after the harvest in January. Perumanallur was reported to have 160 of these labourers employed within its borders.

Christopher Baker rounds the figures for landholders up to 100 when he refers to this survey. He has also chosen to interpret the Goundar 'permanent labourers' as *pannaiyal.* From this position, it is possible to conclude, with Baker, that 160/100 was a high ratio of permanent farm servants, or *pannaiyal,* to landholders, as compared with the nineteenth-century reports from the district. Baker argues that this implies a steep rise in the numbers of permanent farm servants.

However, it is also possible to reach a similar conclusion by relying on the information about the Madhari who joined the farms, most likely as *pannaiyal.* But as the Madhari were few in the village—only 18 families were reported—while the Goundar families numbered 205, other arrangements had to be made by the farmers to secure labourers. Perumanallur was a *kasbah* affected by the depression, almost every farmer was indebted, and no family had been able to save during the previous years. Many Goundars did not hold any land, while a substantial part of the landholders held more than 10 acres of land. These landholders were dependent on having labourers available, particularly so as the factories in nearby Tiruppur were an attractive alternative to a landless Goundar. Therefore, it is likely that the landholders also made permanent arrangements with the landless Goundars. The absence of advance payments would indicate that the deals with Goundar labourers were not *pannaiyal* agreements, while at the same time their existence reveals the farmers' increasing need for long-term settlements between farmers and labourers.[22]

TABLE 3.1. RYOTWARI AND MINOR INAM LAND IRRIGATED IN 1929-30, IN PERCENTAGE

| | *Canals* | *Tanks* | *Wells* | *Other* | *Total* |
|---|---|---|---|---|---|
| Palladam taluk* | 3 | 1.5 | 95.5 | – | 100 |
| Coimbatore district | 18 | 4 | 76 | 2 | 100 |

Source: Cox, 1933, p. 170.

* In Cox (1933), Palladam taluk is named after its most important town, Tiruppur.

The changed cropping pattern not only altered the labour requirements, but also increased the need of water for irrigation. This was a critical factor for the farmers of the highlands. Most of them relied on well irrigation, and new wells were dug, while old ones were repaired. Carrying on cultivation in the dry belt brought the farmers close to a complete dependence on the wells. Palladam taluk was situated in a region that almost completely lacked rivers and streams and where the rains were very unreliable. This fact made the agriculture of the region more dependent on well irrigation than that in the rest of the taluks in the district. The functioning of these wells was a precondition for the expansion of cash-crop cultivation in the region.

Measures were soon taken to increase the capacity of the wells. Oil-fired and steam engines had been introduced on a small scale to extend the cultivated area under irrigation. In 1933, approximately 3,000 acres out of the total of 466,380 acres of irrigated land were watered by pumps. And of the 121 oil-fired and steam engines that had been installed in the district, 13 were functioning in Palladam taluk.[23] But compared with the roughly 90,000 wells that were used in the district, these pumps represented investments by a handful of the most influential and well-to-do farmers in Kongunad. Still, the great majority of the farmers depended on the *kavalai* water-lifts.

There was no taboo that prevented the Goundar from operating the *kavalai*; the farmer could very well himself see that the bulls drew the water properly. But he would not divide up his working hours in such a way that he would have to spend up to six hours a day, every day, by the well. For this, he employed a labourer. These labourers were observed by Cox in 1933. According to him, the farmer would employ the Madhari as *pannaiyal* to make sure that there was always a sufficiency of new and whole leather bags. The links between irrigation, Madhari and *pannaiyal* were thus one of the corner-stones that made the expansion of cotton cultivation possible during the early decades of industrialisation in the district.[24]

Both the Madhari and the Goundar informants confirm this relationship. A Madhari man in Kulathupalayam, who dated his youth by an earthquake in 1902, pastured cattle for a Goundar as a boy. At that time, he learnt how the *kavalai* worked. 'I knew how to drive the bullocks in order to draw water from the well. Thereafter I became *pannayam*. . . . I worked for a Goundar for forty years.'[25]

The Goundar farmers of Semmipalayam kept only Madhari as

*pannaiyal.* Why they so completely outnumbered the Paraiyar as agricultural labourers was explained by the Goundar farmers partly by the use of *kavalai* and partly by the fact that many of the Paraiyar managed to find employment outside the village economy and improve their situation. A distinction between the Paraiyar and the Madhari frequently used by members of the Goundar community recurs also in this interview. The informant constantly referred to the Madhari as 'Harijan' and the Paraiyar as 'Adi-dravida' throughout the interview. The Gandhian term 'Harijan' is in this context a more polite and socially acceptable name for the leather-workers than the downgrading 'Chukkili' that was previously used. Still it indicates their low position as a Scheduled Caste. Adi-dravida has in the same way higher social connotations than Paraiyar. The habit of not referring to both Madhari and Paraiyar as Harijan, but making a distinction between the two, reflects the higher position that the Paraiyar had been able to gain in the area.[26]

These two important changes—the extended need of labour power, and the increased need of water for irrigation by the use of the *kavalai* technique—interacted to reinforce the position of the Madhari in agriculture.

## A Polarised Land Ownership

To finance a workforce of increasing numbers of *pannaiyal,* the cultivation of cotton was based on the existence of substantial farms. As was shown in the Re-Settlement and Re-Survey of 1912 for Palladam taluk, a minority of individual holders, who cultivated more than 10 acres each, controlled three-quarters of the land. The question follows, whether this situation remained throughout the subsequent decades, which would be an important precondition for the employment of *pannaiyal.* A situation in which land would be divided by inheritance between the generations and thereby result in increasing numbers of small farmers would make the employment of permanent labourers more difficult. Also, the increasing indebtedness among landowners might create obstacles to employing a permanent labour force at the farm.

However, the uneven distribution of land appears not only to have been maintained, but also to have been further increased by the results of the growing rural indebtedness which led up to the Government of Madras Acts of the 1930s. The Acts aimed at coming to terms with these debts, but the effects of some of them have been severely questioned. Many small- and medium-scale farmers had become insolvent when the depression caused a dramatic fall in the prices of agricultural products. But the Acts have been accused of being toothless, having only marginal effects in scaling down debts. However, one of them, the Act of 1938, has been pointed out as being supportive to the medium- and large-scale farmers in their efforts to reduce their debts.[27] Also the war years between 1939 and 1945 seem to have served to strengthen the economic position of the large landowners.

The ICS officer who was assigned to the Coimbatore district, John Tudor Gwynn, made an observation in 1906 that reflects the fragility of the small farmers' economies at the time. During that year, the area was struck by a drought that was said to have resulted in famine when two out of three rains failed. The price of fodder for the well cattle rose high, and the small farmers had to borrow money to keep them fed. Gwynn writes to his father that the drought also resulted in unemployment for the daily-wage coolies. Worst affected were the landless Madhari and Paraiyar, who had to live on roots and prickly pear to survive. Particularly hard hit were the Madhari. According to Gwynn, they could not afford to buy water and therefore suffered from many illnesses.[28]

Judging from the land register of 1912, most of the landowners lived within small margins. But, looking at the upper section of landowners, the results presented in Chapter 2 can be made more precise. Within this section, the distribution was not even. A survey of fifteen *kasbahs* in the Palladam taluk, covering 4,028 patta holders, shows that most of the land was cultivated by owners registered for land of medium-sized farms, while a small section of the farmers

TABLE 3.2. DIVISION OF PATTA LAND, SELECTION OF 15 *KASBAHS* IN PALLADAM TALUK, 1912

| *Land rent (Rs)* | *Average farm size (Acres)* | *Patta holders (%)* | *Land held (%)* |
|---|---|---|---|
| -10 | 5 | 60 | 25 |
| 10-100 | 20 | 39 | 64 |
| 100-250 | 135 | 1 | 8 |
| 250-500 | 241 | 0.1 | 2 |
| Total | 12 | 100 | 99 |

Source: Re-Survey and Re-Settlement Registers, Palladam taluk, 1912.

owned an average of 147 acres of land each.[29] As Table 3.2 shows, the medium-sized farms were of an average of 20 acres, which in itself is quite substantial. Thus, the farming community was not a uniform body of smallholders. There was a wealthy minority of farmers who controlled large *pannais*, and the risk of ending up landless and indebted was not a threat to the middle or upper sections of the farmers, but to those owning only a few acres.

From the turn of the century to the arrival of the 1930s depression, rural debts grew. In 1930, rural indebtedness had even become a serious problem. Indebted small farmers fell into insolvency and lost their land to moneylenders, who were either large landholders or urban, non-cultivating lenders. In 1933, Cox compares the situation of the persons dependent on agriculture between the years 1901 and 1921 for the Coimbatore district and concludes that the cultivating landowners were losing ground to the cultivating tenant and non-cultivating rent-receiver or rent-payer. This was reported to be due to the fact either that the small farmer sold his land to the moneylender, for whom he continued to work as a tenant, or that 'an appreciable section' of the landowners had joined the army or taken up employment as industrial labourers or coolies.[30]

This trend is reflected also in the work on the ryotwari tenants by K.G. Sivaswamy. Sivaswamy's bias is strongly pro-tenant and pro-trade unionism, and he is apparently intent on pointing out the present sufferings of the tenants in 1948. While going through the history of the tenants from the nineteenth century, he shows how their rights have been circumscribed and the rents increased in real terms. However, while doing so, his results reveal that growing debts from 1915 to 1938 led to a polarisation of land distribution. The already wealthy farmers could enlarge their holdings, while small farmers lost land. In contrast to the years before 1929, when land could still be sold at reasonable prices, the landowners were forced to sell their holdings and made great losses when the depression had become a fact .[31]

Going back to a situation before this development began, Nicholson recorded an interesting observation in the Manual of the Coimbatore district in the 1880s. According to him, there was a trend in the Coimbatore district for 'labourers' to get hold of small pieces of land. In the Manual of 1887, he both commends and complains about the way the ryotwari system was operating in the district. He writes that it implied a 'complete freedom or non-interference, except in the matter of revenue collection'. This was caused by a slackness in the revenue system. If only the ryots paid their fees, they would not have to 'see the face of the thasildar' No Government official would tell them what to grow or how to make use of their resources.[32]

As a consequence, less good soils got into the hands of poor *patta* holders who, according to Nicholson, cultivated the land in a negligent way without manuring or weeding. The trend to buy more land than the cultivator could make productive, commercial use of was a result of competition for land.[33]

This description of the individual *patta* holder indicates that he never intended to grow a commercial crop. His holding was only a small piece of land which, if he was lucky, would yield him something, which was better than nothing. Considering the results in Cox's Manual, these new smallholders of the 1880s most likely ended up among the indebted tenants that Cox observed in his survey of 1901 and 1921. To cultivate only a small holding carried disadvantages. In large parts of the highlands, commercial crops could only with difficulty be grown without irrigation. As well irrigation was costly, it was hardly an option for a small farmer. One year of failing rains or competition pushing down prices in the local market could be fatal to a small-farm economy. Without the economic resources to make commercial use of the one or two acres owned, the smallholder would easily end up trapped by debts and forced to relinquish the land. Tenancy, as well as coolie labour was then a solution.

The picture of a vulnerable, small-farmer economy, in which growing debts forced them to surrender their property to moneylenders when trapped by economic difficulties, and changed them into indebted tenants, bears a resemblance to that in Breman's study of Gujarat and is in many respects a common phenomenon in Indian history. The immediate reason in Gujarat was a drought in 1899-1900. The cultivators took loans to meet the requirements for survival and were forced into insolvency when they were unable to pay the interest. Land came into the hands of moneylenders, and eventually ended up with the dominant farmers in the region, who came to employ the original landholders as tenants to work on the land they had lost.[34]

However, the comparison between Gujarat and Kongunad is not entirely satisfactory. The fact that the tenants in Gujarat were tribals, further marginalized by the loss of land, and the farmers were Patidars, who continued to enforce their dominance in the region, forms a major difference from the situation in Kongunad. The cultivators in the south Indian highlands who owned only very small plots of land around the turn of the century were most likely not untouchable, landless labourers but members of higher castes. There were no rules against members of an untouchable caste holding land. Nevertheless, it is most unlikely that an untouchable labourer could have become a landowner except in rare cases, as, for example, when he had an official duty as messenger.[35] The Re-settlement Registers of 1912 reveal the extremely small number of landholders among the Paraiyar and Madhari communities.[36] More probable is the assumption that those smallholders, who were forced to give up their lands to become tenants, were for the most part poor Goundars or members of other higher castes.

With regard to the comparison between Kongunad and Gujarat, it is important to note the difference between the relationship of a tribal tenant and a landowning Patidar, on the one hand, and a Goundar tenant and a landowning Goundar, on the other. Where the Patidar would strive to make as much profit out of the situation as possible, the Goundar tenant would find a certain amount of security in belonging to the same caste as the landowner. He would not have been in as vulnerable a situation as the tribal tenant in Gujarat, and he would not end up having the same low social status as a Paraiyar tenant or a Madhari coolie.

Both Sivaswamy and Cox observed the growing indebtedness that led to increased polarisation of land ownership. The 1930s depression, which will be discussed further on, appears to some extent to have further emphasized this trend. The effects of the Second World War on the agricultural economy do not seem to have hampered this development.

During the war years, the economic cleavage between large and small landowners deepened further. In the Enquiry into Rural Indebtedness in the Madras Presidency of 1946, Narayanaswamy Naidu shows that between the years 1939 and 1945 large and medium landowners, owning more than five acres, were able to partially or completely clear their debts to a greater extent than the small landowners, tenants or landless labourers. In contrast, the last three categories showed a larger number of owners who took new loans or became further indebted during the period. Among the 8,530 families included in the survey, coming from all districts in the Madras Presidency, the absolute majority had debts throughout the period.

But while 50 per cent of all the large landowners, holding more than 25 acres of land, were indebted in 1945, the figures varied between 62 and 66 per cent in all other categories.[37]

Profitable prices and Government support made the already wealthy even wealthier through the war years, according to Narayanaswamy Naidu. He specifies three reasons why debts were reduced. The major reason was the sales of land after 1942, when land prices rose. Land sales were estimated to amount to 57.5 per cent of the debt recoveries. Next to the sales, he points to the effects of the Agriculturists' Debt Relief Act of 1938. According to Narayanaswamy Naidu, 12.2 per cent of the loans repaid during the period were the result of the implementation of the Act. The third reason is more vaguely formulated as the 'wartime rise in prices', estimated at 30.3 per cent of the total debt recoveries, and refers to profits made by farmers who were able to benefit from the high prices of agricultural products.[38]

There is yet another interesting result of the survey to be mentioned in this connection. From the collected data, Narayanaswamy Naidu has compiled a table of expenses and income in family budgets, comparing the years 1939 and 1945 for the five ownership-based categories. The results show that the families in the two highest categories were making a substantial surplus in 1945, while the others were ending up with a loss. Over the period, owners of more than 25 acres were increasing their surplus considerably. Owners of between 5 and 25 acres had their surpluses slightly reduced. For owners of up to 5 acres, the period meant going from a small surplus to a small deficit. The tenants and the landless labourers were the big losers, falling from a small deficit for the tenants and a small surplus for the labourers to a clear deficit that may help to explain the increased indebtedness among these groups. Narayanaswamy Naidu concludes: 'The capacity to save and liquidate debt has been strengthened only in the case of big landholders.'[39]

All these different types of evidence may lead us to conclude that a small section of the wealthiest farmers increased further their wealth, while the absolute majority ended up having small plots and farming for subsistence. However, interviews have given information in which conclusions may be made about important divisions between the small farmers. These divisions are not revealed in surveys or land registers. There is a possibility that the rules for the inheritance of land among the Goundars may have served to keep smallholdings together in a supportive way, as was also discussed in Chapter 2. The sons of a wealthy farmer, who at his death took full charge of the land that he had allotted to each of them many years earlier, could continue to support each other. Some of the benefits of a large estate could thus be continued, even though the brothers now cultivated small plots. This would suggest that smallholders, even if they owned only a few acres, who were members of a wealthy family were less likely to end up in insolvency than were those who belonged to a family in which two or three acres constituted the whole of the property.[40]

This suggests further more that the small farmers, whose troubles Gwynn described to his father in 1906, were not all equally hurt by the drought. Between brothers, who had since their own marriages worked on lands allotted to them but owned by their father, there are reasons to assume a praxis of cooperation that continued as a security when the estate was formally divided.

Also the wealthiest farmers were likely to have lived and worked jointly within the family even after the land was divided between the sons, as long as the oldest male member of the family lived and had the final say in land issues. Sivasubramaniyan Goundar's grandfather, Muttu Kumar Samy Goundar, was a village officer and *Ur*-Goundar of Semmipalayam. According to Muttu Kumar Samy's grandsons, he controlled 500-600 acres of land in four villages. His brother Palanisamy was the headman of Sukkampalayam, the main village in the neighbouring revenue village. All this land was considered to be a matter for the family but was spread out over several revenue villages and registered for different, individual patta holders. The land can therefore only with great difficulty be traced as belonging to the same family in the land registers. Sivasubramaniyan's father took up the office as *Ur*-Goundar and village officer for Kumbakoil village. The economy of the farm as a whole allowed him to employ 100-120 labourers; 20 of these were said by another Goundar informant to have been *pannaiyal*. Sivasubramaniyan estimates that his father owned 10-12 bulls for the carts, 20 buffaloes, 50-70 cows and 100 goats. The farm functioned as a joint family unit and only a joint family economy would have allowed this large estate to function.[41]

If we rely on the Goundar informants, the break-up of this system seems to have come about in two steps. The system of keeping the land in the control of the eldest male member and letting the sons settle with their families on the farm functioned until the informants themselves divided the land between their sons. That would generally have happened during the 1950s. At that time, the different sons were allowed to settle in their own houses, rather than under the same roof as their parents. But still the land was cultivated in close cooperation between the family members. The Fixation of the Ceiling on Land Act of 1961, where 15 acres was the maximum limit of land owned, further worked to legally distribute land between family members. However, a situation where Goundar sons cultivated their lands as separate economic units appears to have been a very late development, after the period discussed in this study, when market, land value and labour costs decided a different economic activity.[42]

Over the first few decades of the twentieth century, the trend in the distribution of land indicates that a growing amount of land came under the control of large *pannai* owners. A further polarisation of the distribution of wealth appears to have been caused by the effects of the war years. Scale was an important factor in farming, which gave more opportunities to achieve a profitable cash-crop cultivation and to make an efficient use of the available resources, including labour. A stable farm economy was also necessary for farmers seeking to make investments on the industrial side of agrarian production. From the discussion earlier there is no reason to believe that the increasing rural indebtedness would, as such, have automatically caused the decreasing employment of *pannaiyal* and a growing reliance on casual labourers. Nor would figures showing a large number of smallholders mean that none of them employed a *pannaiyal*, since these figures do not immediately reveal the brothers in a wealthy family who cooperated as farmers.

## Rural Capital in Industry

The general situation in the earlier part of the period studied was that certain castes dominated within different trades. The handloom processing of cotton in Kongunad was basically done by spinners and weavers of the Chettiar and Segundar Mudaliar communities, while the cultivation of the crop had been carried out by Goundar and Kamma farmers. Of course, there were exceptions, but those were for the most part only exceptions.[43] The introduction of industry into the trade began to change this division between castes. When wealthy entrepreneurial groups among the Goundar and the Kamma, making use of local credit, moved into the cotton business and invested in ginning and pressing mills, these major cultivators became closely involved in the urban side of the cotton business.[44] Rural surpluses were transferred and invested in industry, while the investor still held a strong position in the rural economy based on the cultivation of land.

When factories, based on rural capital and the interests of wealthy farmers, grew in the district, it may be assumed that, when labour power was transferred from the villages to the towns, the relationship between the Goundar and Madhari communities was dramatically upset. However, as long as the investments were made from the profits of efficiently running farms, and the factories were able to find a sufficient number of labourers elsewhere, this situation does not seem to have materialised. It appears that the industrial investments that were firmly rooted in farm economies rather served to reduce the risks of a rift developing between agrarian and industrial production, as could have been the result of increasing competition where the industrial sector was growing at the expense of the agrarian sector.[45]

To gain this comparatively firm position, the familiarity of the Goundar with the marketing of cotton was essential, according to Baker. When Baker's conclusion is compared with the situation in Gujarat, as discussed by Breman, the advantages held by the Kongunad farmers become obvious. As in Kongunad, also in the central plains of Gujarat, cotton soon became the principal commercial crop as a result of rising external demand. But, unlike the Kongunad situation, it was the merchants and the money-lenders who profited from the crop in Gujarat. Merchants, acting as agents of the Bombay trading houses, bought the crop from the farmers in advance. The fact that it was sold in the villages, and not in the market, gave the buyers an upper hand and an opportunity to cheat in the negotiations. When the crop was to be collected, the buyer would blame 'inferior quality' as a reason for refusing the crop or reducing the price, and the cultivator would easily become indebted. In this way, the cultivators lost land, while the commercial classes increased their landholdings.[46]

The Kongunad farmers, on the other hand, had acted on the market long before the extended commercialisation of cotton. They had themselves been particular about selling at the right time to gain maximum profit from their produce. There were no merchants acting as middlemen between them and the market. When the Cambodia variety was established and the market expanded, they continued this practice. Baker observes that the farmers were also able to keep their control when a system of commission agents developed in the 1920s. These agents were engaged to sell the crop, meeting the interests of the farmers. This direct relationship to the market made it possible for the farmers to refrain from mortgaging their crops in advance, which would have hindered them from selling at the most profitable time. One of the more characteristic features of the development of the Kongunad cotton market was, according to Baker, the active involvement of the cultivators in the cotton market.[47] J.S. Ponniah observed these agents acting as middlemen between the producer and the market in Dindigul in the 1930s. He estimated that only 25 per cent of the cotton was sold on the spot by the farmer or the village merchant; the rest was taken care of by the *mundi* merchant. By advice and loan-giving, and by storing the cotton and selling it at the most profitable time, they exerted an influence on prices. According to Ponniah, these merchants were trusted by the farmers, even though not all were honest.[48]

Raman Mahadevan agrees with Baker's conclusion, that the involvement in the textile industry of certain sections of the rural cultivators was definitely important. The strong position of Goundar and, particularly, Kamma families is emphasized in his study of the pattern of textile investments and the growth of Indian capitalists in the Coimbatore district. But the significance of the Kamma and Goundar involvement is not seen as a proof of the strong position of the communities, as such, in the textile industry. Of the Coimbatore mills, 60 per cent were owned by cotton cultivators. But, as the number of factories increased, still only a handful of those families owned more than one. In Coimbatore, 16 out of the 32 factories were owned by Kamma families in 1947, but out of the 16 factories, 10 were owned by only three of those families. The major part of all Indian investments in textiles came from a great variety of investors. Apart from the cultivators, mercantile, local bank and handloom interests were behind the textile mills. The rapid growth is, according to Mahadevan, attributable to the commercialisation of agriculture, aided by local credit, and the survival and growth of the handloom industry.[49]

This suggests that the most influential of the rural-based investments were generally made by the wealthiest farmers, who were predominantly of the Kamma community and who could invest capital in factories and thereby consolidate their dominant position, both as *pannaiyars* and as factory-owners. The expanded cultivation of improved commercial crops had provided an important precondition to link the agricultural production to the external market, and the farmers were able to relate to this market as well as to the rural economy of the region. The profit they gained from their industrial enterprise was to a large extent re-invested in the industry and in agriculture; as regards the latter, it was divided between investments and credit.[50] In this way, a small section of the farmers in the Coimbatore district grew to become part of the dynamic capitalist enterprise in the region.

As long as the investments originated from a small section of the farmers and depended on the strength of the farm economies, there is no reason to believe that the development led to the uprooting of the *pannai* system and a transition to employing casual labour. Nor is it possible to conclude that those investments alone initiated a trend in which farmers shifted from rural to urban enterprise. But the farmers, who in the research area were predominantly members of the Goundar community, continued to carry out cultivation on as high a level of efficiency as possible, with regard to both material resources and labour power.

### THE LOGIC OF KEEPING PERMANENT LABOURERS

To summarise the period between 1900 and the 1930s, for the Madhari labourers, the first three decades of expansion of commercial crops and of the industrial processing of cotton rather worked to manifest and reinforce their position as agricultural labourers than to provide new employment opportunities. Around the turn of the century, labour migration, expanded cultivation and changed cropping patterns, that resulted in a situation of relative shortage of agricultural labour, most probably led to the rising numbers of permanently employed labourers on the farms. The increase of irrigated crops and the substantial increase of the number of wells in the district from the mid-1910s to the mid-1920s, served further to increase the need to employ members of the Madhari community on the farms. The results all point to the fact that the Madhari constituted the majority of the increasing number of *pannaiyal* in the agricultural work force.

Members of the Goundar community who needed to supplement their income by working for other farmers were also an important part of the hired agricultural labour force. However, there is no reason to think that these labourers were employed as *pannaiyal*. A *pannaiyal* had to be constantly available to the farmer, which was not possible if the labourer had lands of his own to take care of. As has been shown, Goundar labourers seeking work had easier access to the much-coveted industrial employment than had Madhari labourers, and as Goundar labourers lacked the skills to produce leather items for the landowners, they were replaceable and would therefore belong to the casual work force. To take on a *pannaiyal* carried costs throughout the year, which would make a farmer prefer a Madhari to a Goundar.

Thus, the employment of *pannaiyal* implied a certain economic strength of the farm. To employ permanent labour, it had to be economically sound. The Goundar informants set the limit at 10 acres. There is no reason to believe that *pannaiyals* constituted the entire work force on a farm; employment of permanent labourers was supplemented by that of casual labourers to meet the varying demand of labour throughout the agricultural year. However, the fact that most of the landowners did not reach the limit of owning ten acres in the early twentieth century does not seem to have hampered the growth of the permanent labour force. Neither the inheritance of land nor the growing rural indebtedness seems to have reduced the total number of *pannaiyal* or restrained their growth as a form of agricultural labour. This would suggest that bonded labourers were both economically possible and necessary in the cultivation of most of the farm land, and the farmers controlling this land most likely employed *pannaiyal* until the end of the war.

The investments by wealthy farmers in the textile industry do not seem to have affected the agrarian relations between Goundar and Madhari, to any great extent. Cotton production and rurally based investments would rather have depended on successful *pannai* economies, in which the farmers made efficient use of their resources. Part of the industrial surplus was also redirected to the rural economy.

Small incentives for the Madhari to leave the villages to seek industrial employment and the structural obstacles in the customary laws served to keep the Madhari within the agricultural economy. The factories did not lack labour power, but could keep wages low. These were the reasons why the textile industry in the Coimbatore district in its initial stage did not grow at the expense of agriculture. Labourers did migrate to the towns and to the tea estates, but agriculture was not drained of its labourers. Without the necessary agricultural labourers firmly on the *pannais*, the industrial enterprise of the wealthy farmers would have found it very difficult to succeed.

This situation did not undergo a major change until the late 1930s.

## THE DOWNFALL OF A TRADE

Two events mark the turn of the decade in 1930, both of which had a great impact on the agrarian economy. The world economic depression struck hard at the foreign demand for raw materials, and countries depending on the export of primary products saw failing export incomes, while in some countries, such as India, the domestic market for some products grew. However, the Kongunad medium- and large-scale farmers were able to manage through the depression years. Some even made a good profit. The cotton market in the district was rationalised by increased competition and small producers met with increasing difficulties to sustain, but it was less disrupted than in other parts of Tamil Nadu. Also, in Kongunad, capital was not directed away from the countryside to the same extent as in most parts of the Presidency. Throughout the years of depression, local credit was invested in agriculture. A large portion of this money came from the local cotton mills and cooperative societies.[51]

During the same period, the engineering industry and the introduction of electricity brought a change that in the longer-term perspective faced the Madhari agricultural labourers with a competition up to then unknown. In 1924, the Government of Madras launched the large-scale Pykhara project in the Nilgiri hills, where water power was to provide large parts of the Presidency with electricity. Six years later, at the peak of the depression, the first generator was turned on, and eventually power was connected to the villages and electrical pumps were installed on the farms.

The depression itself does not seem to have had any substantial effect on the relationship between Goundar and Madhari in the villages or in agriculture. Still, those years were of such importance to the farmers and the agrarian economy that some brief comments about the impact of the depression on cotton-producing farmers in Kongunad will be made before entering into the developments which did make a difference in the Goundar–Madhari relationship.

In the mid-1920s, the tide turned against the producers of primary goods, in India just as in many of the other colonial countries. Until then, demand had reached high levels and prices had risen. But now the supply of primary produce was not met by an equal level of demand.

Among the textile producers in general in India, the mill-owners in

Bombay felt the recession particularly hard. In the economic upswing after the First World War, they had made large-scale, capital investments in machinery. This became a disadvantage in the stagnation of the 1920s, when the Bombay mills turned out to have idle capacities and achieved only a low productivity in a situation of over-capitalisation. Under increasing foreign and national competition and increasing labour protests, several mills closed down.[52] The textile producers urged protection from foreign competition, but the British Government responded late. The free-trade doctrine still held a strong position, and was departed from only after 1930. When restrictions were finally put on trade, they were to be given with 'imperial preferences'. These were preferences that turned out to be British rather than Indian when the subsequent agreements were worked out in detail.[53]

In the 1910s and early 1920s, merchants from Bombay approached the cotton-producing farmers of Kongunad to purchase raw material. The World War caused a sudden surge in demand for cloth, and the long-staple cotton that could be produced in this region was in great demand. Merchants were even reported to have come with bags of money to the villages, offering credit on condition that the farmers grew the Cambodia variety.[54] This credit, as described by Baker, is not to be compared with the system of mortgaging a harvest in advance to a merchant. The demand from Bombay was much too erratic. It seems rather to have been a way for the Bombay merchants to make a deal with the farmers and assure themselves of supplies of high-quality cotton in a situation in which the mills were under pressure.[55]

The European countries, facing the recession in 1930, took steps to reduce the damage done to their economies, and the prices of primary products dropped. Measures were taken in India to support the price level, but soon enough the effects of the world depression were also felt by the farmers of Tamilnad.[56]

But not all products met with the same difficulties. Europe was recovering from the First World War, and agricultural production had begun to rise again. Therefore, the Indian export goods that faced European competition were more likely to lose their foreign demand than those that could only be produced outside Europe. In that way, in spite of falling prices, cotton was not as severely affected as, for example, wheat. Baker relates that the world production of cotton even rose between the years 1926-30 and 1930-8 by 6 per cent.[57] Still, cotton-export prices fell dramatically from the mid-1920s to 1930, to remain on a low but fluctuating level throughout the following decade.[58]

For Indian farmers in general, the depression led to a difficult situation. They found themselves caught in a trap between declining agricultural prices resulting in lower incomes, and payments of rents, taxes and the cost of implements, which remained on the same level as before the depression. Rothermund discusses the link between agricultural credit and the control of the grain and cash-crop market. In a situation in which the trader was also the creditor, he would generally not seek to force the debtor into insolvency, as long as the interest was paid. But when the depression became a fact and the value of the security for the loans dropped, the trader-cum-creditor would immediately sell his stocks and reclaim the money from his borrowers. For the cultivator, facing a 50 per cent fall of the agricultural prices in only a few months in 1930 and seeing credit dry up, while costs were still on a high level, the depression could mean disaster.[59]

But, in contrast, in spite of the depression, the cotton-cultivating farmers in the Coimbatore district appear to have managed fairly well during the 1930s. Some of them responded to the recession by taking a step forward. Investments of rural capital had already been made in the textile industry when the depression became a fact. Such investments increased and the industry boomed during the thirties.[60] And even though a small number of families dominated the industry, as the market was rationalised by hardened competition, a large number of farmers made smaller investments in ginneries and sometimes also spinning units and thereby became involved in the industrial side of textile production.[61] Baker ascribes the progress of the textile industry in Coimbatore to the emerging, large-scale availability of electric power and of capital that had become idle as a result of diminishing profits from lending and trading in agricultural raw materials. In the late 1930s, mill production increased throughout the nation as a whole; only the Bombay mills did not grow in quantitative terms.[62] When foreign demand declined, the Indian market expanded. Baker estimates that one-third of the cotton produced in the Madras Presidency was purchased by mills in the Presidency alone in the late 1920s. Ten years later, the proportion had risen to two-thirds.[63]

The extended world production of cotton during the years of depression was also apparent in the Coimbatore district. The statistics provided in the district gazetteers show a substantial expansion between 1925-6 and 1935-6, both in the cotton produced and in the acreage under cultivation of the crop.[64]

The fact that the cotton trade was relatively prosperous during those years does not mean that all the farmers in the Coimbatore district survived on the same level throughout the depression. Different crops met with different results when sold and exported. Groundnuts show a vulnerability that never affected the cotton production. The extent of the area sown and the yields per year for the whole of the Madras Presidency fluctuate dramatically over the years of depression. The figures fall in 1929-30, recover in 1930-1, fall again in 1931-2, to rise during the following two years, and fall once again in 1934-5 to a level below the area sown and the annual yield in 1925-6.[65] In the year 1930-1, in a time of increasing food-grain prices, the price of groundnuts dropped by 75 per cent, leaving the farmers who depended on this crop in financial trouble.[66]

In the Coimbatore district, groundnut cultivation was concentrated in Pollachi taluk, south-west of Palladam. In 1925-6, 46.5 per cent of all land under groundnut cultivation in the Coimbatore district belonged to Pollachi taluk. In 1930-1, the year of the steep price fall, the proportion of land under groundnuts had risen to 53.5 per cent. The farmers who were dependent on of the sale of this produce were hard hit by the depression, while the neighbouring farmers, relying on cotton as the commercial crop, managed fairly well.[67]

## A Substitute for Manpower

The increased demand for raw material by the textile industry and thereby the expansion of cotton production were dependent on a further development of irrigation. Extended watering of the fields was crucial, and more water had to be lifted out of the wells. New wells could be dug and old ones deepened. But there were limits to the manual, water-lifting technique. Increased capacity could only be achieved by new technology. The old *kavalai* technique, with its leather bags, was becoming an obstacle to further expansion.

However, agricultural production was not the prime issue when the large, water-power plant in the Nilgiri mountains was planned. The initial inquiries about changing over to electric propulsion were made by the Government to the factory owners and the South Indian Railways.

In September 1929, the Pykhara water-power project was

sanctioned by the Secretary of State, and in 1930 the first generator was turned on. The project itself had commenced in 1924. Pykhara was a large-scale project. In 1926, the aims were still to transmit electric power the 418 kilometres to Madras to use it for the railways and the municipality. But the major obstacle was to find enough consumers of the electric power made available. The Chief Engineer for Irrigation in the Madras presidency, C.T. Mullings, presented rather vague ideas in 1926 about the best use for the electric power. He was willing to sell it for any purpose that paid. However, to provide power for water-lifts had not been considered, since it was only expected to result in a loss. To transfer current to small areas and for small-scale purposes was considered far too expensive.[68]

Mullings's initial scepticism soon had to be reconsidered. Already in the early 1930s, power was distributed to villages for agricultural purposes; in the 1940s, electric-power lines were put up also in some of the more remote villages. In the case of Palladam taluk, the main transmission lines ran in its outskirts, and villages in large parts of the taluk lay at a distance. However, economically and technically, the installation of pumps was possible during the 1940s, but such installations were not made on farm land until the early 1950s. As compared with large parts of the Madras state, 1950 is still early for rural electrification.

In 1929, the main interest of the Government was in persuading the factory owners in Coimbatore to use electric power. However, shifting from one source of power to another in the factories resulted in a need for investments in new machinery, and the Government of Madras feared that industrial demand would not be sufficient. They turned to the South Indian Railway authorities, but without success. The railway company considered the electrification of the railways to be too risky an investment to make.[69] The Government was also reported to have met 'considerable opposition' when they negotiated with the textile-mill-owners in Coimbatore to change their old engines for electric operation. Ten years of activities in the Electricity Department were summarised in the 1937-8 annual report, and the author writes: '... the vested interests of oil and coal suppliers and oil engine manufacturers all doing their utmost by temporarily reducing prices to dissuade consumers from converting'.[70] To face this competition, the Government made the conversion of loans available to mill-owners. In this way, money could be advanced without delay to both new and old mills for the purchase of electrical machinery and equipment.[71] Already in 1934-5, all the mills but one were operated by electricity.[72] During the following years, there was an increase in the number of mills, and by the beginning of the 1950s, 55 per cent of all textile mills in Tamil Nadu were situated in Coimbatore. The town had become a major textile centre, next in importance to Ahmedabad and Bombay.[73] The dam-building project in Pykhara generated investments in infrastructure. Roads, bridges, railways, hospitals, etc., had to be built in order to carry out the project.

From 1930 onwards, the installations of electrical power show a steady increase in the district. In 1933, when all three generators were working at Pykhara, the Department of Electricity was established and took over the work of the Department of Hydro-electric Development.[74] Transmission lines ran from Pykhara in the north to Anamalai in the south and Erode in the north-east. In order to secure demand for electricity and to promote the mechanisation of agriculture, the Government of Madras now approached the larger landowners and farmers with information and propaganda. The arguments focused on the possibilities of improved farming by the use of electric power instead of manual labour.[75]

As early as 1932-3, six agricultural areas were receiving low-tension electric power.[76] This electricity was used for operating agricultural pumps to lift water out of the wells for irrigation purposes. According to a bulletin issued by the Department of Industries in the Madras Presidency, a manually worked *kavalai* could lift 2,000 gallons or 9,092 litres per hour, while a small pump of one and a half horsepower could lift 3,000 gallons or 13,638 litres per hour.[77] This was an

TABLE 3.3. INSTALLATION OF AGRICULTURAL ELECTRIC PUMP SETS, COIMBATORE DISTRICT

| *Year* | *Total installations of agricultural pumps* | *Villages reached by electricity* |
|---|---|---|
| 1934-5 | 97 | No data |
| 1935-6 | 269 | <30 |
| 1936-7 | 543 | 90 |
| 1937-8 | 970 | 121 |
| 1938-9 | 1429 | 160 |
| 1939-40 | 1810 | 176* |

Source: Administrative Reports of the Electricity Department for the years 1934/35-1939/40.

* The lower increase is said to have been an effect of World War II, causing prices to rise and making imports of industrial goods uncertain. (1939/40, p. 1.)

investment that could have repercussions on the farmer, as the wells were not proportioned for this kind of use. In 1937-8, the Department of Electricity expressed worries about the lowering of groundwater levels,[78] and the Department of Industries, after having praised the electric pumps to the skies, reported pumps overheating when installed in the deep wells of the Coimbatore district.[79]

In the first phase of rural electrification, electric power was distributed to the areas closest to the main transmission lines and, in spite of initial difficulties, the number of installations increased in the 1930s. Installations were motivated by the possibility of increasing production by getting access to more water and reducing labour costs. They were a long-term investment.[80] After the initial years, during the Second World War, other arguments were added to these to support efforts to find an alternative way to bring the water to the fields. Between 1939 and 1945, not only the prices of crops, but also the prices of cattle rose.The cost of a bullock team was estimated to have risen from 150 rupees to 1,000 rupees during the war years by the Enquiry into Rural Indebtedness in 1946 (inflation not considered). The costs of cattle feed rose by three to seven times. Prices of implements, such as timber and iron, to repair and maintain a *kavalai* increased, as did also the prices of hides and skins.[81]

The farm lands in Palladam taluk were not crossed by any of the main transmission lines running from Pykhara, and it was another ten years before electric power reached these villages. Both Madhari and Goundar informants remember the fear that people felt towards the electricity. Government representatives had to gather the farmers in the villages and market-places to convince them and canvass support.[82] Seventy-four-year old Narayana Goundar of Semmipalayam remembers going to the village of Karamathai for a festival in the early 1950s. Everywhere, he met with people who were talking much about electricity. A rumour went round that an electric pump was going to be demonstrated at the Panchayat union office, and Narayana Goundar, not believing that water could possibly come out of a well by itself, went to see it. In 1954, he was the first person in his area to be connected to the electric-power system.[83]

Between 1947 and 1953, the district was struck by a severe drought, and in the most drought-prone areas, such as Palladam, agriculture was running at a low level. But still, as is shown in Table 3.4, the peak in electrical installations for agricultural purposes came in 1951-3 in Palladam taluk. In the same year, the Season and Crop Report noted with some satisfaction that the farmers had availed themselves

TABLE 3.4. CONNECTIONS TO VILLAGES FOR AGRICULTURAL PURPOSES FROM PYKHARA ELECTRIC SYSTEM, 1950-7

| *Taluk* | *Coimbatore* | *Palladam* | *Pollachi* | *Avanashi* | *Udamalpet* | *Dharapuram* |
|---|---|---|---|---|---|---|
| 1950 | — | 1 | 1 | — | — | — |
| 1951 | 6 | 13 | 9 | — | 1 | — |
| 1952 | 8 | 10 | 5 | 14 | 2 | — |
| 1953 | — | 10* | 3 | — | 1 | 3 |
| 1954 | — | 3* | 1* | 1 | 1 | — |
| 1955 | — | 5 | 11 | 6 | — | 10 |
| 1956 | — | 5 | 9* | 2 | — | 2 |
| 1957 | — | 8* | — | 1* | 1* | 9 |

Source: Government of Madras, Department of Public Works, Indexes 1950-7.
* Includes connection in which power was supplied to several villages.

in increasing numbers of Government facilities for improved farming.[84]

During the drought, the prices of cattle feed had risen high and made the maintenance of cattle extremely difficult. Even though the government granted subsidies for the sinking of wells and gave interest-free loans for different agricultural purposes, drawing water by draught animals became expensive: As a result of the Department of Agriculture supplying agricultural input at controlled or concessional rates and leasing out tractors and petrol pumps, the Season and Crop Report concluded that the use of electricity for agricultural purposes, the reclamation of waste lands and the raising of short-term food crops had become evident.[85]

'Propaganda for the use of power machinery was intensified' in 1951-2, according to the Season and Crop Report.[86] During the early 1950s the district as a whole alone accounted for nearly half of all the electric pumps installed in the state of Tamil Nadu. In 1956 the number had fallen to below one-third of all installed pumps. But throughout the 1950s and 1960s, Coimbatore was a leading district in the number of pumps installed.[87]

C.T. Kurien stated that the increasing availability of water from electric pumps and the expanding distribution of tractors were major factors in the agricultural change in Tamil Nadu during the period 1950-80. He notices a close connection between increased subsoil irrigation by electric pumps and an increased use of tractors. Tractors and trailers began to replace carts and bullocks. In his district-level survey, he also observes the correlation between the high increase of the number of pumps and tractors and the prominent wet-cultivation districts. The exception is Coimbatore, where wet crops are less prominent. Still, the number of tractors distributed in the district was among the highest in Tamil Nadu. Kurien observes that the district 'has traditionally had a lead in tractors'.[88]

There was a noticeable change in the village when the electric transmission line was connected. Since the Government in Madras urgently needed consumers of electric power in order not to end up with a large deficit on the Pykhara power plant, rural electrification came quite rapidly, partly with Government support. The initial costs of installation prevented small farmers from switching from *kavalai* to electric pumps. But for farmers who could afford these expenses, it was a long-term investment which paid off in reduced costs of labour and bulls. More importantly, the pumps could be used both day and night, more water could be taken from the well, and consequently a larger part of the land could be irrigated and yield a second harvest or be sown with a cash crop.

However, these immediate benefits were most visible from the Goundar point of view. From the Madhari point of view, the immediate benefits turned out to be immediate disadvantages. The electric pumps, that could water more land without the consideration of wearing out bulls in the midday sun, not only came to replace cattle and manpower, but also the trade ascribed and allotted to the Madhari as leather-workers. Over a period of approximately two to three decades, there was no longer the same need for leather buckets, as the *kavalai* ceased to be the principal technology for lifting water. It was not the demand for leather products, as such, that vanished; sandals were still made in thousands for the higher castes. It was one of the most important products of the leather-workers in the agricultural production process that was replaced by industrial goods. As a result, the Madhari's specific identity, as being the only group who could provide the necessary buckets for the irrigation works, and were therefore an indispensable part of the agricultural production, was undermined.

Both interviews and contemporary documents testify to the negative effects felt by the Madhari. Rajamanickam of Arulpuram, who worked as a *pannaiyal* in his youth, recalls that the *pannaiyal's* work was reduced. Stitching the *kavalai* had yielded an income that disappeared as a result of the electrification. Until then, the hides had been given free of charge to the Madharis of Arulpuram, but gradually they had to buy them from the Goundar, since hides had come to make a profit when sold to the growing leather industry. Rajamanickam associates this loss with a social gain for the community, as they were less often called Madhari or Chakkili in the same degrading way as before. But the financial loss was more immediately felt.[89]

The bulls of the *kavalai* were generally supervised by Madhari men. This task had given the labourers work for several hours every morning and evening. The new electric pump sets also needed supervision, and once in a while lubrication. This was not too difficult a task to perform, but it was rarely entrusted to the Madhari. As Abraham of Manidiripalayam recalls, the Goundar himself switched the current on and off.[90] This does not imply that the Goundar immediately ceased to employ Madhari men as agricultural labourers. Though manpower was gradually replaced in the work of drawing water, agriculture still depended on manual labour. But there was no longer a natural necessity to engage the Madhari, no more than to employ members of any of the other castes among the agricultural labourers.

The Rev. Anders Andrén reported from the area in 1955 as follows:

> ... these poor villagers living under pitiable conditions in scattered villages. They have to work hard in the fields for their masters without adequate salary. Yet they have to be content with the salary given to them and they most of all fear to be without work. The number of unemployed in the villages seems to increase and this situation creates a great problem. Electric water pumps, tractors and other modern equipment have become the substitute of men and this fact reacts upon the outcastes who have already so many difficulties. They know very well what starving is. Though the conditions as regard to food supply have improved considerably since the six years of famine, the standard of living has not come up to that level which prevailed before the famine.[91]

As early as 1967, the Madhari had begun to speak about the good old days, when there was a demand for tanning by the old methods, for the drawing of water and for tent-making, and when more field work was available. Now, in 1967, electrical pump sets and threshing machines had reduced real wages and the amount of work available. Days could pass when there was no work to be found.[92]

The Reverends Olle Jonsson and J.S. Victor investigated the situation of the Madhari in the villages surrounding Arulpuram mission station in 1962. The aim was to evaluate the preconditions for future development work among these people, with particular stress on their skills in leather-work. Walking about in the villages, they found the tanning industry completely in decay. In 1994, Olle Jonsson remembered that they had found old tanning basins intact, and in the ceilings of the Madhari houses they had found the tanning knives stuck under the beams. When asked 'When did you last work in tanning?', the Madhari men had replied: 'In my father's time.'[93]

A similar development has been described by John Harriss in his work on capitalism and peasant farming in North Arcot district, which is a district bordering on Coimbatore. Irrigation was mainly performed by the leather-working community in the area, the Chakkiliyar. Two different manual techniques were used to bring the water from the wells to the fields. However, neither the *eeram*[94] nor the *kavalai* technique could withstand the competition of pumps, and from 1957, when the Madras Electricity Board took over from the private electricity companies, widespread electrification and diffusion of electric pump sets began. The 1960s was a decade of rapid electrification in North Arcot.

The consequences of this change, as observed by Harriss in the 1970s, showed a reduction of male labourers in agriculture, while the number of female labourers increased. 'Attached' male labourers, working under conditions similar to those of the *pannaiyal* in the Coimbatore district, had operated the *kavalai* water-lifts, and electrification made them redundant. However, as a result of the increased irrigation made possible by the more efficient pumps, the acreage of land under paddy cultivation could be expanded. The high-yielding variety of paddy that was sown increased the demand for labour in weeding and harvesting. Consequently, since these parts of the production process were carried out primarily by female labour, women were employed in larger numbers.[95]

Returning to the Coimbatore district, there seems to have been another negative consequence for the Madhari of the introduction of electricity into the villages. The information has been revealed in interviews, but it has not been possible to confirm it elsewhere. After electric power replaced bullock power and lorries and buses gradually replaced the bullock carts, the need for cattle was reduced. Over the years, the big herds diminished and, by the end of the period studied, even manure had begun to be replaced by chemical fertilisers.[96] However, interestingly, this downward trend in the number of cattle, which was so visible to the Madhari labourers and the Goundar farmers, has not been recorded in official statistics. Throughout the century, irrespective of economic depression, drought and the shift to using electric power on the farms, the number of cattle and buffaloes given in the Season and Crop Report changes only very little and with no trend in any direction. This fact throws some doubt on the accuracy of the figures.[97]

The result of a reduced cattle stock became more and more evident to the Madhari, who had been allowed to pasture their own cattle without cost, together with the Goundars' cattle, in their fields. This provided the fields with more manure and made it possible for Madhari labourers to have their own cattle. When the farmer ceased to have cattle in large numbers, the Madhari could not keep cattle any more, since they could not afford the fodder.[98]

As part of the *urimai*, the rights and duties that may explain part of the relationship between the Madhari and the Goundar, the Madhari had access to a share of the produce and to the meat from the dead cattle. When the necessity of keeping cattle in agriculture diminished, this right lost some of its validity.

To conclude, the introduction of electric power and mechanical equipment on the farms affected the lives and livelihoods of the Madhari in more than one way. As the pumps began to replace the *kavalai* water-lifts, they also replaced the agricultural task that was as a rule entrusted to the Madhari, that of irrigation. But as mechanical equipment not only replaced this occupation, but also the widespread use of cattle in agriculture, something that was also in the care of the Madhari labourers, the Madhari began to lose an important part of their rights, in the terminology of Chapter 2, their *urimai*. With fewer cattle in the villages, they would less often receive meat and would have fewer opportunities to keep cattle of their own.

This development can be suspected to have had major consequences for remuneration and employment conditions. But, before going further into that, the drought that struck the region at the height of the connection of electric power to the villages and the consequences created by the lack of rain will be discussed.

## NOTES

1 Cox 1933, p. 239; Baker 1984, pp. 268-74. The Nilgiri Mountain Railway opened in 1899, connecting important plantation areas with urban trading and industrial centres, and Palghat was reached not only from the east, but also from the north-east and the south-east by 1915 and 1932 respectively.

2 IOR, Baramahal Records 10.8.1794, §30, and comment by the Board of Revenue on this paragraph.

3 In the 1880s, new implements and methods and improved cotton and other seeds were tried in the Government model farms. But the Department of Agriculture complained that, unless the Government gave subsidies or could offer prices higher than the market prices for the

produce, the cultivators would not run the risk of using an unknown seed. Several experiments were carried out, and exhibitions were taken to the villages to influence the cultivators to change from the old varieties of cotton. Report on the Operations of the Department of Agriculture 1884/85-1889/90, see particularly 1882/83, pp. 10-11, 1883/84, pp. 16-18. See also 1884/85, p. 16, where the introduction of 'soil-breaking' ploughs was reported to have been received with hesitation but was accepted after demonstrations and had begun to show good results on black cotton soils. Nicholson 1887, p. 233; Baker 1984, p. 267; Rothermund 1993 (1988), p. 45.

4 Madras District Gazetteers, Coimbatore, 1966, pp. 269-70.

5 The Dindigul and Palni areas, in the extreme south of the highlands, were regions where unirrigated Cambodia cotton could be grown and even predominated among the cotton varieties in the 1930s. This was caused by the fact that the plentiful rains in the hills percolated through the soil and gave the necessary moisture to the neighbouring plain. Ponniah 1934, p. 394; Baker 1984, pp. 267-8.

6 Cox 1933, p. 161.

7 Cox 1933, p. 166.

8 Spate and Learmont 1967 (1954), p. 762; Mahadevan 1992, p. 9; Baker 1984, p. 272.

9 Mahadevan 1992, p. 20; Baker 1976, pp. 184, 187.

10 Cox 1933, p. 160; Baker 1984, pp. 267-8. In the whole of the Madras Presidency there was an increase of cash-crop cultivation from 25 per cent of the cultivated area in 1911 to 33 per cent in 1931. Baker and Washbrook 1975, p. 215.

11 DRCC, Re-Survey and Re-Settlement Registers, Palladam Taluk, 1912, a selection of twenty-five *kasbahs*.

12 Only two other taluks in the district came close to the figures of Palladam taluk for *cholam* and cotton. Udamalpet taluk cropped about the same amount of cotton, compared with other crops, as Palladam. Coimbatore taluk achieved the same result for *cholam*. Cox 1933, Table IX, pp. 25, 81-5, 159.

13 See also Chapter 3. Cox 1933, p. 148.

14 Evans 1995, pp. 172-4.

15 See, for example, Mandiripalayam 31.1.1995, interview.

16 Baker 1976, pp. 184, 187.

17 Hjejle 1967, p. 106, referring to a report by the Collector of Trichinopoly, 1846.

18 Census of India 1901, 1911 and 1921:1901, Vol. XV, Madras I, pp. 25-6; 1911, Vol. XII, Madras I, p. 25; 1921, Vol. XIII, Madras I, p. 51.

19 Baker 1984, pp. 209-10.

20 In contrast to the Season and Crop Report of the Madras state, referred to later, and the district Gazetteers, Cox's Gazetteer for the Coimbatore district gives taluk-wise figures. Between the years 1897 and 1930, the

number of wells increased by 32 per cent, from 65,461 to 86,207. Cox 1933, pp. 171-2; Ganesamurthi 1935, p. 272.

21 From 1902 to 1916, the area of cultivated land watered by well irrigation was around 300,000 acres. From 1917, a trend began in which this area increased to more than 400,000 in 1922-4. After 1926, the extent of land watered by well irrigation was stabilised at that level. Season and Crop Report for the years 1902/3-1933/34.

22 Ganesamurthi 1935, pp. 271-2, 277; Baker 1984, p. 209.

23 Cox 1933, p. 173.

24 Cox 1933, p. 149.

25 Lindberg 1969, p. 72.

26 Semmipalayam 1.2.1995, interviews, Sivasubramaniyan Goundar and Narayana Goundar.

27 Madras Agriculturists' Relief Act (Madras Act IV of 1938). Rothermund 1992, pp. 122-3.

28 SAA, Gwynn Papers, Box 1:36, No. 30, 4.6.1906, letter to 'Dear Father'.

29 DRCC, Re-Survey and Re-Settlement Registers, Palladam taluk, 1912, a selection of the following *kasbahs*: Vadugapalayam, Kasbah Ayyampalayam, Pongalur, Thongattipalayam, South Avanashipalayam, Vadamalaipalayam, Kamanaickampalayam Krishnapuram, Kettanur, Elavanthi, Velarasikallipalayam, Palladam, Naranapuram, Madapur, Sembipalayam, Ittivirampalayam.

30 Cox 1933, p. 148.

31 Sivaswamy 1948, pp. 18-25.

32 Nicholson 1887, p. 166.

33 Nicholson 1887, pp. 178-80.

34 Breman 1985, pp. 92-3.

35 *Tandalkaran*, an office generally performed by a Paraiyar, using his *parai*, a drum resembling a tambourine.

36 DRCC, Re-Survey and Re-Settlement Registers, Palladam taluk, 1912.

37 The data for the enquiry were collected by stratified sampling from villages in all districts in the Madras Presidency. Report of the Economist for Enquiry into Rural Indebtedness 1946, p. 38. See pp. 92-4, Statement I, for details of the data collection.

38 Narayanaswamy Naidu bases his data of prices for nine crops for the years between 1938 and 1945 on information given in the Season and Crop Report. Report of the Economist for Enquiry into Rural Indebtedness 1946, p. 55.

39 Report of the Economist for Enquiry into Rural Indebtedness 1946, pp. 49-50.

40 Mandiripalayam 2.2.1995, interview; Jacob 1996, interview.

41 Semmipalayam 1.2.1995, interviews, Sivasubramaniyan Goundar and Narayana Goundar.

42 Mandiripalayam 2.2.1995, interview, Ramasamy Goundar; Semmipalayam 1.2.1995, interviews, Sivasubramaniyan Goundar and Narayana

Goundar; Yanagisawa 1996, pp. 251-2.

43 That is, Devanga Chettiar, Kaikolar or Segundar Mudaliar, Kongu Vellalar and Kammavar (the latter are sometimes named by the title given to originally Telugu communities: Naidu or, in Tamil, Naicker). Cox 1933, p. 152; Thurston 1909, Vol. 5, p. 138.

44 Washbrook 1974, p. 29; Baker 1984, pp. 272-3.

45 Baker 1984, pp. 267, 275, 347.

46 Breman 1985, pp. 88-9.

47 Baker 1984, pp. 267-70.

48 *Mundi* = wholesale trade. Ponniah 1934, pp. 296-7.

49 In a table, Mahadevan shows the relative positions as between the major Indian industrial groups in the Coimbatore district from 1915 to 1948. It reveals the strong position held by the three Naidu families. Mahadevan 1992, pp. 33-5, 40, 45-6, Table V, p. 37.

50 Baker 1984, pp. 213-14.

51 Baker 1984, pp. 272-4, 333. See also Harriss 1983, p. 11.

52 Rothermund 1992, pp. 136-7, 139.

53 Rothermund 1992, pp. 141, 146-7.

54 Baker 1984, p. 268.

55 Baker 1984, pp. 168-9.

56 Baker 1984, pp. 116-17.

57 Baker 1984, p. 119, referring to figures given by the League of Nations, *World Production and Prices, 1925-34*, pp. 37-8.

58 The highest level reached in the mid-1920s: Rs. 0.7 (Index 100); 1925: Rs. 0.5 (71); 1929: 0.35 (50); 1930: 0.22 (31). Prices listed in *Bombay Millowners' Association Annual Report* 1931, p. 186. Rothermund 1992, p. 81.

59 Rothermund 1992, pp. 79-81, 92. Baker states that, while mortgages on landed property could reach 70 per cent of the estimated value, land prices halved between the years 1929 and 1931. Baker 1984, pp. 296-7.

60 Baker 1984, p. 350, Table 17. See also Baker 1976, p. 182.

61 Mahadevan 1992, pp. 33-5; Baker 1984, p. 272.

62 Rothermund 1992, p. 161; Baker 1984, pp. 251-3.

63 Baker 1984, pp. 272-4, 333.

64 In tons/acre for the year 1925/26: 97,900/300,000; 1930/31: 109,400/336,000; and for 1935/36: 113,310/348,000. Madras District Gazetteers, Coimbatore, 1966, pp. 269-70.

65 Tyabij 1995, p. 39, Table 2.1.

66 Cox 1933, p. 160; Madras District Gazetteers, Coimb., 1966, pp. 269-70.

67 Cox 1933, p. 25, Table IX; p. 83, Table IX; p. 160; Tyabji 1995, pp. 36-41.

68 Royal Commission on Agriculture in India 1927, pp. 519, 525, 527; Dept. of Hydro-electric Development 1929-30, pp. 1-3.

69 Dept. of Hydro-electric Development 1929-30, pp. 1-3.

70 Dept. of Electricity 1937-8, p. 2.

71 Dept. of Electricity 1933-4, p. 1.

72 Dept. of Electricity 1934-5, p. 1.
73 Harriss, Kannan and Rogers 1990, p. 4.
74 Dept. of Electricity 1932-3, p. 1.
75 Dept. of Industries, Bulletin no. 35:1932, p. 6.
76 Dept. of Electricity 1932-3, p. 5.
77 Dept of Industries, Bulletin no. 35:1932, p. 1.
78 Dept. of Electricity 1937-8, p. 5.
79 Dept. of Industries, Bulletin no. 35:1932, p. 6.
80 Dept. of Industries, Bulletin no. 35:1932, p. 6.
81 Report of the Economist for Enquiry into Rural Indebtedness 1946, p. 47.
82 Semmipalayam 1.2.1995, interview; Mandiripalayam 31.1.1995, interview.
83 Semmipalayam 1.2.1995, interview, and iron plate on the electricity switchboard on his farm.
84 Season and Crop Report 1953/54, p. 24.
85 Season and Crop Report 1949/50, p. 35.
86 Season and Crop Report 1951/52, p. 34.
87 Kurien 1989 (1981), Table 3:19, pp. 56-8. The district's share as a percentage of the total distribution of electric pumps in Tamil Nadu was, according to Kurien's table, 1951: 47.6, 1956: 29.53, 1961: 24.91, 1966: 21.83. The figures for 1951 and 1961 have been corrected according to calculations based on the actual number of pumps given in the table.
88 Kurien 1989 (1981), pp. 35, 60.
89 Arulpuram 26.1.1995, interview.
90 Mandiripalayam 31.1.1995, interview.
91 Reports of unemployment began to come in during the drought. From 1950/51, the Season and Crop Report gave information of the growing numbers of unemployed agricultural labourers. CSMA, FaR, Board of Pioneer Evangelism 1955, p. 1; Season and Crop Report 1950/51, p. 1.
92 Lindberg Collection, Staffan Lindberg Field Diary, Vol. 2, p. 28, Vavipalayam 21.6.1967, pp. 34-5, Mandiripalayam 21.6.1967, pp. 38-9, Kullampalayam 22.6.1967; Lindberg Collection, P. Solomon Field Diary, Veerapandi 29.5.1967.
93 CSMA, MBa 1962:158*a* and *b*; Jonsson, 1994, lecture.
94 A *eeram* or a *picota* is a technique by which water is drawn from a well by a large lever or well-sweep. A *picota* cannot be used in a deep well.
95 Harriss 1982, pp. 67-9, 97.
96 Kurien 1989 (1981), p. 36.
97 The consequences of a reduction of the numbers of bulls in the villages will be further discussed in the coming chapters. Madras District Gazetteers, Coimb., 1966, p. 271; Season and Crop Report 1976/77, p. 157.
98 Mandiripalayam 31.1.1995, Interview, Subban James. See also the Royal Commission on Agriculture in India 1927, p. 551, for details of how cattle were shifted between different fields in rotation in order to provide manure.

CHAPTER 4

# The Drought

To remember an event once experienced and place it in time, in a situation in which calendars and dates are used for telling the future, not the past, requires comparisons with other contemporary events. While Independence might be unknown to the older Madhari people, the great drought was an event that could not be mistaken. It was a landmark in memory, things are said to have happened before or after the famine. Questions like 'When were you born?' or 'When did you move into this area?' may be given the answer, 'During the famine.'

Six years of drought, from 1947 to 1953, dug deep into the rural economy. Without rain, there was little to harvest and little agricultural work and the profits from agricultural produce in general were reduced. The effects on the separate agricultural classes proved to be very different. The means of survival for the propertyless agricultural labourers diminished in their home villages. But even among these, some managed fairly well, while others were worse off. The differences depended on what alternative possibilities could be realised, and on what strategies could be adopted to counter the loss of work in the fields.

Also between the small and medium farmers, on the one hand, and the large farmers, on the other, different results for the famine years have been found. Those farming on a bigger scale appear to have been able to make profitable use of the Government's subsidies for making improvements in agriculture and of rising prices for agricultural products. The small farmers, on the other hand, seem to have lost in the competition.

Dry periods were not unknown to the people of the highlands, weak or failing monsoons occurred rather frequently. The first reactions to the failing north-east monsoon in late 1945 reflect this familiarity with the climate. The Rev. Stephen noted that 'a greater number than usual' of the labourers left the villages. Apart from the majority, who were the seasonal migrants of the tea estates, there were others who joined them or left for other villages or moved into the towns. Stephen adds assuredly: '... this migration is only a temporary one and will not affect our work permanently'.[1]

Local society was not taken by surprise but was prepared and was used to keeping stocks of grain in case of failing crops. It was not that life went on as usual after the failure of a monsoon but that there was no immediate threat to survival. Labour on daily wages could generally be found elsewhere, and there was still work for the *pannaiyal* in the farmers' service. But as the monsoons of the next six years brought only very little rain, there were no longer any means of paying wages in kind. For the poor who remained in the villages, private or public relief was often the only way to survive.

The two, yearly, monsoon rains fed the dry soils of the highlands. The results of the harvests depended on those rains. The little water that fell during the other parts of the year had very little effect on the agricultural output. Groundwater irrigation ensured high-quality cash crops, vegetables and good millet harvests. But as only a minor part of the land was irrigated, the major part of cultivation depended on the monsoon rains. The different distribution of rain is shown in Map 5.

The two monsoons cover slightly different areas in the district. The south-west monsoon in June to September gives more water to the southern parts, while the north-east monsoon in October to December gives rainfall also to the western and northern parts of the district. This is due to the geographical situation, where the mountains in the west hinder the onset of the humid winds in June, making them release most of the rain on the western side of the mountain chain. In Coimbatore town the south-west monsoon was better known for its strong winds than for its rain.[2] These areas were rather dependent on the more reliable, but at the same time weaker, north-east monsoon.

The fact that the Coimbatore district received weaker rains from 1946 to 1953 can be seen in Graph 4.1, but a complete failure of the monsoons is more difficult to observe. This is explained by the way information was collected for the Season and Crop Report. In the yearly statements for the Coimbatore district, this area was reported as one unit, all the data being generalised for the district level. This information did not take into account the differences between the geographical zones within the area. Throughout the drought years, the hills received normal rains, and in the southern regions up to Pollachi, even though weak, the rains appeared from time to time. In the Map 5, 'Average annual rainfall', shows clearly the variation of rainfall between the dry centre and the hills, depending on topographical conditions and location. It was not in the hills and the immediately neighbouring regions that the drought left its deepest marks. The severe consequences were to be found in the central part of the district, situated in the rain shadow from the western mountains. This was the region from which reports were sent that described villages that had been completely without rain for six years. These reports came from the Lutheran missionaries, some of them working in the villages around Palladam and south of Coimbatore, some of them working further south in Pollachi and Dindigul.

The contradiction between the generalised and detailed information can be observed also in the Season and Crop Report itself, without comparing it with another source. 1946-7 was reported as a normal year. Rainfall was above average, as can also be seen in Graph 4.1. At the same time a 'marked decrease' and 'reduction' were reported for the most important crops grown on the plains of the highlands, i.e. cotton, *cholam*, *korra* and gingelly.[3] Three of those were crops that needed regular watering to make a profitable harvest.

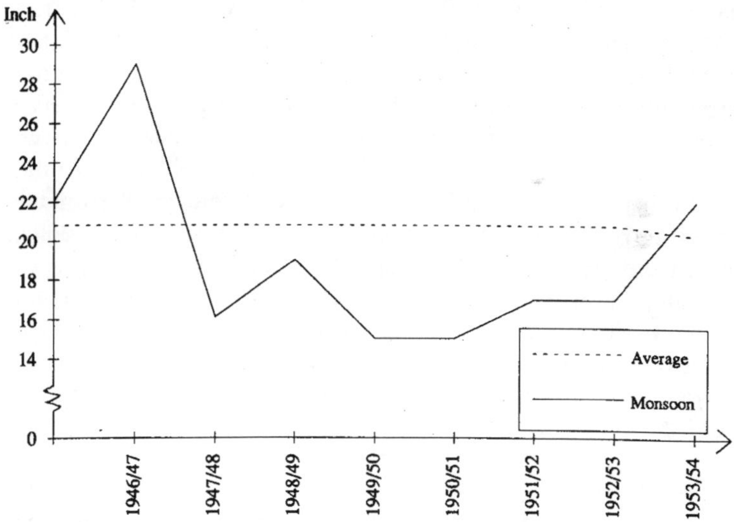


GRAPH 4.1. MONSOON RAINS FOR THE COIMBATORE DISTRICT, 1944/45-1954/55, AS COMPARED WITH THE AVERAGE FOR THE PRECEDING 50 YEARS

Source: Season and Crop Report of the Madras Presidency/State, Department of Statistics.

Looking at the rural situation from the point of view of industrialisation during the drought, the trend to bring industrial goods to the villages continued. There was rather a further expansion during the 1950s. Distribution of mechanical equipment and electricity for agricultural purposes were aided by Government subsidies. Farmers adjusted themselves to the changing market conditions, and social and labour relations were remodelled. One could say that this happened *in spite of* the drought. But the issue could also be turned round, and the question could be formulated thus: Did the drought hasten this process? Did failing crops enforce a further rationalisation of the agricultural production? Was the relationship between the Goundar and the Madhari affected in a special way *because of* the great drought?

## A PROFITABLE DROUGHT

The 1947 north-east monsoon was late and weak in the Coimbatore district, and the crops withered.[4] The following year was reported to have been just as dry. Madras was not the only state to suffer from failing rains in the forties. Many parts of India were affected, and Bengal was hardest hit by the severe drought. During the initial years of the drought, food crops were rationed according to different levels depending on the results of the harvest in each district. Of two neighbouring districts, one could be classified as 'deficit' and the other as 'surplus', which made it very profitable to smuggle food grains across the border, and the black market grew. In Coimbatore, a deficit district, the Government of Madras controlled all trade in food grains.[5] But rationing was seen as an obstacle to economic growth by the central Government and was to be removed before the end of 1948. Thereafter, the states were to reduce their demands on the central Government.[6] By December 1947, price control was removed in four districts in the Madras state, and by December 1948 'free trade' was completely restored in the state.[7]

The effects were immediate. When the price control on rice was lifted in January 1948, prices doubled in Coimbatore district. Not until the Government opened grain stores was it possible for consumers to purchase rice at the previous price. Rice in the Government stores was rationed, and only limited amounts were available.[8] Food-grain prices were already high as a result of the war. Particularly after the fall of the rice-producing countries in south-east Asia, prices rose in India. Now the failing crops resulted in a marked increase in the prices of all agricultural products, but in particular of the commercial crops. Also, a slight rise in land prices was recorded.[9]

As a consequence, the amount of land under cash-crop cultivation increased. Among the major, cultivated, food crops in the Coimbatore district between 1945-6 and 1950-1, paddy, Bengal gram and a local millet variety increased in cultivated area. But in spite of being grown on larger portions of land, Bengal gram did not show any increasing yields in the sub-total for the district. The millet variety was increasing but was only cultivated on a very limited area. The increased yield from paddy cultivation continued but slowed down. Between 1945 and 1950, the increasing results for paddy were less than half of the increase over the previous five years. Even though paddy expanded in acreage, the total yield per hectare fell.[10]

1949 was the third year of failing rains in the Coimbatore district, and the consequences in food and water shortages, as well as scarcity of work, were severely felt by the people living in the dry belt of the highlands. The missionaries in the region could not avoid noticing the grave effects that the drought had for the Scheduled Caste villagers when they visited the congregations. These were almost all to be found among the Madhari and Paraiyar villagers. They were the 'people' that the author of the following passage was referring to when he described the situation in the Palladam area in his report.

> The Coimbatore district and the northern part of Madura hardly got any rain at all. By the end of the year the wells dried out, the crops withered, and for the first time within living memory the newspapers declared that famine threatened the fertile South India. People are starving in the Palladam area. Cattle and poultry are being sold, and the population capable of doing work emigrate. Hardly one fourth of a village population remains.... From the villages in the Coimbatore district thousands seek work on the plantations in the mountains.[11]

Also the Season and Crop Report speaks of labourers migrating away from the drought-stricken villages. These labourers were said to have left for the towns, and the author reports on Government relief work in construction, road repairs and well-digging. But just as in the report for the previous year, the 1948-9 records give information about what might seem to be a paradox. Side by side with paragraphs relating the difficulties that the failing rains caused the landless labourers, farmers were reported to have grown more cotton, tobacco, sugar and groundnuts than in the previous years.[12] These are commercial crops that require regular irrigation, unless the rains are normal, and are not very likely crops to have been cultivated during a drought. Obviously, all the wells did not run dry, and there were farmers wealthy enough to be able to expand their cash-crop cultivation and profit from the rising prices.

An interesting trend is revealed in the Season and Crop Report during the following drought years. For all the years until 1952, rising prices for commercial crops were recorded for the districts struck by drought.[13] 'Larger landholders' were said to have profited from them. They were not only able to break even, making enough profit to cope with the rising prices of agricultural implements and consumption goods, but also managed to create a surplus and repay their debts.

A comparison of the area under cultivation in the Coimbatore district of the fifteen major crops between the year that showed the first sign of the coming drought, 1945-6, and one of the most severe drought years, 1950-1, shows that in spite of the lack of rain, groundnuts and sugar cane had substantial increases in acreage. Though the yields from the crops did not increase to the same extent, favourable prices can be expected to have made up for the smaller harvests per unit.[14]

For the medium farmers, who also grew commercial crops but who did not control such extensive holdings as the large farmers, the reports give the impression that during the initial drought years they were able to manage without having to lower their standard of living. In the year 1949-50, the farmers were described as having faced a complete failure of the monsoon. Insect pests and diseases attacked the standing crops, and the cattle feed was poor. In the following year, when the larger landholders were said to have partly repaid their debts, costs were described as having cancelled out profits for the majority of landholders who could not cope with the steep rise in the costs of cultivation and maintenance of cattle and who suffered from the short supply of agricultural implements and consumer goods. In 1951-2, a growing number of them could not meet the requirements but had to take up loans to pay the interest on former debts.[15]

The division between larger and smaller landholders is vague in the Season and Crop Reports, but the author of the reports obviously thought that the dividing line was determined by the scale of cultivation. Large-scale farming implied less risk-taking, the margins were broader, production costs had become lower than the profit per unit, and thus the large landholders were able to expand through out the drought years without getting further indebted. Subsoil water made it possible to carry out a limited amount of cultivation, in spite of the absent monsoons. The intensively irrigated, garden cultivation, with its flexibility, permitted farmers to concentrate on the more profitable, commercial crops, since this form of cultivation was suited to adjusting to such rapid changes.

As was discussed in the previous chapter, in the late 1940s, the Government had for several years supplied the farmers with information about the benefits of the electric pumps, and demonstrations had been held in the market-places. The peak of the first wave of electrical connections that were made for agricultural purposes in the Palladam taluk coincides with a period when cultivation was on a low level. The years 1951 to 1953, when several of the revenue villages around Palladam and its main roads received electrical connections, are recorded as the worst of the drought years. 1952 was claimed to be the worst of them all.[16] Some rain was received in 1953 and eased the conditions for the villagers. Late in that year, people were seen returning to the home villages from the estates in Nilgiri and Valparai, but still the reports speak of famine.[17]

The Enquiry into Rural Indebtedness calculated that 50 per cent of the landowners holding more than 25 acres were free from debts when the drought hit the Madras state, and another 22 per cent of them had improved their economic positions by partially clearing their debts. When price control was lifted and it became profitable to grow the commercial crops, water was urgently needed to irrigate these crops. Therefore, not only the fact that the *kavalai* was both costly and less efficient and that the Government subsidised the installation of electrical pumps, but also the effects that the drought had on prices most likely helped to encourage farmers to change from the old *kavalai* to electrical water-lifts. Having repaid their loans, the larger farmers were able to shift to the new technology of lifting water that made the expansion of land under irrigation physically possible.[18]

These initial connections and pumps reached the villages when many of the labourers were away because of the drought. The new technique was labour-saving and was in the long-term perspective one of the important steps taken by the farmers that made it possible for them to break away from employing permanent labourers.

The economic capacity to produce a surplus was necessary but does not appear to have been sufficient to achieve remunerative cultivation during the drought. Different crops predominated within different regions in the district. By observing the correlation between the expanding crops and the major crops for different local regions, the regional difference can be observed. The expansion in cultivated area was accounted for by groundnuts and sugar cane. The area under groundnut cultivation grew by more than 20 per cent between 1945-6 and 1950-1 and sugar cane increased by 40 per cent over the same period. Even though the increases of the yields for the different crops were not as large, they were substantial. But those crops were not among the most important ones in the driest regions of the district. The major base for groundnut cultivation was situated further south, around Pollachi, a region that was less affected by the drought than the central highlands. In the Palladam area, groundnuts were not as common; in this region, cotton and *cholam* predominated among the grown crops. Over the same period as measured for sugar cane and groundnuts, *cholam* decreased, in acreage as well as in yield. The area under cotton cultivation did expand but much less than before the drought.[19] Therefore, one cannot deduce, from the general conclusion that the larger farmers profited from favourable prices when they changed to commercial crops, that the scale of the farm economy determined the outcome. It may have created favourable preconditions for making a profit. But the conclusion has to be qualified by considering the climatic conditions and geographical locations of the different areas within the district.[20]

## A DISASTROUS DROUGHT

The annual reports from the different mission stations in the district make depressing reading. The Rev. Yngve Frykholm exclaimed in 1950 that it was hopeless to preach to starving people. The villagers were so weak that they remained seated when he entered the village, apathetic and silent, without replying to him. The Rev. Bertil Envall described dry fields, empty wells and deserted villages: 'Often elderly people and small children were left behind in utter distress.' The villagers did not have the strength to stand even for a few minutes. Maria Säfvenberg received people at Karunagarapuri mission dispensary who had swollen bodies and palms white from anaemia. Several reports complained about the medical consequences of eating wild plants. Aloe roots were boiled and eaten, and people with severe stomach pain sought medical help at the mission stations.[21]

The people hardest hit by the drought were those that the missionaries had dedicated their lives to working among, and naturally one can expect a tendency to exaggerate the situation. A well-written report, giving eloquent descriptions of starving, indigent people, can be suspected of having been aimed at appealing to the hearts of the fund-givers.

The need for water was urgent, particularly in the villages, where the wells used for drinking water had run dry. The mission reports from the drought years give vivid descriptions of the situation. But even without the drought, missionaries realised the need for wells of the Scheduled Caste villagers. In particular, social boundaries and taboos about drinking water made the Madhari who lacked a well in their hamlet very dependent on the Goundar farmers. If the farmer wanted to enforce his will, he could easily put pressure on them by preventing them from getting water out of the common well of the village. That will be further discussed in Chapter 5. The point in this connection is that there were social reasons, as important as the drought itself, why the Church of Sweden Mission initiated a well-boring project in 1954.[22] The leading ideas of the project were established before the drought began and were aimed at meeting a combination of social and physical needs.

Therefore, there is no simple, cause-and-effect relation between the annual reports from the field during the drought and further external funding. Moreover, additional funds could not be applied for by way of annual reports. The only foreign aid that the mission distributed in the district because of the famine originated from the United States, through the Church World Service. The bias that might be found in the reports is therefore not likely to have been caused by the authors' desire to make an impression on the home board.[23]

On the other hand, a bias is sometimes visible in the reports. This can be assumed to have come from the situation in which the missionaries worked. When the missionaries formulated their reports, there was a risk that they would generalise their statements from a limited situation that was familiar to them and claim that the description was valid for a larger region. They worked in the most drought-prone area of the district and moved from village to village to meet either the congregation members or their Hindu relatives. They went in search of the landless Madhari and Paraiyar villagers in areas where nothing grew for lack of water, and in every year that passed more and more people left the villages in search of work. The descriptions of the effects of the drought in the villages may very well be correct and not purposely exaggerated, but they are only valid for the villages in the dry zone of the district. They were description of the Scheduled Caste settlements, and in particular the Madhari villages.

The consequences of the drought for the Madhari may be

summarised in words as simple as the Rev. Stephen used in a report of 1945: 'No rains—no work; no work—no food'.[24] The 1945 monsoons were, on the whole, above average in the district, but locally, in the driest regions south of Coimbatore, they had failed. The following 1946 south-west monsoon was a complete failure.[25] The next few years can be followed in all the subsequent mission reports from the Coimbatore district: no rain for 'the third year in a row', 'the fourth year of failing rains', 'the failure of the monsoon for the fifth year'.[26] The missionaries saw Madhari and Paraiyar labourers gradually lose their work opportunities, and the Scheduled Caste village populations reduced to half, or even to one quarter, as a result of migration. At the beginning of the drought, missionaries witnessed the heads of households leaving the villages and leaving the wife, children and parents behind, in order to find work and income to support the family. Later on, whole families migrated.[27]

The first few years did not have any drastic consequences for the landless labourers. Even though there was a scarcity of food, the labourers were able to find temporary solutions to their problems. In Semmipalayam, immediately west of Palladam, both Madhari and landless Goundar labourers were accustomed to joining the seasonally migrating, labour force heading for Pollachi further south and for Dadagam west of Coimbatore. Unlike the Palladam area, Pollachi was more fertile and not as drought-prone. During forty days in July to September, Madhari and Goundar labourers from the village would leave for Pollachi to harvest groundnuts. Sivasubramaniyan Goundar, the *Ur*-Gōundar and Panchayat President of Semmipalayam, estimates the number of migrant labourers to have been 75 per cent of all the village labourers in the 1940s and 1950s. But it was only the coolie labourers that left the village for seasonal work; the *pannaiyal* had to remain on the farms. The groundnuts harvest fell in a period when there was no agricultural work in the home village and nothing to keep the casual labourers from leaving. The Semmipalayam *Ur*-Goundar describes the coolie wages during the harvest as good; according to him, they were a share of one-fifteenth to one-tenth of the harvest. Going to Dadagam, on the other hand, afforded work during the December to January, *cholam* harvest. But only one-quarter of the labourers from Semmipalayam used to go there seasonally. When the drought struck in 1946, there were labourers, among those who went to Pollachi every year, who stayed there until the monsoon rains fell again. Most of them returned to their home village after the drought, but a number of them—one-third of the migrating labourers, as estimated by Sivasubramaniyan Goundar—also settled in Pollachi.[28]

When asked in an interview if all the labourers were allowed to leave Semmipalayam village during the drought, including the *pannaiyal*, the farmer Narayana Goundar replied:

'We also let them go. It was difficult to keep the cattle as well.'
'Did they go to the estates?'
'Yes, people did go there. The *maistri* would come and take them.'
'Did you not object when the *maistri* took the people?'
'How could I? We had no coolie for them. There was no rain, so we let them go. We sold most of the cattle, and kept one or two for ourselves. So we could not have a group of people as we used to have. We let them go.'[29]

For the landless labourers, who already had an alternative source of income elsewhere as seasonal, migratory labour or in mere, supplementary, coolie work, the means of survival during the drought were more easily found. When there were no harvests and the farmers did not even risk their grain by sowing their fields, the labourers accustomed to circular migration tried to find work throughout the whole year in the areas to which they were used to go. Labourers were recorded as having migrated southwards to Pollachi or to the east to the Tiruchi district, where crops could still be grown. There was also an extended migration to the tea estates in the hills. The missionaries often described those labourers who migrated regularly as 'more forward' or 'more active' than those who remained in the home village.[30] But even though they may have been active in seeking alternative sources for survival, more than as a matter of personality, this situation most likely reflected the different labour relations that they were part of and their previously established contacts outside the villages. Casual labourers had weaker ties to the village and its farms than had the *pannaiyal* and could therefore easily leave.

This is one of the more important reasons why the Madhari more often than the Paraiyar were found still living in the villages after several years of drought. Thus, when a CSM document related that half of a village population had left in order to find work elsewhere, it cannot be concluded that 50 per cent of each of the two communities had migrated. The proportion of Paraiyar villagers among the migrants was most likely larger than that of the Madhari.

Added to the fact that permanently attached labourers were found among the Madhari, and not among the Paraiyar, there were also other ties that made the Madhari hesitant to leave. Over several generations, the relation between irrigation, Madhari and *pannaiyal* had worked as part of an insurance for successful cultivation by the Goundar farmers. It had given the Madhari an undisputed role in production, and it had linked the two castes in this particular region to each other in a mutual, uneven dependence. During the drought, the objective causes of this relationship had diminished; without rains and harvests, there was hardly any water to be drawn from the wells. But the subjective ties were still there. The understanding that 'the Madhari were the people who operated the water-lifts and managed the irrigation' and that 'a farmer cultivating a reasonable amount of land needed Madhari labourers' did not vanish like the rains. For the Madhari, the step out of the village was a much greater one than for the Paraiyar, as they did not have previously established workplaces to go to. For them, the step out of the village had to go beyond their subjective ties to the Goundar.

But, as is indicated in the interview with Narayana Goundar, keeping cattle was related to certain labour requirements and in particular to *pannaiyal*. When cattle had to be sold and there was neither enough work nor food available, also the *pannaiyal* were allowed to leave. In this way, the drought in a sense forced the Madhari out of the villages. But it could also be said that this provided them with an opportunity to leave and establish connections with other trades.

Still, the option to leave was, first and foremost, an option for the Paraiyar. They were to a large extent already involved in the circular migration of labourers to the tea estates, and those without employment on the estates generally had relatives working there. Seeking to join them was not a far-fetched decision.

Throughout the drought, *maistris* arrived in the villages and markets to gather labourers for the planters. As the years of drought passed, also some Madhari coolie labourers joined. By all informants, it is described as exceptional when a Madhari joined a group of labourers gathered by a *maistri*. Abraham of Mandiripalayam was one of those 'free hands' who had previously worked at the estates and who now walked together with a *maistri* to Attamalai to pluck tea and clean the vessels used to fertilize the plants. On the way to the estate, the number of labourers increased, as more and more people joined the party. Abraham says that 'villages' joined on the way: 'We were hundreds of people, a big group.' The *maistri*, who was from Kallipalayam nearby, gave an advance of between 10 and 100 rupees, according to the background of the person, 'a bribe' in the words of Abraham.[31]

Uppilipalayam was a Madhari village that had lost its drinking water in 1950. According to the missionary living immediately next to the village, half of its population had left 'for the hills or elsewhere' in search of work. The informants in Uppilipalayam provide important, complementary information, when they specify that it was only one family that left the village to find work on a tea estate. All the other migrants were among those who had moved elsewhere, which meant coolie work in Tiruppur in connection with the factories. Already in 1948-9, there was a noticeable tendency among the agricultural labourers in general to find refuge and casual work in the towns.[32]

Estate work was an exception also to Abraham. It did not even last the whole of the drought. In one of the years, when he went to harvest paddy further north, he turned to a solution that was more common among those of the Madhari who found sources of income outside the home village. News about casual labour being available in a certain place in the district spread rapidly among the villages, and, like Abraham, who had heard about good wages being paid in the Atur paddy harvest, people from the nearby villages joined the place of work.[33] The casual work that was given by the Government—repairing roads, constructing factory buildings, deepening wells—was also one of the short-term solutions that attracted coolie labourers, even though the deepening of wells was not the kind of work that a Madhari man would hope for. The interviews, and to a certain extent also the annual mission reports, give the impression that this form of casual labour was a more widespread solution to the Madhari villagers than going to the estates.[34]

The effects of the drought on those among the Scheduled Caste villagers who did not immediately leave their homes in the late 1940s can be observed in the increasing death-rates. Cholera, smallpox and plague were recorded during several years and for different villages. It is unlikely that people starved to death, but the results of malnutrition, which lowered the resistance to diseases, caused higher death-rates during epidemics. 1950 appears to have been particularly difficult, and in the following year the absence of epidemics is understood as the result of immunity acquired among those who had survived smallpox and cholera the previous year. The death-rate for 1951 among the Christian congregations was still at twice the level that it had been two or three years earlier.[35] However, the fact that there was no famine, in spite of the six-year-long drought, bears witness to the change of the economy since the nineteenth century. Half a century before this drought, a period of six years without rain would have meant disaster. In the villages, one or two years of drought could have been endured, with the stocks kept by the landowners, but even less than six years without rain in the last century would most likely have resulted in a famine. However, in the late 1940s, the infrastructure was developed to such an extent that food could be transported over long distances and relief work could be quite effectively organised.

For those without opportunities to leave, the distribution of gruel was organised during the worst years. The gruel was made from different grains mixed together with water and was made sour overnight. Portions were often measured by a coconut shell and served from a trough. The Madhari informants remember the liquid as unpopular, but it kept the hunger away. It was distributed by both public and private means and seems to have reached the major villages along the main roads.[36] When the gruel was not available, wild plants and cattle feed were substituted for food grains. The residue of groundnuts, when the oil had been pressed out, was usually given to the cattle, but now it became food for the poorer villagers.[37] The most desperate solution to counter the famine was recorded by a missionary in 1951, when she related that there were hundreds of homeless villagers dwelling in the streets of Coimbatore or at the roadside.[38] The Rev. Bertil Envall once witnessed a mother selling her child at the Tiruppur railway junction. She had no food for the child, and when she left on a train with a sum of money, the child was carried away by someone else. But Envall believes that this was uncommon. The situation was very difficult for those without means, but not so desperate that they were commonly forced to find a solution by selling a child.[39] The overall impression from both interviews and annual reports is that Scheduled Caste villagers, whether Madhari or Paraiyar, either migrated to another place to carry out casual work that they had heard about before leaving, and believed that they had a chance to get or they never left the home village.

## WHEN RIGHTS CEASE TO HOLD

The period of drought appears to have been decisive in the rapid decline of the employment of permanent labourers in the form of *pannaiyal.* Not that the drought acted as the *prime mover* in the outcome, but it appears to have created conditions that made it easier for the farmers to cease employing permanent labourers in agriculture.

1. Electric-power lines along a street in Coimbatore, 1934.
Photograph: Ebbe Wängsjö

2. Woman grinding outside a Goundar house near Palladam in 1934.
Photograph: Ebbe Wängsjö

3. Madhari women near Kinnathukadavu working in the fields during the *cbolam* harvest. 1934. Photograph: Ebbe Wängsjö

4. Children collecting cow dung for fuel and manure while pasturing cattle. 1935. Photograph: Ebbe Wängsjö

5. Two *kavalai* water-lifts. 1939. Photograph: Ebbe Wängsjö

6. Detail of a *kavalai*. The copper container and leather tube by which water is discharged into the irrigation canal. 1933. Photograph: Ebbe Wängsjö

7. Madhari women and girls deepening the irrigation canal to obtain drinking water. Pollachi. 1954. Photograph: Anders Andrén

8. Woman and girl taking water from an irrigation canal. Pollachi. 1954. Photograph: Anders Andrén

9. Madhari men in a village between Pollachi and Kinnathukadavu welcoming missionaries by playing drums. The 1930s. Photograph: Ebbe Wängsjö

10. Musicians at a baptismal ceremony near Palladam. 1931. Photograph: Ebbe Wängsjö

11. Auction at a harvest festival in Karunagarapuri mission station in 1943.
Photograph: Ebbe Wängsjö

12. The Rev. G. Stephen and William Daniel, Candidate of Ministry in the TELC, visiting a Madhari hamlet in the early 1950s.
W. Daniel dressed a according to western style.
Photograph: Ebbe Wängsjö

13. The Lutheran missionary Harald Frykholm instructing Paraiyar boys in physical exercise on the flat roof of Palladam church. 1932. Photograph: Ebbe Wängsjö

14. Musicians in a procession during baptismal ceremony. 1948. Photograph: Anders Andrén

15. Lutheran evangelist instructing Madhari villagers near Palladam in Bible stories. 1935. Photograph: Ebbe Wängsjö

16. The story of the good Samaritan retold for Madhari villagers in 1935. Photograph: Ebbe Wängsjö

The effects of the situation on the propertyless labourers were immediate. Their forms of survival had rapidly changed, as the period not only made living costly and difficult, but also marked the shift to a labour-saving technology that replaced leather-work. 1947, the first year of the more widespread drought, was still marked by high prices of consumption goods, left over from the Second World War. In 1953, when the rains returned, the electric-power pumps had begun to reach and be installed also in major villages distant from the main electric-transmission lines.

The high food prices would not worry a labourer who could rely on payment in kind. But during the drought also those labourers would find difficulties. In those cases in which some work was still required but no crops were harvested, there was obviously nothing to distribute as wages in kind. At the same time, a wage in cash would lose its value when food prices rose.

As the results will show, wages in cash came to be more relevant to agricultural labourers after the drought than they had been before it. This was due to the fact that there was both a gradual shift from payment in kind to cash payment, and a drastic decline in the employment of *pannaiyal*.

In interviews, the question 'What work did you do?' often got the reply *Cumma*, 'nothing'. 'But then, how did you survive?' 'Oh, I planted and weeded in the Goundar's fields when he asked me.' This answer did not mean that the labourer took on planting and weeding as odd jobs. The question, which was obviously badly put, was based on the assumption that all kinds of work are 'work'. But to have laboured for survival turned out to be more familiar to the older informants than understanding labour as part of a formal employment.

For those labourers dependent on buying food in the market, the margins for survival seem to have decreased during the 1940s. This was the post-depression period, when the world was at war, and India was fighting its final battles for independence. In the Coimbatore district, prices were high, and the most necessary items—rice, sugar, kerosene—were rationed. The Lutheran missionaries in the district, who otherwise seldom made comments on such issues, complained grievously about prices, ration cards and wages in their reports from 1945 to 1947.

There is only very vague information about the level of agricultural labourers' remuneration in the central highlands in the mission reports. For a comparison, a brief note may be made about the salaries of the workers employed at the missions during the war years.

The Reverends Stephen and Diehl were concerned about the living situation of mission-employed workers. If teachers' and the lower-paid workers' salaries in the mission compounds lagged behind those of employees in the towns, it would be difficult to persuade them to stay with the mission. Stephen estimated that the cost of living had risen three to five times since before the war. Diehl had compared the price index for India with the European countries, the results turning out to India's disadvantage. Even though India had been spared from the war, Diehl understood that the indirect consequences had been considerable.[40] The following year, he described what he called a genuine need for the continued demand for higher wages. This statement is followed by calculations, in which a teacher's salary of 12 rupees per month in 1939 was estimated to have corresponded to a salary of 30 rupees in 1946. In this difficult situation as understood by Diehl, the demands for rises of wages were seen as just, even though it was an expression of the 'craving desire for money' and was matched by a colourful description of the 'deep-rooted indifference' among the 'socially low-standing groups' to social and economic advances.[41]

Anna Irbe, who arrived in the district in 1927 and was now in charge of Karunagarapuri mission station south of Coimbatore, had a somewhat different view. In her report of 1947, she complains about how the mass awakening among the lower classes had caused the wages of coolies to increase to four times above the level at which they were before the war, while wages for teachers and clerks had only doubled. It was now 'almost impossible' to get domestic servants in distant places like Karunagarapuri. Prices are described as 'notoriously high'.[42] Irbe may have been somewhat hostile to labour movements, something which she reveals in several of her reports, but her estimate of the doubling of the teachers' salaries corresponds well to the figures in Diehl's report. The teacher who earned 12 rupees in 1939 received, with the addition of the Government allowance of 16 rupees as a result of the period of high prices,[43] 28 rupees in 1946. If Stephen was correct in his estimate, that living costs rose three to five times during the war, coolie wages kept pace with the inflation, while teachers' salaries lost ground.

From 1944-5, the Season and Crop Report continually remarked on the high wages paid in cash to agricultural labourers, as compared with the pre-war years. However, in 1944-5, it was remarked that, in spite of the higher wages paid, the increases of these wages were generally less than the prices of food grains.[44]

However, there are strong reasons to believe that it was only after the drought that the major part of the Madhari agricultural labourers were remunerated in cash rather than in kind. The report by Ganesamurthi in 1935 describes the payment of wages in kind to the Madhari.[45]

In 1945, before the drought, the Rev. Knutsson described remuneration in kind when he reported on the payment to the Madhari labourers. He found that the Madharis were '... actually slaves of the caste-people, but fairly well supported by the *Gowndas*. In times of need they are getting nearly everything they ask for'.[46] There was a striking difference between those labourers who depended on cash payment and those who could turn to the Goundars as patrons. This was the right of the Madhari in local society, as observed by Knutsson, and particularly an option for the pannaiyal. The Season and Crop Report for 1944-5 confirms the advantage of being remunerated in harvest shares. While agricultural labourers who were paid in kind were unaffected by the inflation, those who were paid in cash saw their wages lose value. When prices of food grains continued to rise, grain wages remained the same.[47] But in the following year, there were failing harvests in the area and the first signs of the coming drought appeared that cut a wide swathe through the promise of patronage protection.

Also immediately after the drought, payment in kind appears to have remained on a substantial level. A Government survey of the Madras state in 1954 estimated that 66 per cent of the total work-days among agricultural labourers were paid in cash, 22 per cent were paid in kind, and 12 per cent as a combination of cash and payment in kind. Perquisites were given on 28 per cent of all work-days. The average income for male, casual, agricultural labourers was estimated at 15.5 annas per day (or 0.97 rupees[48]). The female labourers were recorded to have earned 9.5 annas (or 0.59 rupees). Added to those wages were the perquisites that were given on certain occasions throughout the year.[49]

The wage rates given in the survey are on a slightly lower level than the figures provided by the Agro-Economic Research Centre of Madras University. According to their estimate, a male agricultural labourer earned 1.29 rupees in 1954-5 and female labourers earned 0.73 rupees.[50] Christopher Baker, who refers to the Agro-Economic

Research Centre survey, notes that wage rates for agricultural labourers were on a higher level in the highlands than in the rest of the state and that a simultaneous migration from other districts into the highlands occurred.[51] But it is risky to compare different wage surveys, as the methods used for collecting and generalising the data generally differ as between investigations. This is particularly so as regards the way perquisites and wages in kind have been valued. The significance of the results is rather to provide an indication of the general wage levels and to show that wages in kind were still paid to a substantial extent.

However, immediately after the drought, the number of *pannaiyal* had become strikingly small. In 1933, Cox had estimated the agricultural labourers permanently employed as farm servants at 28 per cent of the labour force, while 72 per cent worked as casual field labourers.[52] Until the mid-1940s, the Madhari were still necessary for agricultural production and were not replaced on the farms. There is no evidence to support a fall in numbers of *pannaiyal* before the drought began. When the rains fell again and cultivation of the land could be carried out on the full scale, the labourers moved back into the villages, but only a small number were taken on as *pannaiyal.* Of the six million agricultural labourers in the Madras state as a whole, 5 per cent were recorded as 'attached' labourers in the Agricultural Labour Inquiry of 1954.[53] As this is a figure generalised for the whole of Madras State, it is a rough estimate for the Coimbatore district. On the one hand, the estimate includes areas where the employment of permanent farm labourers was less prominent, and the figure for the Coimbatore district may have been slightly higher. At the same time, attached labourers were more common in some of the wet rice-cultivating districts of the state than they were in Coimbatore, which would level out the differences. However, even though 5 per cent is a rough estimate of the number of permanent labourers in relation to casual labourers for the Coimbatore district, it indicates a dramatic fall in the employment of *pannaiyal* since before the drought.

In the 1960s, after the first phase of electrification in the villages of Palladam taluk and 14 years after the drought, Staffan Lindberg's documents provide a much closer look at the Tiruppur-Palladam area. These documents reveal the same proportions between casual and attached labourers as in the state-level survey of 1954. In the villages where he carried out his investigation, he collected basic data to get an idea of the population statistics in the area. The figures were collected from thirteen villages 'by asking the people, if possible the headman, while walking and checking every house'. The information given about the occupation of the head of the household shows that 80 per cent of the respondents found their means of survival as agricultural labourers and 11.5 per cent earned their livings from other trades, while information was lacking or the respondent had answered that he did not know for 8.5 per cent of the heads of the households. Of the respondents employed as agricultural labourers, 5 per cent were *pannaiyal.* But it is worth noticing that in seven of the villages no *pannaiyal* was recorded at all, while one village sticks out from the rest, where as much as 26 per cent of all the respondents working as agricultural labourers stated that they were employed as *pannaiyal.* Individual deviations explained by local circumstances could thus stand out from the general trend.[54]

In 1970, permanent labourers were still employed in the Coimbatore district. A sample survey of the district for the years 1970-1 to 1972-3 specifies the relation between casual and permanent labourers by the scale of cultivation. The different labour categories are measured by the inputs made and are recorded for each of five categories of farm size. This reveals an important difference between farms of different sizes. The study shows that, of the total input made of human labour, the amount spent on casual labour was 92 per cent for the smallest holdings and dropped in each of the categories to 75 per cent for the largest holdings. The figures for permanent labour showed the reverse trend. For the smallest holdings, it was recorded to have been 8 per cent, thereafter steadily increasing in each category to reach 25 per cent for the largest holdings[55] (see Table 4.1). It should be observed that this shows the input and not the percentage of real numbers of labourers. Permanent labour carried more costs than casual labour, which explains the figures that may appear to be too high for the permanent labour force. The fact that large farmers spent 25 per cent on their permanent labourers out of the total labour costs does not mean that those labourers represented 25 per cent of the total, hired, labour force. They were rather much less. What the table reveals is that in the 1970s the situation still prevailed that the larger the farm was, the higher was the amount of permanent labour employed.

To a small farmer, permanently hired labour was not an issue. He would manage his cultivation with family labour and hire casual labour during the peak periods. But to rely on casual labour had long since

TABLE 4.1. PERCENTAGE OF INPUT MADE ON HUMAN LABOUR FOR DIFFERENT FARM SIZE, 1970-1 TO 1972-3, COIMBATORE DISTRICT

| *Farm size, in acres* | *0 - 4.9* | *5 - 8.25* | *8.26 - 14* | *14.1 - 26* | *26.1-* | *All farms* |
|---|---|---|---|---|---|---|
| Hired casual labour | 92% | 91% | 86% | 78% | 75% | 80% |
| Hired permanent labour | 8% | 9% | 14% | 22% | 25% | 20% |

Source: Studies in the Economics of Farm Management, p. 60, in Kurien 1989, p. 80, Table 4.12

been an opportunity also for the larger farmers in 1970. Labour scarcity was no longer a problem and, considering the small number of permanent labourers employed, the figures in the sample survey clearly show the economic logic of farmers relying on casual labourers, if possible. *Pannaiyal* had by that time lost its former importance for cultivation as ensuring labour and irrigation of the fields. In spite of this, the larger farms did not completely depend on casual labourers, but still kept some *pannaiyal.*

In the 1960s, wages paid in kind appear to have been exceptional. The statistics on income provided by Lindberg indicate that cash payment by far exceeded payment in kind in the Palladam–Tiruppur area in 1967. According to Lindberg's results, the remuneration for *pannaiyal* labour was at the time basically paid in kind, while coolies received cash payment. This would support the conclusion that the shift to let wages in cash predominate in the remuneration of agricultural labour related to the reduced employment of *pannaiyal.*

A *pannaiyal* in Veerapandi may stand as an example. He earned 130 rupees per year, of which 120 were paid in kind. Casual labourers were, on the other hand, paid in cash, except during harvests, and only occasionally were they presented with gifts in kind at festivals round the year.[56] A rough estimate can be made from Lindberg's statistics on the number of labourers in his research area who received wages in kind in 1967. Unfortunately, the categories in his tables lack some details, and wages in kind have been recorded together with the answers from labourers who did not know what kind of incomes they had. But taken as a rough estimate, the tables show that only a little more than 13 per cent of the respondents declared that they received incomes in kind or that they did not know.[57]

After the drought, the development of real wages was obviously something that became relevant to the Madhari labourers. A time-series of real wages for agricultural labourers in Tamil Nadu, beginning in 1951-2, has been provided by C. T. Kurien. Prices of second-sort rice have been used as a deflator, since food grains were considered the most appropriate choice to measure real wages for rural labourers. The table shows a fluctuating but falling trend. The real wages for male field labourers fell to 72.9 per cent in 1970-1 from the base year 1951-2. The real wages for female field labourers fell to 79.8 per cent during the same period of time.[58]

Wages in kind were obviously preferred to wages in cash for the labourer. At the same time, the employing farmer would rather have preferred to give cash wages.

To keep up wages, the casual labourers around Palladam had to adopt a different strategy than that of the permanent labourers. For a daily wage coolie in the Palladam area in the 1960s, the working day did not start in the same way as for a *pannaiyal.* The permanent labourer would begin early in the morning, cleaning and feeding the cattle. The daily coolie, on the other hand, would spend hours waiting by his house, not being sure of earning an income at all on that day. The Madhari coolies kept to a strategy of not going to the Goundar to ask for work. To get reasonable pay, they waited outside their own houses for the Goundar to come to them. Approaching the landlord could bring down the payment to half, which in 1967 would have been to 1 rupee, enough for one litre of *cholam* grain.[59]

The effects of inflation for casual agricultural labourers can be traced also in the Lindberg material from 1967. The Madharis in Kethanur, next to Palladam, recalled that ten years earlier they received eight annas a day for coolie work, which was equal to four litres of *cholam.* In 1967, the price of *cholam* was one rupee per litre. Having a daily income of Rs. 2-2.50, the daily pay of 1967 was equal to only two litres of *cholam.*[60]

But these figures are not completely reliable. When the Madhari in Kethanur recalled that they earned only eight annas a day, they probably underestimated their income in 1957. The Agro-Economic Research Centre of Madras University reaches the same conclusion as recorded in Lindberg's notes for the level of wages for male field labourers in 1967 in their Wage Rate Series. But, for the year 1957, it is claimed that male field labourers earned 1.28 rupees and not 0.5.[61] The notes in Lindberg's diary indicate that the information about both price and wage levels was taken from the informants. Still, it is not possible to judge whether the villagers were actually able to buy a large amount of *cholam* in 1957 or whether—which is more likely—they remembered being able to buy four litres of *cholam* but could not recall the correct wage level. If the wage-level data for 1957 in the Wage Rate Series are taken into account, a calculation based on this data and Lindberg's notes can be made. The result would then show that the price of *cholam* increased by a factor of four in the Palladam area, while wages doubled between 1957 and 1967. But such estimates should be regarded with much caution, and it suffices to conclude that it indicates that real wages in the Palladam area fell over the decade previous to 1967.

At the same time, missionaries remember noticing a trend among the Madhari to a growing desire for cash payment. Steadily improving communications facilitated the opportunities for agricultural labourers to find casual work in the towns. But a consequence of buses reaching more and more villages was that the labourers had to use money. And once in the towns, there were plenty of consumer goods to buy that were not available in the villages. Over a period of time, the desire for cash payment might have turned into a need of money to meet the daily requirements.[62] But the need of money does not seem to have been equal to a desire for casual employment.

Subban was the thirty-year-old Madhari referred to earlier who worked as *pannaiyal* for a Goundar in Veerapandi in 1967. For this, he received 30 *vallam* and 10 rupees a year.[63] As *pannaiyal*, he had to be available at any time day and night, whenever the Goundar called. This gave him a low daily income, which was compensated for by other gifts of necessary items that he could expect from the Goundar. Subban preferred this arrangement to being an agricultural coolie, and all those of his community sitting around him agreed. They much preferred the bonded, but secure, work as a *pannaiyal* to the coolie work they were compelled to do.[64] This position of the Madhari resembles Kathleen Gough's findings in her Tanjavur study. Gough concludes that when bonded labour rapidly declined, the labourers preferred to be taken on as *pannaiyal* rather than as coolie labourers. This yielded one-year contracts and an assured supply of grain in a situation of increasing competition for work.[65]

Subban's statement is important. Throughout the surveyed period, from the early twentieth century onwards, there are no indications that point to a struggle among the Madhari to become wage labourers who could move about as 'free' individuals on the labour market. The reason for this is not to be found in better payment or in the fact that they benefited from better treatment. But, unlike the casual labourers, they were not just an extra resource of manpower to be hired during periods round the year when the need for labour increased. The *pannaiyal* of the late 1960s was employed full-time and appears to have been able to count on some of the rights included in what Tage Holmberg observed in 1956 as the *urimai*—the rights and duties of the Madhari in relation to the Goundar. The results earlier indicated that those rights were closely related to remuneration in shares of the produce and were therefore also related to payment in kind. To have rights in dead cattle would only matter as long as cattle were kept in substantial herds. In the late 1960s, when wages were generally paid in cash and the big herds belonged to history, the effects of the *urimai* system had therefore in reality ceased to work. Some of the benefits of the system, such as being provided with resources when needed, still appear to have been attached to the *pannaiyal* employment. But there is no evidence to support the existence of a situation in which the Madhari as an agricultural labouring community could claim shares in kind in the produce of the village.

This leads to the conclusion that *pannaiyal* did not disappear as an unaltered form of labour relation. A description of *pannaiyal* made by the *Ur*-Goundar of Mandiripalayam puts the statements from the Madhari men in Veerapandi in a different light. Ramasamy Goundar explained that the *pannaiyal* was like a *maistri*, who supervised other labourers and stood in for the Goundar landowner as a trusted servant. Also Goundar labourers were supervised by the Madhari *pannaiyal*. When the Goundar was not present, the Madhari *pannaiyal* handed out wages to the daily coolies.[66] Ramasamy Goundar may have emphasised only the advantages of being a *pannaiyal*. But what he described was not a *pannai* system; it was not a description that referred to a situation before the drought. This *pannaiyal* was an overseer.

The *pannaiyal* of the 1960s is sometimes described as a privileged labourer. Not only did he have a secure income, but his closer relationship to the farmer also gave him a different position in relation to the other labourers. The Rev. Anders Andrén had the impression that the *pannaiyal* labourers held a favoured position and that they functioned as supervisors of the coolie labourers.[67] The *pannaiyal* served as a retainer and faithful servant.

E. Jacob stresses the weak position of the *pannaiyal* in relation to the Goundar farmer. If the Goundar wanted to delay wages or paid less than the amount agreed upon, the *pannaiyal* had no one to complain to. But while he lived at the mercy of the Goundar, the *pannaiyal* held a favoured position in relation to the casual labourers employed by the farmer. Also the Goundar coolie labourers were commanded by the Madhari *pannaiyal*—though in a milder tone of voice.[68]

The Goundar farmers themselves stress the formal side of *pannaiyal* by emphasising that they generally worked on one-year contracts. The loans that the labourers received were seen as financial settlements separate from the labour relation. The farmers accepted the fact that an indebted labourer could not leave the farm unless he had repaid the loan. But in the understanding of the Goundar farmers of Semmipalayam, this need for physical control that resulted in labour for the lending farmer was explained by the lending of money. They would not accept that lending money was a means of controlling labour.[69]

When Subban and his friends discussed *pannaiyal*, it was not as a memory of a better and perhaps a glorified past. On the contrary, they were able to compare existing casual and *pannaiyal* employment and came to the conclusion that the *pannaiyal* employed had the advantage of not being exposed to the insecure labour market.[70] Throughout the surveyed period, no opportunities have been found for the Madhari outside agriculture that have acted as incentives to direct more than a few individuals among them away from the farms. Unlike the Goundar farmers or the missionaries, no one among the Madhari informants or among those interviewed by Staffan Lindberg understood this 'privilege' of being a *pannaiyal* as being anything but the privilege of having a secure income.[71]

As there were Goundars who owned factories, the question immediately arises why they did not see to it that Madhari men from their villages were employed as industrial labourers, particularly as unemployment is reported to have spread among the labourers during the late 1950s. This would most likely have given the factory-owner a loyal labour force. But this seems not to have been the case. There is no evidence that Madhari men were employed as industrial labourers as a result of their relationship with the Goundars. On the contrary, missionaries relate how, at times, they tried to find industrial employment for Madhari villagers. But, in spite of promises, their efforts were in vain. The missionaries' own interpretation of this is that the Madhari could never be punctual, and therefore it would have been impossible to have them working in shifts.[72] It may also have been due to more skilled labourers already being available to the factory-owners, labourers who had roots in the towns and factories, personally or through relatives, at the time when the need for alternative employment rose among the Madhari. Left over was the unskilled coolie work outside the factory buildings, where Madhari men could be seen loading and unloading lorries and carts.[73]

At the end of the period surveyed only one form of employment remained intact and apparently on the same level as previously. Child labour on one-year contracts, as a mortgage for a loan to the parents, was still the rule among the Madhari. Ever since they first took up work among this group of people, the missionaries reported difficulties in giving the children primary education. As children worked eight to ten hours a day looking after the cattle, they were exhausted in the evening, and if they showed up at all in the village chapel for night classes, they were likely to fall asleep.[74]

It has not been possible to find figures from the central part of the highlands that show the extent of child labour among the Scheduled Castes in general and the Madhari in particular. Statistics have rather been gathered on a more general level. The information given in the Agricultural Labour Inquiry of 1954 gives a general idea of the situation for the whole population immediately after the drought. The estimates in the Inquiry show that 3.6 per cent of all children laboured. It is not a far-fetched assumption that those children were basically members of a scheduled caste. Of these, one-fifth, or 19 per cent, were recorded as 'attached'.[75]

Again, Lindberg's notes provides a close view of the situation. When Staffan Lindberg went through the school records in Kullampalayam in 1967, he found them to be in perfect order. The pupils were mainly Goundar, but nine Madhari children were registered for the second and third standards. Nevertheless, they were not at school. These children had simply given their names, but they very seldom showed up, according to Lindberg.[76] As a rule, as soon as the children were old enough, they were sent to pasture the Goundar's cattle. In Vavipalayam, all the Madhari were agricultural coolies in 1967; only their children were tied to labour as the result of a debt. As one of the parents explained: 'Our children have to work and earn for the family.' For this, they received midday meals in addition to the fixed payments.[77]

The Lindberg material, as well as the mission documents, give numerous examples of child labour. One of these emanates from

Tiruppur, where the Madhari community living in the slum area had originally moved to the town in order to make it possible for their children to get education. But there were only two children, one boy and one girl, who attended school. The rest of the children worked.[78] The 100 rupees that the parents received in advance for one year's work could not be given up for their children's education.[79] In Vavipalayam, the son of a Madhari man could not fulfil his father's dream that his son should be educated, since his father had been forced to give his son 'as a pledge' to a Goundar for a loan of 120 rupees.[80]

The information in the Lindberg Collection and the mission documents would rather prove that the general figure in the Agricultural Labour Inquiry is completely misleading as a measure of the amount of child labour among the Madhari.

## SIX YEARS OF RAPID CHANGE

The major impression from studying the years of drought in the highlands is not that the drought itself created a new kind of rural development. It rather accelerated or forced a development in which the important factors were already established before the drought struck.

Surveys of rural indebtedness show that the wealthiest farmers had to a substantial extent been able to strengthen their farm economies during the first half of the 1940s. In the late forties, when price control was lifted, they seem to have been able to further expand by profiting from the production of commercial crops. They took a risk when they sowed during a severe drought. Water was extremely scarce, and a large part of the labour force had migrated. To continue to farm by the same methods as before was therefore likely to end in a failure. But when electric power was connected to the farms, it improved the prospects of success, as the electric pumps made more water available.

As was observed by C.T. Kurien and discussed in Chapter 3, at the time when electric pumps were installed on the farms in the Coimbatore district, also tractors began to be purchased. Before the drought, the Government had started to argue for the mechanisation of agriculture. But it was during the drought that mechanical equipment and electricity were installed in any substantial way, in particular, on the large-scale farms. In the district, the mechanisation of agriculture began during the drought and thereafter continued at a comparatively high level.

Both cattle and *kavalai* were beginning to be replaced when pumps were installed and tractors purchased. While a reduced number of *kavalai* would basically affect the Madhari labourers, tractors came to have consequences also for small farmers who made an extra income from ploughing others farmers' fields. Of course, this shift did not come about immediately, and initially only on the larger farms. But the events during the drought reveal the fragility of the Madhari's means of survival at the time. Simultaneously, they were dependent on the Goundar as their patron, and on a form of agriculture that required their particular services. When the rains failed for six years, this created extreme conditions that appear to have hastened a process that was begun already before the drought.

After the drought, the results point to *pannaiyal* being employed in much smaller numbers. When the labourers who had migrated returned to the villages to take up work, as a rule they had to rely on casual work. The results also indicate that the form of remuneration changed. Wages were rather paid in cash than in kind, and the wages in kind seem to have related to the form of labour contract. Most likely, the *pannaiyal* basically continued to be paid in kind, while the casual labourer as a rule was paid in cash. Exceptions to the trend occurred. Labourers may have been given food and clothes at festivals, according to customary rules. Harvests may in some places have been gathered by labourers who could claim a share. However, the general trend does not indicate the preservation of such forms of payment, but a change-over to payment in cash. During the following two decades, real wages fell.

The right to claim a share of the village resources had sustained the survival of the Madhari labourers. The older people quoted earlier did not 'work' but survived by their labour. When *pannaiyal* ceased to be re-employed and wages were paid in cash and for each workday, this right was undermined. It lost its substance.

## NOTES

1 CSMA, MBa 1946:357, p. 2.
2 CSMA, MBa 1948:525, p. 1.
3 Season and Crop Report 1946/47, pp. 1, 3. Gingelly: Lat. *Sesamum indicum.*
4 Season and Crop Report 1947/48, p. 1; CSMA, MBa 1948:525, p. 1.
5 To turn each district into a food unit and ban all private movement of food was a measure resorted to by the Government during the war years

and the immediately following drought beginning in Bengal in 1942 and 1943. In the Madras state, this led to widespread smuggling across district borders. The Madras state as a whole was normally deficient in rice, wheat and millet. Before the war, food crops were imported from Burma. IOR, District Officers' Collection, H. J. Downing, p. 18; The Famine Enquiry Commission. Final Report, 1945, p. 5; TNA, Food 1947, Civil Supplies—Foodgrain, Derationing and Decontrol Policy—Orders passed, Memoranda 1, 2 and 3; Hunt and Harrison 1980, pp. 217-21.

6 TNA, Food 1947, Civil Supplies—Foodgrain, Derationing and Decontrol Policy—Orders passed, Immediate telegram No. 10053, from Ministry of Food, Govt of India.

7 TNA, Food 1947, Civil Supplies—Foodgrain, Derationing and Decontrol Policy—Orders passed, Council of Ministers, Fort St George 3.12.1947, Food Policy—Madras Govt's Decision—Intimation to the Govt of India.

8 CSMA, MBa 1949:489, p. 5.

9 Report of the Economist for Enquiry into Rural Indebtedness 1946, p. 46; Season and Crop Report 1948/49, p. 11; TNA, Food 1947, Civil Supplies—Foodgrain, Derationing and Decontrol Policy—Orders passed, Ref. No. 076199/UII/47(CS)d/19.12.1947.

10 The millet variety is Varagu or Kodo Millet (Lat. *Paspalum scrobiculatum*). Madras District Gazetteers, Coimbatore, 1966, p. 270.

11 CSMA, Unsorted documents, CSM in India 1949, p. 3.

12 The figures of the Board of Revenue reveal that government expenditure on famine relief in the Coimbatore district was negligible (800 rupees) in 1949/50 while, during the following years, expenditure varied dramatically between more than 800,000 and less than 122,000 rupees. From 1950 to 1954, the district occupied the second and third places in the Madras state to receive famine relief. Season and Crop Report 1948/49, p. 11; Quinquennial Statistical Abstract for the Madras State, 1949-50 to 1953-4 (1958), Table 23.

13 Those were Coimbatore, South Arcot, Chittoor, and Guntur. Season and Crop Report 1948/49, p. 11.

14 Madras District Gazetteers, Coimbatore, 1966, p. 270.

15 Season and Crop Report 1948/49, p. 11, 1949/50, p. 35, 1950/51, pp. 35-6 and 1951/52, p. 33.

16 CSMA, MBa 1953:551. See also Table 3.4.

17 CSMA, MBa 1954:320, pp. 3, 4, 8.

18 Report of the Economist for Enquiry into Rural Indebtedness 1946, p. 38.

19 Madras District Gazetteers, Coimbatore, 1966, p. 270.

20 Season and Crop Report 1948/49-1951/52.

21 *Katralai kilangu* = Agave root (Lat. *Angustifolia*). CSMA, MBa 1951:544, p. 1; CSMA, MBa 1951:521, p. 2; CSMA, MBa 1951:520*a*, p. 1; CSMA, MBa 1951:544, p. 1; CSMA, MBa 1951:550, p. 1.

22 The well-drilling project is further discussed in Chapter 5. CSMA, MBa 1954:320, p. 2; Frykholm 1970, p. 135.
23 CSMA, MBa 1952:544, p. 1.
24 CSMA, MBa 1946:357, p. 2.
25 CSMA, MBa 1946:357, p. 2; Season and Crop Report 1945/46 and 1946/47.
26 CSMA, MBa 1950:551, p. 3; CSMA, MBa 1951:545, p. 1; CSMA, MBa 1952:544, p. 1.
27 CSMA, Unsorted documents, CSM in India 1948, p. 3; CSMA, MBa 1952:544, p. 1; CSMA, MBa 1950:551, p. 3.
28 Semmipalayam 1995, interview, Sivasubramaniyan Goundar.
29 When the term 'coolie' is used by Narayana Goundar, it refers to any kind of agricultural work on the farm given to labourers. Semmipalayam 1995, interview, Narayana Goundar.
30 CSMA, MBa 1946:357, p. 2; CSMA, MBa 1952:544, p. 1.
31 Mandiripalayam 31.1.1995, interview.
32 CSMA, MBa 1951:520a, p. 1; Uppilipalayam 26.1.1995, interview, Vedamani; Season and Crop Report 1948/49, p. 11.
33 Abraham went to Atur near Salem, which was an area that did not suffer as much from lack of water as the central parts of the highlands. Mandiripalayam 31.1.1995, interview.
34 Season and Crop Report 1948/49, p. 11.
35 CSMA, MBa 1946:357, p. 1; CSMA, MBa 1952:544; Envall 1995, interview.
36 The gruel was known as *totti kanji*, since the coconut shell was locally known as *totti*, which literally means 'cap'. Uppilipalayam 26.1.1995, interview; Mandiripalayam 31.1.1995, and 2.2.1995, interviews; Kuppandampalayam 1995, interview; Ingefrid Envall 1995, interview; Season and Crop Report 1951/52, p. 33.
37 Mandiripalayam 31.1.1995, interviews with Abraham and Subban James.
38 CSMA, MBa 1952:550, p. 1.
39 Envall 1995, interview.
40 CSMA, MBa 1946:357, p. 3; CSMA, Unsorted documents, CSM in India 1945, p. 1.
41 CSMA, MBa 1947:413, p. 3.
42 CSMA, MBa 1948:508.
43 CSMA, MBa 1947:413, p. 3.
44 Season and Crop Report 1944/45-1951/52:1944/45, p. 6; 1945/46, p. 6; 1946/47, p. 6; 1947/48, p. 9; 1948/49, p. 11; 1949/50, p. 35; 1950/51, p. 36; 1951/52, p. 33.
45 Ganesamurthi 1935, p. 277.
46 CSMA, MDc 2.6.1945, from the Mission Director to Knutsson. The italics are mine.
47 In a detailed description of labour conditions for *pannaiyal* from the 1950s, the missionary Sigfrid Estborn estimated that the yearly wages

varied between 4 and 10 measures to a total of 64, or 1/16 to 1/6 of the harvest. The Panchayat President of Semmipalayam estimated that 'good wages' for the same period varied between 1/10 and 1/15 of the harvest. Jonas Ulrici, working in Arulpuram and Sulur, estimated the *pannaiyal's* remuneration at 1/16 of the annual harvest. Estborn 1959, p. 37; Semmipalayam 1995, interview Sivasubramaniyan Goundar; Ulrici Collection, (2) document beginning 'Census 1971'; Season and Crop Report 1944/45, p. 6.

48 Sixteen annas equalled one rupee.

49 Agricultural Labour Inquiry 1954, p. 47.

50 Agro-Economic Research Centre of the Madras University in Kurien 1989 (1985), p. 96, Table 5.5.

51 Baker 1984, p. 210.

52 Cox 1933, p. 148.

53 Agricultural Labour Inquiry 1954, p. 258.

54 Lindberg Collection, Census. The thirteen villages surveyed are situated in two areas, one south of Palladam town the other south of the more industrial Tiruppur.

55 *Studies in the Economics of Farm Management*, p. 60, in Kurien 1989 (1985), p. 80, Table 4.12.

56 Lindberg Collection, Staffan Lindberg Field Diary, Vol. 1, p. 12, Veerapandi 16.6.1967.

57 The different tables Lindberg provides are somewhat difficult to handle. The table on 'Weekly income' has been divided into three levels of cash payment and a fourth category indicating 'income in kind or don't know'. This fourth category has not been estimated in rupees, and there is no discussion about how he has treated those labourers who received payment both in cash and in kind in his table. Neither is this category found in the table on 'Monthly income of households'. In the latter table income has been measured in rupees only. Also, the two tables do not exactly correspond on the different income levels, which makes them difficult to compare. Lindberg 1969, p. 110, Table 39, and p. 111, Table 40.

58 Kurien 1989 (1985), p. 99, Table 5.7.

59 Lindberg Collection, G. Kasturi Field Diary, Kethanur 12.5.1967, confirmed by Lindberg Collection, Staffan Lindberg Field Diary, Vol. 1, p. 37, Kethanur 14.5.1967.

60 Sixteen annas were equal to one rupee. Lindberg Collection, Staffan Lindberg Field Diary, Vol. 1, p. 38, Kethanur 14.5.1967.

61 Kurien 1989, p. 96, Table 5.5.

62 Envall 1995, interview; Jonsson 1996, interview.

63 *Vallam* is a measurement of volume for grain and other dry materials. According to Lindberg's notes, one *vallam* of the grain given corresponded to 4 rupees.

64 Lindberg Collection, Staffan Lindberg Field Diary, Vol. 1, p. 12, Veerapandi 16.6.1967.
65 Gough 1977, p. 277; Gough 1978, pp. 43-4.
66 Mandiripalayam 2.2.1995; see also Jacob 1996.
67 Andrén 1993, interview.
68 Jacob 1996, interview.
69 Semmipalayam 1.2.1995, interviews, Narayana Goundar and Sivasubramaniyan Goundar.
70 In Veerapandi, where Subban lived, Lindberg's assistants failed to note that he worked as *pannaiyal.* In the Census, in two of the 51 households in Veerapandi, the name of the family head is Subban. They are recorded as being 22 and 25 years old and are registered as 'agricultural coolie'. Lindberg Collection, Census, pp. 6-7.
71 Lindberg Collection, Staffan Lindberg Field Diary, Vol. 1, p. 38, Kethanur 14.5.1967.
72 Andrén 1993, interview.
73 Ulrici 1993, interview; Jonsson 1996, interview.
74 As will be discussed in Chapter 5, no new schools were started in Madhari villages by the CSM. CSMA, MBa 1938:448; CSMA, Unsorted documents, CSM in India 1947, p. 8.
75 Agricultural Labour Inquiry 1954, p. 78.
76 Lindberg Collection, Staffan Lindberg Field Diary, Vol. 2, p. 42, Kullampalayam 23.6.1967.
77 Lindberg Collection, Staffan Lindberg Field Diary, Vol. 2, p. 29, Vavipalayam 21.6.1967.
78 Lindberg Collection, Staffan Lindberg Field Diary, Vol. 2, p. 26, Tiruppur 29.6.1967.
79 Lindberg Collection, Field Notes, Vol. 2, p. 56, an interview with Madharis in Agronom, i.e. Akaranam, village carried out by E. Jacob. Staffan Lindberg Field Diary, Vol. 1, p. 29, 9.5.1967.
80 Lindberg Collection, G. Kasturi Field Diary, 17.5.1967.

## CHAPTER 5

# Encompassing the Mission

'We kept them low' was a statement made by Goundars over and over again in interviews, and it summarises well the contents of many of the missionary reports about the Goundars' treatment of the Madhari throughout the period of missionary involvement in the rural Coimbatore district. The Goundar control of the Madhari, both as labourers and as a separate and well-defined community, placed low in the local social hierarchy, appears generally to have been firm. As was discussed in Chapter 2, during the early decades of the twentieth century there were institutions at work that regulated social relationships between groups of people with regard to caste and control over land and labour. These institutions were rooted in customary law and placed the Goundar community at the highest level, while the Madhari were found at the bottom end.

The Madhari were both part of the system and dependent for their survival on staying within it. Also, the identity ascribed to them as 'the Madhari' or 'the Chukkili' was explained in local society by the fact that they were the leather-workers as well as the Goundars' labourers. However, already in the early 1930s, there were signs of growing mobilisation among the Madhari to approach another authority that had long been established in the district. The Madhari turned to the mission.

Mobilisation is the main theme of this chapter. The question of mobilisation and organisation among the lowest sections in Indian society has been dealt with in many previous studies. However, sometimes there has been a tendency to divide this question into (at least) two different subjects of debates in which the participants rarely meet. One of the debates has focused on social and political movements in which members of Scheduled Castes have organised politically and socially over a larger region for common goals. The other has basically moved within the discipline of mission studies and has concentrated on mass-conversion movements. Such movements have also been analysed in social and economic terms. However, they have often been either treated as special cases or the researcher has been interested in the socio-economic consequences of conversion or the reasons for adopting another religion. There are exceptions from such mission-centred perspectives; the division is not so clear-cut.[1] However, to integrate the analyses of conversion movements further into the history of growing popular organisation and into the general, socio-economic history is a fruitful way to proceed. The points of departure need to be moved outside the 'mission sphere', but the presence of mission activities should still be considered important for social and political mobilisation among the Scheduled Castes or the 'untouchables'.

Two of the missions that had been working in the highlands since the nineteenth century came to be deeply involved in the rural areas. These were the Church of Sweden Mission (Evangelical Lutheran) and the Wesleyan Methodist Missionary Society (hereafter CSM and MMS[2]). The MMS had established itself at Nagapattinam on the coastline east of the Coimbatore district in 1820. Gradually, they had worked their way westwards, making Tiruchirapalli their headquarters in 1847. But their work developed only very slowly.[3] A handful of Swedish missionaries had worked for the Leipzig Evangelical Lutheran Mission until the Church of Sweden Mission Board was formed in 1874 and the Church of Sweden authorised its own mission.[4] Both missions had established stations in the highlands at the beginning of the twentieth century, the MMS in Dharapuram and the CSM in Coimbatore. Their work was generally urban-based, and their congregations grew as a rule by individual conversions.[5]

The turning-point was dated 1913 by the MMS. That year was regarded as the beginning of the kinship-based conversions on a large scale within their area. Whole families or even all the members of a particular caste in a village came to the missionaries to ask for baptism. At this early stage of the movement, these converts were Paraiyar. The first of them who turned to the MMS had relatives who had converted as a result of the work of the London Missionary Society.[6] This was the same kind of group-based conversion movement that is generally called a 'mass movement', and it has been observed by several authors in studies of different periods of south Indian history. Such conversion movements were directed both towards the Christian missions and towards Islam.[7] Characteristic of this kind of mobilisation for conversion was that the presumptive converts initially took the most active part, not the mission workers. The converting communities acted consciously and collectively. Thus, the untouchable castes 'encompassed' the mission.

The first signs of this movement, reported by the CSM missionaries, were recorded in annual reports and in local baptismal records, when baptisms took place in Tiruppur and Pollachi pastorates in 1924. These converts were members of the same caste as the converting families in Dharapuram.[8] As had been the case in Dharapuram, also in the central part of the Coimbatore district, members of the Paraiyar community were the first to convert. A few years later, members of the Madhari community began to ask for baptism. However, as will be discussed later, these were different movements with regard to mobilisation. While the Paraiyar movement had most of the general features of other mass-conversion movements, the Madhari movement had characteristics of its own. These can only be understood by keeping the particular social and labour relations of the Madhari in mind.

The fact that representatives of foreign missions arrived in the villages and section-wise admitted large numbers of members of the untouchable castes into a Church as followers of a new religion raises many important questions, particularly as the mission workers were generally called on by the Madhari community in the village, rather than the mission workers themselves taking the first initiative. The most important and general question related to this study can be formulated as follows: Did the presence of mission representatives in the villages make a difference to the relationship between the Goundar and Madhari communities? As was discussed in Chapter 2, this relationship was one of power and subordination, of control and dependence. The change of religion is thereby not 'merely' understood as a change of gods. The presence of 'outsiders' who came in order to build up a relationship with the Madhari would put the Goundar community in a position in which they had to decide how to regard the mission and its workers. The question raised is whether the presence of mission and of mobilisation within the Madhari community to approach the mission altered the relationship between the Goundar and Madhari communities. Before going into a deeper analysis of the Madhari mobilisation, the ways in which the movement spread will be discussed. Thereafter, the question of mobilisation will be more closely examined and discussed under three main headings: Integration, Control and Conflict, and Ideology and Identity.

### INTEGRATION

First of all; in order to have any influence or to matter in the local situation, the mission or its workers would have to become integrated to some degree into local society. Of course, just being there and not being immediately kicked out are signs of integration in the widest sense of the word. However, the question to be dealt with here concerns integration in the more conspicuous meaning of the term. Could the mission, as it was manifested by its representatives, establish itself as a social institution to which people could relate? Were the mission representatives able to integrate into local social life and relationships and become a recognised party in the local society?

In speaking of the missions as 'institutions', they should not primarily be thought of as administrative and organised entities. The firm impression given in the sources that this study is based on shows that it was hardly as institutions in this sense that the missions appeared in the villages. It seems unlikely that villagers applied to *the Church of Sweden Mission* for assistance of any kind to be given by the local missionary. The missions were rather better known as the individual missionary—'Ulrici *durai*' or 'Envall *durai*'—who arrived with an outside authority that backed the individuals concerned. At the same time, it has to be emphasised that the missions were not equivalent to their missionaries, either in the sense that they were men or women of great personal powers who moved around independently as 'small islands' in society or in a more concrete sense. The majority of the mission workers were not European missionaries. Much more numerous were the Indian pastors, evangelists and bible women. Especially the two last-mentioned were often drawn from the local region.[9]

The theme of Integration will embrace different aspects, to elaborate the question how the mission workers were received in the villages and how they were represented by their material resources and by their actions.

### CONTROL AND CONFLICT

Another set of questions focuses on the Goundar control of the Madhari. These can be summed up in the question: Did the mission involvement in the villages and the Madhari's decision to convert serve to reinforce the Goundar–Madhari relationship or did it imply a threat to the prevailing division of labour and power? Of course, it is also possible that it may not have made any difference at all, but, as described by most writers on mass-conversion movements, also in the highlands the large-scale conversions by members of the untouchable castes were accompanied by conflicts with the employing landowners. The causes of these conflicts may have turned out to be different in different cases. The relevant question here is whether explanations may be found in the existing relationship between the Goundar and Madhari communities and in the Goundar exercise of control over the Madhari. This is therefore not a question that is limited to the prevailing labour relations, as they were manifested over different periods, but includes a discussion of the dominant position of the Goundar in local society with regard to the Madhari community. This means that a discussion of labour relations in the more economic sense will go hand in hand with a discussion of power relations in the more social or political sense. As a consequence, the search for answers to the question of mission involvement in local social relationships will lead into the context of local social and economic power structures. This will be discussed under the heading of 'Control and Conflict'.

### IDEOLOGY AND IDENTITY

Thirdly, whether expressed in themes or practices, did the ideology of the mission present a viable alternative to an ideology that ascribed the lowest position in the social hierarchy to the Madhari, as well as their identity as leather-workers and agricultural labourers?

In the concluding section, the focus will be on ideology and identity. However, it is only in a limited aspect that these issues will be discussed. The main object is the ideology embraced by local society, as it was expressed in its institutionalised practises, in sets of rules and behaviour. Identity will also be understood in that perspective, as the identity ascribed to the different members of local society. The discussion will therefore mainly deal with human actions, not ideas. The self-identity of members of different communities will not be in the main focus of the discussion. However, it will sometimes be elaborated on, but the empirical basis for a thorough discussion of self-identity or conflicts between a societal or dominant ideology and ideologies carried by different communities is too weak.

When the mission established its presence in the region, its representatives expressed an ideology that occasionally came into conflict with expressions of a societal or dominant ideology. Their ideology was expressed in both words and deeds, and the missionaries constantly made their standpoint clear to the village people they met. But words and deeds do not always match. The missionaries appear to have been very careful not to come into conflict with the Goundar community. When missionaries relate how they assured the Goundars that they were not out to change the local order, that the farmers would continue to be farmers and that the labourers would continue to labour for them, the response they received is surprising. The missionaries said that all they wanted to do was to evangelise and baptise people and form congregations. How did it come about that such aims received a violent reply from the farming Goundar? The apparent lack of conflicts related in the reports after the mid-1950s is also noteworthy.

In a situation with no open conflicts, ascribed identities and a societal ideology may co-exist without disturbance or being questioned. They become a part of everyday language, are taken for granted and thereby further reinforce identities and existing hierarchies. Therefore, ideology does not necessarily have to be a set of ideas that is consciously embraced by a person but may also refer to prevailing social practices, in which both dominators and dominated are unaware of the ideological implications. However, that does not necessarily imply that ideology and identity carry inertia and are carried unconsciously by people for times without end. Where structural contradictions exist between groups of people, a dominant ideology and its different expressions may from this perspective be questioned when conflict arises.

In the way ideology is understood in the subsequent text, the link between themes and practices is important. The aim of a dominant ideology is understood to conceal contradictions that relate to the control of the means of production and of social power and influence. Ideology will thereby legitimise the status quo.

This position opens up a discussion of the consequences of missionary involvement in the rural Coimbatore district and its influence on the Goundar–Madhari relationship.

However, there are some limitations in the material when it comes to the question of ideology. The expressions of ideology in practice in both the economic and the social spheres have clearly come to the surface, as has also been briefly discussed in the previous chapters. However, it has only been possible to study the dominant ideology in the local society of the past in an indirect way, through the eyes of an outside onlooker or in the memories of Goundar or Madhari informants.

Among representatives of the Subaltern Studies collective of historians, this situation has not been treated as a weakness of the material that would create obstacles to drawing conclusions about what went on in the minds of persons other than the author of a certain set of documents. In an early contribution to the Subaltern writings, Ranajit Guha researches into peasant insurgency in India under colonialism. He aims at writing the history of the peasants as a history in which the peasant is the subject and does not play a minor part in the history of colonialism or Indian nationalism or any other history in which they are given the rôle of an object and a subordinate part. More specifically, Guha searches for the 'general form' of peasant insurgency in India, in which the peasants in the whole of the subcontinent are aware of their depressed situation under colonialism and strive to end it. To interpret peasant insurgency as spontaneous, unorganised uprisings is to take an elitist view of history; the insurgency must be understood as essentially rational and organised, argues Guha. Methodologically, he starts from the idea that insurgency was 'the necessary antithesis of colonialism'. In the British colonial documents, he finds evidence for the peasants' subordination. It follows that subordination cannot be recognised without acknowledging also insubordination. When a ruling culture affirms dominance, it reveals the 'Other', resistance. Indigenous India thereby becomes the complete opposite of the British colonial power. It is argued that, as counter-insurgency derives from insurgency, official and unofficial documents, even though elitist in character, can be taken to reveal the presence of the rebel. Assuming that the antagonism between the dominator and the dominated was firm and the perceptions mutually contradictory, the values and norms expressed in the documents can be reversed and thereby uncover a 'subaltern mentality'.[10]

Striving to find evidence of the history of people who did not leave documents behind is not only commendable; it is necessary. However, as discussed in Chapter 1, I would prefer to rely on visible evidence in the first place, rather than start with the theoretical assumption that the ideas held by the subordinate class are a reversed construction of norms or ideas embraced by the author of a document.

As regards the study of the relationship between the Goundar and

Madhari communities, the reference to the Subaltern methodological position presented here is not entirely correct. The mission workers were not dominators of either the Madhari or the Goundar communities. The dominant party in this case lived in local Indian society; they were the Goundar. Just as in the case of the Madhari, no texts about the Goundar–Madhari relationship have been found that were written by Goundar authors. In this connection, it may also be stressed that the Goundar community was not united by class but that there was an economic hierarchy dividing the community, and they were not all able to enter into a *pannaiyar–pannaiyal* relationship with the Madhari labourers.

It is hardly possible to arrive at firm conclusions about the mentality of a party by relying only on statements by an opposite party. There is an immense risk that a vast number of factors, of which the writers of the documents were completely unaware, may have been conducive to the actions taken and the 'mentality' held by the peasants. Such conclusions have a strength as probable assumptions that may lead to further research. But, as conclusions, they must be taken with much caution, as they are hypothetical and lack confirmation in other types of material.

## ORGANISING ALONG KINSHIP LINES

Before going into the earlier, structured discussion on integration, control and ideology, it is necessary to look more closely into the kind of conversion movement that developed in the Coimbatore district and the work of the Lutheran and Methodist missions.

The two missions, the MMS and the CSM, reacted somewhat differently to the community-based conversions. They both appear to have been overwhelmed by the onset of converts from untouchable castes. But while the Lutheran missionaries did their best to 'catch up' with the movement, while struggling against scarce financial resources, the Methodists set about systematically categorising the converts not only by caste (or community), but also by sub-caste or kinship lines. Just as systematically, they tried to reach members of the same sub-caste as the already converted Christians. By 1925, all *Sangu* or Conch-shell Paraiyar, except 300-400 in and around Dharapuram, were reported to have become Christians through the MMS. The movement was growing among the *Paccaivalaiyal* or Green Bangle Paraiyar, as well as in two sections of the Madhari.[11] In the annual report of 1926, the author explains that 'a mass movement works perpendicularly through one particular out-caste, and not horizontally from one out-caste to another'.[12] In contrast, when caste is mentioned in the CSM reports, it relates almost always to the general level, the Paraiyar.[13]

Interviews with CSM missionaries show that, at least after 1940, they were not unaware of those subdivisions. The Methodists, for their part, were not untouched by money problems. Just like the CSM, they had to deal with shrinking resources.[14] The point is that there seems to have been a difference in approach and method. 'Our policy is quite definitely to discourage isolated baptisms', the MMS stated in 1940. The author relates that people were not baptised unless most of the community in a village were prepared to join. This reveals a systematic method of emphasising the kinship character of the conversions, adopted in order to reach new converts and make new congregations stronger to resist outside attempts to enforce reconversion.[15]

But while the MMS strategy, whether successfully implemented or not, appears to have been to reach, regionally and kinship-wise, every village where a certain caste or sub-caste community lived, before seriously entering the next region or sub-caste, the CSM admitted all who turned to them with what were thought to be sincere motives. Though they often commented on it, the CSM does not seem to have systematically followed the 'community- or caste-trail', in order to reach as many as possible of a certain sub-caste at this early stage of the community-based movement. The MMS were rather irritated by the 'free-lance pioneer work' of the CSM among the untouchables in their neighbourhood. This work fell short in both organisation, staff and methods and had a negative effect on the MMS work, according to the Standing Committee in Dharapuram.[16]

Later, in 1940, the Lutheran pastor assigned to Pollachi indicated as an interesting observation how the new converts made great efforts to 'enlist' relatives in other villages. In that year the newly baptised Paraiyar of Sinna Negamam influenced the Paraiyar community in nearby Chandrapuram, with whom they had relations by marriage, to convert. Twenty-five heads of families, who represented about 65 persons, from Chandrapuram were brought to Karunagarapuri mission station to be enrolled as catechumens.[17]

This kind of note, conscious of the kinship logic of religious affiliation, is rarely found in the CSM documents. It should be noted

TABLE 5.1. CHRISTIAN POPULATION IN COIMBATORE DISTRICT

| *Census of India* | *Total pop.* | *Yearly change per thousand persons* | *Christian pop.* | *Yearly change of Christian pop. per thousands persons* | *Net change of Christian pop. to total pop.* |
|---|---|---|---|---|---|
| 1901* | 1,979,464 | | 18,887 | | |
| 1911 | 2,116,564 | 6.7 | 19,550 | 3.5 | –3.2 |
| 1921† | 2,219,848 | 4.8 | 28,308 | 37.7 | 32.9 |
| 1931 | 2,445,064 | 9.7 | 46,840 | 51.6 | 41.9 |
| 1941 | 2,809,648 | 14.0 | 68,593 | 38.9 | 24.9 |
| 1951 | 3,293,204 | 16.0 | 74,493 | 8.3 | –7.7** |

Source: Census of India.‡

* In 1910, the Karur taluk was transferred to Tiruchirapalli district. If Karur is included, the total population of the district reaches 2,201,752. This is the figure that is given in the Census of 1901; however, the figure has been revised in the Gazetteer of 1933. Cf. Census of India, Madras, 1901, Part 3, Table 1, p. 7, and Cox 1933, p. 1.

† Between 1921 and 1931, the borders of Palladam taluk were changed. The total population was thereby reduced by 23,765 persons. In Table 5.1, for the year 1921, these persons are included. Cox 1933, p. 70.

** The reasons for this decrease are discussed later in this chapter and in Chapter 6.

‡ The proportion of Christians to the total population in the Coimbatore district shows an increase from 0.85 per cent in 1901 to 2.26 per cent in 1951.

that this observation was made by an Indian pastor, the Rev. G. Stephen, who was known among the Lutheran missionaries for working on 'community-lines', by the same methods as were used by the Methodists. This was known to be exceptional in CSM work. Stephen was also the only one who consistently gave information about the sub-caste affiliation of converts in his reports to the CSM Board.[18]

By 1935, when the Methodist church the year before had recorded a growth from nearly 2,500 to 15,100 members in 20 years in the Dharapuram circuit,[19] the annual report reveals that the missionaries expected all Paraiyar, whether *Paccaivalaiyal*, *Sangu* or *Samban*, to convert as a consequence of the movement being kinship-based.[20]

This situation also explains why requests for baptism did not propagate from a geographical centre outwards to village after village but came from villages sometimes far apart as a result of marriage relationships. As stated earlier, when the movement spread westwards in the highlands from Dharapuram, both Tiruppur and Pollachi, which were 50 kilometres apart, recorded Paraiyar converts in 1924.[21]

In 1925, when the Methodists admitted converts in an area reaching from Udamalpet, south-west of Dharapuram, to Karur, north-east of the town, the first members of Madhari communities had begun to ask for baptism. As with the Paraiyar, these requests came from whole sections of Madhari in one village after another and were based on a common decision by the members of the group.[22]

The same trend began in the Palladam and Tiruppur area in the early 1930s. The first baptism among the Madhari community was recorded in 1933, after two years of contact with the Madhari of Karundanputhur and Kerdenjouthoor. At that time, it was reported that 'practically all' Paraiyar in the Palladam pastorate had already converted.[23] 'The movement spreads by itself', explained the CSM missionary in Palladam, Harald Frykholm, in 1931. The first from among the Madhari had sought contact with the CSM representatives, and Frykholm was hopeful. He expected the Madhari soon to follow the example of the Paraiyar and become Christians.[24] In 1933, J.J. Ellis, of the MMS, gave an explanation of the fast-growing movement that made it sound as if natural forces were at work. In 1923, the *Sangu* Paraiyar movement was at its peak. 1933 had turned out to be another peak year, this time caused by the Madhari. Ellis exclaimed that they were not able to hold them back, as the newly converted Madhari themselves prepared relatives to request baptism. Dharapuram and Udamalpet showed the highest figures in the statistics.[25]

Opinions in the two missions on the new group of converts were similar: the missionaries were glad to receive them, but they could cause problems. The Madhari were much more numerous than the Paraiyar in the areas where the missions worked, and their economic situation was more precarious. They were more tied to the villages and to agriculture, and would find it difficult, if not impossible, to earn a living anywhere else. To such material judgements were added statements of the Madhari's ignorance and low morals. To work among the Madhari was believed to be difficult and financially onerous.[26]

Both the Methodists and the Lutherans expressed their preference for converts among the higher castes. According to a CSM missionary in 1931, high-caste converts would not join in such large numbers as the untouchables, and they would immediately be financially self-supporting. High-caste converts would also be able to evangelise among high-caste Hindus. Paraiyar evangelists would not so easily be accepted among them.[27] In a major MMS report on the mass movement in 1935, it was stated that, before the movement had begun, the aim of the Methodist mission had been to convert the middle-class communities. But in a report from 1926, the author stated that from what he knew, there had never been a mass-conversion movement among the high castes, either in the Methodist mission or in any of the others.[28]

In 1946, an explanation was given as to why there had been a stagnation in the growth of members in the Palladam pastorate from the early 1930s to 1943.

> The stagnation was to some extent caused by a conscious restraint on the part of the mission towards the large group of leather-workers. We felt incapable to open the doors wide, as the Methodists in the Dharapuram area did, . . . Our experiences with the leather-workers' character and development possibilities were depressing, and we lacked possibilities to give them the leadership and training that would have been needed.[29]

Both CSM and MMS reports indicate that the contact between the presumptive converts and either of the missions was as likely to originate from the mission workers as from the villagers. In cases in which no mission worker had been in contact with a particular village, representatives of the community could be sent to the mission station and request baptism for its members. If the whole community was involved, the decision was likely to be taken in the community's council of elders. This decision could be a result of marriage relations with Christians but could also be influenced by boys in the community who had spent time in a Christian boarding-school or attended courses at the mission stations. The latter situation was rather rare in the case of Madhari children, as they seldom went to school.[30]

Frykholm reported in 1932 about the first Madhari converts in the Palladam area. A few months after baptismal education had been taken up in their village, requests for teachers came from three new Madhari villages. During Christmas 1932, a deputation from one of these villages came to the mission station, saying that they had already built a palm-leaf shed. All that they wanted now was a teacher from the mission.[31]

'A group of men could be standing in a corner of the compound when I got out of the house in the morning', remembers Bertil Envall, who worked in Pollachi, Palladam and Arulpuram between 1944 and 1953. 'When they saw me, they tied up the *lungi* and approached.' The name of their village was usually unfamiliar to Envall, but they had come to ask for a teacher in order to get baptised. Relatives of theirs had benefited from conversion, and now they wanted to have contact with the mission themselves. An evangelist was generally sent to make a first visit in the Madhari *cheri* and to ask permission from the Goundar elder to meet with the Madhari.[32]

Jonas Ulrici, who took up work in Palladam in 1941, relates that at the beginning of his work in the area, he did not pay attention to the Goundars when he approached the Madhari *cheri*. But from experience he learnt to visit them first, in order to avoid conflicts.[33] As a rule, the CSM missionaries seem to have sought to reach an understanding with the Goundars of the village before entering the Madhari part of the village.[34]

From what has been said, it is important to note that both Madhari and Paraiyar acted on a caste-basis and, judging from the MMS reports and those CSM reports that discussed the movement in detail, their collective actions were based on sub-caste or kinship divisions. The initiative appears to have come from either of the missions or from villagers who had been influenced by people other than the mission workers. Kinship-based conversions were not initiated by the missions in the first place. They were rather troubled by the risk of baptising people with mixed faiths or more material than spiritual motives. But, once the movement had begun, methods where mission workers themselves approached villagers could further encourage Hindu relatives of Christians to convert.

Comparisons with the Paraiyar are to some extent fruitful in trying to understand the Goundar–Madhari relationship. But from this point onwards in this chapter, the emphasis will be placed mainly on the Madhari community. As has been previously discussed, the history as regarded the Paraiyar took a different path than that as regarded the Madhari, and I shall leave the former to focus on the acts of the latter.

## INTEGRATION

In going deeper into the questions of integration, control and ideology, the scope of the investigation will again be limited to the geographical centre of the highlands. As in Chapters 2 to 4, the developments in the area extending from Tiruppur in the north and approximately 60 kilometres south-west and stretching 40 kilometres from east to west will remain in the focus of the study. This means that the MMS material will basically be left aside. But rather than making a comparison between the missions, it has turned out to be more fruitful to follow up the developments in the chosen region. Nowhere in the MMS reports has evidence appeared that indicates that the relationship between the Goundar and the Madhari in the Dharapuram area was of a fundamentally different character from that in the Tiruppur–Palladam–Coimbatore area. Also the kinship-based conversions follow a similar pattern.

There is also another reason that would complicate any attempt to compare the MMS and the CSM in this respect. That is the different characters of the two sets of documents, particularly the annual reports. The details on sub-caste that are given in the MMS reports discussed earlier may give the impression that these reports were more detailed in general. Unfortunately, that is not the case. Where a certain event in a village is described, the name of the village is seldom given, and the description covers mainly congregational life in a more spiritual sense. 'Persecution' from the landowners as a means of enforcing reconversion may be briefly related. But rather than associating this with labour relations, the coming harvest, the exercise of power or the like, the authors conclude that 'the faith of the newly baptised congregations were sorely tried' or that 'it has generally served only to reveal the glory of God in the lives of His disciples'.[35]

An event that invites further questions was related in 1936. This is one of the more exceptional cases in which the village was mentioned by name. In Sulliporikkipalayam, 'riots' were said to have taken place between the Goundar and the Madhari. Nine of the Madhari men were arrested, and a court case was filed. While the men were awaiting their trial, their houses were burnt to the ground, and some of the women in their households were (falsely, according to the author) accused of theft. After six months, all the men but one were released. They all remained Christian.[36]

Of course, it may be possible to trace such events by going through court records and by holding interviews in Sulliporikkipalayam. That may make it possible to get answers to questions such as 'What caused the riots?', 'Why were the nine men arrested?', 'Did the mission act on behalf of the Madhari community during the conflict?' 'Were sentences passed upon the Madhari men?' and 'When the eight men had been released, had the Goundar and Madhari communities reached an agreement or was one party the obvious winner?' That is not the point. What is generally lacking in the MMS reports in this regard is the mere observations made by an outsider, such as the missionary. The reports give the impression that, rather than relating events in detail, they served to show how well the poor, newly converted Christians bore with persecution and how Christ triumphed in their lives.

Progress in the evangelical efforts was emphasised, and 'growing harvest' was a common expression.

This is not to say that the MMS reports completely lack details on social or economic conditions or that such pieces of information are legion in the CSM reports. But while they occur more randomly in the MMS files, one can find them rather frequently in CSM documents. In conducting a discussion about labour and power relations, the latter is, of course, to be preferred.

The fact that mission workers have provided the most ample documentation of the villages and their inhabitants obviously reduces the range of different informants, especially as the geographical region was divided between the different missions and, in this particular area, the Church of Sweden Mission had a 'monopoly'. That may lead one to conclude that the information gathered will be extremely one-sided.

However, it is necessary—and it is only correct—to consider the different mission workers according to their different backgrounds. There is a clear division between European and Indian authors. The Indian mission workers writing reports and letters were not many, but they were very influential in the work they carried out, and their opinions mattered a great deal in the decisions taken in the different committees and boards in the mission work in India. As was discussed in the 'Introduction', the risk of misinterpreting an observed situation is much reduced among the Indian mission workers and pastors. Secondly, these authors tend to observe social interactions between different actors in the villages, and there is no reason to believe that important parts of the existing social relationships escaped them.

It will also be useful to mention a second level of divisions between authors. This is further discussed under the section 'Social Status' but should be considered in a discussion of the sources. Among the European missionaries submitting reports, some worked in the highlands, while some did their main work outside this region. Most of the missionary authors belonged to the first category, while the bishop, Johannes Sandegren, was stationed in Tiruchirapalli, and from there made visits to all the pastorates of the Church. That he was an outsider in the highlands should not be taken to mean that he was completely uninformed. Johannes Sandegren was born and raised in India and had a vast knowledge of south Indian society as such. But he might not have been as sensitive to the particular village context as were the missionaries stationed in the district or as was Bishop David Bexell, who worked for decades in the region. Sandegren's presence was also associated with particular interests of the Church and with decisions in the Church Council or other minor committees that were to be enforced. There were also divisions among the Indian mission workers. As members of different castes, they did not have the same access to the different communities in the villages. This fact may have influenced their reports.

Thus, although they had the Church of Sweden Mission or the Tamil Evangelical Lutheran Church as employers, and their different reports eventually ended up in the same archive, I intend to read and interpret these authors according to their different backgrounds.

To begin with, the following discussion will be focused on the initial years of kinship-based conversions among the Madhari. For the CSM this means the 1930s and 1940s. These were years when the interaction between the CSM representatives and the local people became intense. The presence of missionaries was not unknown to the villagers. They had worked for several decades in the region, but suddenly they made a difference.

From one point of view, the decision to convert will at a certain stage have to take place in the mind of the individual person. But, as has been discussed, the characteristic feature of these conversions was not the individual decision, but the collective action. The fact that conversion took place on kinship lines in sections or whole groups of members of a certain community in a village, and not by a series of individual decisions in scattered villages, made the presence of mission workers a matter for the whole of local society, and not only for the individual family.

Also, a situation in which the mission, which had been present in the Coimbatore highlands for many decades, suddenly became an important institution for villagers without the mission changing its work or its approach indicates a change in the situation in the villages. To discuss 'integration' does not presuppose a static, immovable situation into which outsiders 'integrated'. It rather appears as if ongoing change, economic and social, opened up the possibility of the integration of the mission workers into the villages. In the relationship between the Goundar landowners and the Madhari *pannaiyal*, the mission appears as a refuge and a 'tool' for the Madhari with regard to their relationship to the Goundar.

This situation gives rise to questions on the level or degree of integration into local society that the mission or its representatives were able to achieve. Without becoming a party to be considered by the different parties in the locality, there is no reason to believe that the presence of the mission had any significant impact on the relationship between the Goundar and Madhari communities. Without integration, the mission or its representatives would only represent a religious order in which the Madhari found spiritual consolation that had no impact on local social relations. Any level of integration would mean that a new party had entered into the social life of the village. In order to further develop the question of integration, the following discussion will focus on areas of interaction with regard to social status, physical representation, material resources and mediation.

## Social Status

In a village, social status was generally not a matter of doubt. When the mission workers arrived, they also were treated according to the social code. However, in contrast to the village inhabitants, they were outsiders. With some exceptions, they had no previous personal links with people in the villages. This can be assumed to have given them a certain space, in the sense that they were not tied into the local social structure in which the village inhabitants placed themselves and regarded each other in terms of social status.

From the results, it is important to note that the mission workers were not treated as a homogeneous group. They were not received in the same way as 'representatives of the mission'. Europeans and Indians were met differently, and caste mattered. The latter appears to have made a difference, to the extent that it may be assumed that European missionaries and high-caste pastors were received with more equal respect than were Indian high-caste pastors compared to Scheduled Caste pastors, evangelists and bible women. But education also added to social status. Being an educated man, even though of a Scheduled Caste, could bring a more respectful treatment from members of higher castes. However, there is nothing to show that affiliation to the mission or education anywhere replaced caste barriers.

As was stated earlier, the CSM mission workers made a habit of asking the leading Goundar for permission to begin work among the Madhari community in his village. Nowhere is it indicated that the missionary consciously tried to replace the Goundar as the patron of the Madhari. 'On the contrary', states Bertil Envall, 'we told the Goundars that "we have not come to change your relationship. We want them [the Madhari] to continue to do their work. We are not going to tell them to do their work less honestly or hard when they become Christians, just the opposite."'[37] Considering the violent reply that the mission workers and the presumptive converts sometimes received after that first encounter, the statement may sound peculiar. This invites the assumption that, even though they accepted the mission workers into their village, the Goundar community still felt threatened by their presence.

From interviews, it appears that the mission workers were received with regard both to the mission they represented and their caste. Of course, the latter does not apply to European missionaries, but they also seem to have been received with regard to their status as Europeans.

As a rule, bible women and evangelists were members of the Paraiyar community and came from the area, while pastors in the earlier part of the century were more likely to come from higher castes, such as the Vellalar, Chettiyar, Nadar or Servai. Later, when a substantial number of the Paraiyar community had passed through the mission schools and seminaries, the majority of the pastors in the district were Paraiyar.[38] In the villages, caste mattered. In Nallakalipalayam, a village near Arulpuram, all the Madhari converted in 1948. The Rev. E. Jacob, a native of the village, gives an interesting description of the mission workers.[39] The pastor in Mandiripalayam was A.S. Muttiah.[40] The place was itself a centre of the conversion movement south of Palladam. Jacob was young at the time when Muttiah was stationed in Mandiripalayam, and therefore his knowledge about the pastor stems from discussions with Jacob's father-in-law, who worked as an evangelist in the Palladam region.

> Muttiah was middle class, a Nadar. Therefore he could go in between the Goundars, and he was working among the poor people. He was like a mediator. If he went to the Goundars he would not be misunderstood. He could command respect from the Goundar. Suppose that I go there, I will be misunderstood, I will be treated as any other man although I have my education.[41]

Jacob had personal experience of the latter from the time when he worked as an assistant to the sociologist Staffan Lindberg in 1967. Lindberg and his four assistants carried out interviews during a couple of months in villages around Palladam, while staying in Mandiripalayam. On 9 May, Lindberg wrote that Jacob had suddenly run away for fear of the Goundar in Mandiripalayam.[42] On the day before, after some concluding remarks about a troublesome interview in his diary, Jacob wrote: 'By that time one woman came and recognised me, because she is from my village, and asked: "Which is your native place?" I had to tell a lie: "I am from Kinnathukadavu". Actually I am native of Nallakalipalayam in which many people of Mandiripalayam have relatives. This [person] is in one way or other related to me.'[43]

Immediately, the word was spread that Jacob had relatives in the Madhari *cheri*. The following day, after having finished an interview, Jacob and Kasturi, another of the assistants, went to take a bath in a field well, when a 'stout man' arrived and asked 'peculiar' questions. This was enough for Jacob to realise that the news had spread—a Madhari man had taken a bath in one of the Goundar's wells. And Jacob decided to 'build the dam before the flood came' and ran off to nearby Kethanur. It took great efforts to persuade him to continue his work in Mandiripalayam.[44]

Jacob's description of Muttiah as a mediator who could communicate with members of different castes without encountering problems resembles the Mandiripalayam *Ur*-Goundar's description of the situation. When Ramasamy Goundar was approached by Muttiah in the late 1940s about selecting land for a new *cheri* for the Madhari and digging a well in the *cheri*, Ramasamy contacted the Collector of Coimbatore, Morris, and land was allotted. Neither Ramasamy nor anyone else in his community would participate in the congregation that was founded among the Madhari. But, as the chapel that was built in the *cheri* was separated from the Madhari settlement by a minor road, Ramasamy could, when so requested, come and garland prominent visitors in the chapel. Missionaries were never invited to his house, but occasionally he would eat with them at the parsonage, provided the missionaries brought the food with them. The pastor had to assure him that no food was cooked by the Madhari.[45]

Envall points to the importance of caste to explain why Muttiah was well received among the Goundar. But education and conciliatory behaviour added to his reputation, according to Envall.[46]

Jacob's father-in-law, C.P. Masillamani, was of the Paraiyar community and an educated man. As an evangelist, Masillamani worked together with Bertil Envall when he was stationed in Palladam and Arulpuram. Jacob explains that the Goundar were suspicious of the missionary at the beginning and that sometimes stones were thrown at him. Among the Madhari, there was no throwing of stones, but still a distance was kept: 'My father-in-law would be accepted because he was dark in complexion, but the Reverend Envall would not be so easily accepted. They would bow down and say *toottiram* or something, but they would stand at a distance.'[47]

Bertil Envall relates that he always went to the *Ur*-Goundar's house on his first visit to a village, to pay his respects. He emphasises how important it was to act according to the social code. No teacher could walk through the main village with his shoes on, as teachers were generally of the Paraiyar community. If they came on bicycles, they had to step down when a Goundar approached. If they did not push the bicycle, they might find that it had been roughly handled when they were about to leave. But the Paraiyar teachers seem to have been allowed to keep their shirts on, something that was not permitted to the Madhari around 1950. 'They could keep that honour, even if they were Adi dravida. I know that I have walked together with them, and they have always been fully dressed.'[48] The teachers were also often called on by the Goundar to read and write. In a village, the teacher might be the only literate person.[49]

As an interviewed person relies on his or her memory when past events are related, the information will be a construct of an observed reality. In its essence, the information given in interviews may not be a 'larger' construct than that given in written annual reports or in correspondence, since they all rely on a person's memory of the past. The difference is in time. More than in documents written on the night of an event or a month later, there is a risk in an interview that the informant may construct a 'personality' out of a person. Someone known for many years is remembered for having had a certain character, rather than for what he or she actually did or said. But if we disregard the qualities attributed to the individual persons and consider only the information given about social barriers that have been indicated as being upheld in social contacts, the interviews give some indications as to how mission workers were received in the villages.

From the interviews, it seems that social status was decided by affiliation to caste and to the mission in combination. The Indian mission workers appear not to have been able to become completely associated with the mission as an institution and thereby to escape from the social rules of caste. Education may have added to an individual's reputation, but the different categories of mission workers do not seem to have been thought of as one and the same or as 'of the Church of Sweden Mission'. From the interviews, we are rather led to believe that being an educated person infused some respect that may have raised the individual's status. Being an outsider and not immediately known or related to someone in the village may also have provided an opportunity to communicate in a more 'unbiased' way. But nothing that has been said proves that education or being from outside the region made caste affiliation insignificant.

Returning to the mission reports, the way in which mission workers were met generally corresponds well with the information in the oral material. The only noticeable difference comes in the descriptions of the way in which missionaries were received on visits to the villages. This may have come about as a result of the fact that the reports were written by missionaries. The situation in which the missionary stayed in the background, as described by Jacob, does not resemble the picture given in the mission documents.

In the reports, the Rev. Stephen stands out more than the Rev. Muttiah as a man who 'could talk to anyone' and who mediated between Goundar and Madhari. In that sense, Stephen may seem to have been an exceptional case among the pastors mentioned in the CSM documents. But the frequent occurrence of his name in the CSM files is explained by his long-term involvement with the mission. While Muttiah arrived at Mandiripalayam as a retired pastor, Stephen worked in the district for 20 years. During that time, he had responsibilities that can be compared to those of missionaries. For a time, he was in charge of a part of a mission station and wrote reports to the CSM Board.[50]

Stephen was of the Servai community, a higher caste, just like Muttiah, and was also held in high esteem in local society. The status this gave him made it possible for him to mediate in conflicts. In cases in which a Goundar had been cruel or had beaten a Madhari man without cause, Stephen managed to secure compensation (a fine) for the beaten man. The informants' statements agree that that would not have been possible if he had been of a lower caste.[51]

## Physical Representation

When representatives of the mission arrived at a village, they became known as individuals to the villagers. They came with outside authority and acted in ways that sometimes interfered with daily life. But the mission workers were not the only manifestation of this outside authority. Its presence was visible in several ways, some of which were independent of the presence of mission workers. Immediately after the introductory visits, a building was erected to house the baptismal instruction. This was not necessarily a mud-brick building, but more likely a palm-leaf shed. New ceremonies and rites were introduced. These were not shared by the rest of the village but were exclusively practised by the Christians. The baptismal ceremony was turned into a festival, in which the Madhari would play the instruments that they used in the village temple ceremonies, a procession was held and, in cases in which the Goundar community was not hostile, they would be invited as honoured guests.[52]

Eventually a chapel was erected. Until then, most holy places in the Madhari *cheris* had been cult centres, often with a stone or some dressed-up, wood carvings under a tree, where offerings could be made. Temple buildings were more rare. A temple, a building to enter at the holy place, was rather associated with religious worship among the high castes.

Stephen was a man for great festivals. But he was not alone, or even the first in the CSM, to initiate Christian festivals that resembled the large, colourful and noisy, Hindu festivals. As early as in 1925, Johannes Sandegren argued for the introduction of festivals to replace the Hindu festivals and the 'half-heathen entertainment' of the Catholics. If the Lutheran Church appeared dull and boring, he feared that the converts would relapse. But the festivals should be respectable; the congregation members should be taught to give and therefore collections were an important part of the celebration.[53] Anna Irbe noticed that the Christian Paraiyar missed the Hindu festivals badly, as they were the only 'bright spots' in life. But at Karunagarapuri, with the help of Stephen, the Christian festivals were made into lively happenings.[54] They were held every year and grew to become big events. Even in the difficult drought-year of 1952, he arranged a festival in which 1,500 people were said to have received a meal and 300 Goundar came for the event. On this and other occasions, Stephen made the Goundars contribute something to the expenses of the celebration. In that way, the mission could collect resources from the powerful people in local society and distribute them to the poor. To be able to do that required a certain amount of authority that was acknowledged by local society.[55]

Ceremonies, daily services, the building of chapels and the visits of evangelists or pastors all manifested the presence of a new party with an authority derived from outside the village.

### Material Resources

The obvious poverty of the Madhari made the question of material aid unavoidable. Mass-movement converts have sometimes been accused of being 'rice Christians', which meant that they had converted for material and not spiritual reasons. They were, so to speak, not true Christians. This is a normative position, sometimes slightly moralising. The question 'Did they come for material *or* spiritual reasons?' presupposes an ideological (or theological) position in which the human being is divided into body and soul. The underlying assumption may go even further and indicate that the mission's responsibility covered the saving of souls, while caring for the body should be a matter for local society or the state; anything else would constitute the buying of souls. On the other hand, if the question is turned into a research question, it disregards the possibility that people may have come for *both* material *and* spiritual reasons and that they may not have divided life into two sections, one physical and the other spiritual, at all. However, let us leave the moral aspect of this question aside and concentrate purely on the research question.

The CSM entered with resources into the villages. However, the documents show that, rather than being spread freely around, these resources were given with restrictions and a developmental purpose was embraced by the mission. The overall aim with regard to the Madhari, irrespective of the outcome, can be summarised as 'self-reliance'. One of the explicit purposes for lending was to enable the Madhari to become free from other debts that constituted obstacles to their social and economic progress. It may therefore be concluded that, in whatever form the resources appeared to the Madhari, in terms of integration, the fact that their actions were aimed at self-reliance implies that the CSM's distribution of resources was designed to produce a deep integration into rural relations.

There is also a firm impression that the Madhari realised no other alternative than that presented by the mission. They do not appear to have had any possibility of bargaining with either the mission workers or the Goundar farmers, as members of other communities sometimes could. In the matter of education, the Madhari community appear to have been less successful than the Paraiyar. The CSM also approached members of the two communities in different ways.

When converts made explicit material demands, the missionaries reacted with irritation. Among the MMS converts, the Koravar caste was often describes as pushing for material benefits. In 1927, the Koravar in Kongunad were reported to have reconverted when the 'material benefits of their new faith were less, and the disabilities attached thereto greater than they had expected'.[56] In the CSM reports, the Valayar had the same reputation. In 1946, these reports were written in an optimistic tone. The Valayar was a new group in which sections had decided to convert. They held a much higher social position than the Madhari and lived in 'neat houses and move freely with all inhabitants of the village'. Several hundreds had been admitted in that year, and three to four times as many were expected to join. But the satisfaction did not last long. Soon they became known for stealing and for illicit distilling, and Bertil Envall reports in 1948 from Palladam that the Christian Valayar had spent most of the year in jail. Their 'strong caste-feeling' was also troublesome. According to Envall, they had worked their way up from having been among the untouchables to 'a kind of low caste' and appear to have been 'particularly eager to mark their distance to the outcaste'. In Valacu, they did not allow untouchables to enter the church, and when Envall insisted that the Paraiyar Christians in Agrarapudur should attend the inauguration of the church, the Valayar Christians in the village became indignant.[57] In 1951, the conflict between the Valayar and Paraiyar Christians as regarded church attendance was resolved when a portico was built to enable the Paraiyar to enter the church.[58]

The specific stipulation of the Valayar that they would accept only high-caste teachers from the mission, together with the facts that the CSM lacked resources and that the Valayar congregations would have to wait for months for a visit, made them approach the Roman Catholic Church, which was at work in the district. In 1947, the author exclaims that the Catholics had already baptised far more of the Valayar than had the Lutherans and that they offered education as well as food and clothes without fees. As a rule, the Catholic Church was regarded as a 'threat'.[59] But annual reports give the impression that members, or 'villages', of the Valayar community crossed the border between Christian and non-Christian affiliation more than once. Most of the Valayar converts lived around Sulur, between Coimbatore and Tiruppur, and the missionary stationed in Sulur, Jonas Ulrici, complained repeatedly about drinking, theft and quarrels among the Valayar Christians. Villages could relapse and, occasionally, once again return to the Church.[60]

Also between the Madhari and the Paraiyar, caste feelings were strong. Being socially and economically on a higher level, the Paraiyar refused to have anything to do with the Madhari. But the contempt appears to have been mutual. Without going more deeply into the reasons for this dislike, the fact is that it created complications for the congregational work. In a small number of villages, both the Madhari and the Paraiyar communities were Christians. But only in a very few of them did they agree to share the church building. It happened that the CSM erected two chapels in the same village, one in the Madhari and the other in the Paraiyar settlement.[61] Some observers note that, after having become Christians, the Paraiyar moved to another settlement. In Mandiripalayam, Ramasamy Goundar related that the Paraiyar converted and went for higher studies, which meant that they left the village. In Ganesamurthi's study in the *Madras Agricultural Journal* of 1935, he observed a population decrease. This he found to have been caused by a general emigration to the expanding, commercial cotton centres and by the emigration of the whole Paraiyar community from the village as a result of conversion to Christianity.[62]

When the Constitution (Scheduled Castes) Order was promulgated by the President of India in 1950, it included a third paragraph that read '... no person who professes a religion different from Hindu shall be deemed to be a member of a Scheduled Caste'.[63] As a result, conversion to Christianity carried the consequence of exclusion from the Government financial support reserved for members of Scheduled Castes. From the local government authorities, the argument followed that Christians would receive such benefits from the missions and did not need this form of Government support. Just like Subban James, one of the interviewed persons in 1995, Madhari converts had both a Hindu and a Christian name. In 1951, the year after all but Hindus had been excluded from the category of Scheduled Castes, the missionary in Pollachi believed that Government hostels for schoolchildren might begin to admit Christians if only they changed their names back to the old Hindu names. If such a situation were to emerge, he suggested firm action by the mission. However, it is difficult to judge whether the law was differently applied in the Coimbatore district immediately after its ratification, compared with the 1960s, or whether the worries of the mission workers had been exaggerated. According to Olle Jonsson, who worked at Arulpuram from 1961 onwards, the practice of the law was somewhat arbitrary. He relates that, according to the quota for Scheduled Castes, 'Harijans' owning land could receive Government-subsidised oxen. However, 'Harijan' was understood as being equivalent to Hindu. But if only the Christians would give their Hindu names when applying for this benefit, they would in practice not be excluded from the Scheduled Caste category.[64]

The Koravar and Valayar cases show some similarities that stand out as against the Madhari. The Koravar did not get the expected benefits and reconverted. The Valayar left the Lutherans for the Catholics to get their higher status acknowledged.

Individuals among the Paraiyar may have left the Lutheran fold to gain material or social benefits. But in contrast to the other two, the absolute majority of the converted Paraiyar remained as members of Lutheran congregations. A common description in the mission reports throughout the period is that Paraiyar converts were most keen on raising their social and economic status. They were apparently conscious of and careful to uphold the barrier between themselves and the 'lower' Madhari community.[65]

The Madhari were not described as eager for benefits. The descriptions of them were rather more understanding. Either they were considered too poor, and their needs too obvious, or their 'slave mentality' was understood to make them abstain from such demands. In the words of the missionaries, they were described in a most passive way. The fact that a large number of the Madhari conversions were made by people among whom no mission worker had ever worked does not seem to have influenced the missionaries' understanding of the Madhari as victims in need of outside assistance.

However, compared with the situation of the Paraiyar, Valayar or Koravar communities, the Madhari do not seem to have been in a position to bargain for benefits. They may have joined in the hope of getting a well of their own, but in most cases the offer from the evangelist appears to have been their only alternative, besides remaining with the status quo. The Catholics did not work in the rural Tiruppur–Palladam region, and to 'go to the Harijans', i.e. to ask for Government help as Scheduled Caste Hindus, implied a level of organisation and a possibility of moving from the villages that cannot be associated with the Madhari in general.[66]

In order to prevent conversion for the sake of immediate benefits, the missionaries introduced a system of fees in the late 1940s. When baptismal instruction was begun, every married couple paid one rupee, which was equal to one day's income. At the baptismal ceremony, another rupee was paid.[67]

Even though the Madhari did not have the power to bargain for benefits, both relief work and 'economic uplift' were directed to them. The reason why the Madhari first came to Karunagarapuri mission station in 1936 was to ask for food, according to the missionary Elna Wimmercranz. A failure of the rains had caused a lack of food and, on the promise of repayment after the groundnut harvest, the Madhari were allowed to borrow money. The following day, more members of the Madhari community arrived at the station. Wimmercranz wrote that a dog had pushed down the image of their god, and now they too wanted to become Christians.[68] The fact that people turned to the mission station in their need of food is quite understandable, but it would have been interesting to know whether the story about the clumsy dog was the sole reason given by the Madhari for their conversion. That would have given an answer to the question whether the Madhari arriving on the second day were in fact out to get material aid as well or whether they had come to someone who was expected to provide for all needs, either material or spiritual.

In the Pâraiyar conversion movement, education and medical aid were important features. This was part of the mission strategy from the start; 'Christian faith is nothing without education and care for the neighbour's bodily health', explained Anna Irbe at Karunagarapuri.[69] But the contrast between the Madhari and the Paraiyar *cheris* is striking. As a rule, a school was started among the Paraiyar converts, while this was not the case with the Madhari. This may be explained by lack of resources in the CSM. After the war, in 1946, the teachers' salaries had increased. Between 1939 and 1946 living costs were calculated to have increased by four times and teachers' salaries doubled. At Karunagarapuri, the teaching staff was reduced, and only a few new schools were started in the villages.[70] The inflation struck after the peak of the Paraiyar conversion movement, while the Madhari movement was still on a high level. This implies that schools could be built in the Paraiyar *cheris* but that the Madhari were left without.

At the same time, even if schools had been built on a large scale for the Madhari, it appears unlikely that they would have been filled with Madhari pupils. To secure an income for the family, the children were sent to pasture the Goundars' cattle, and rather than starting schools that would remain empty, the missionaries tried to send the Madhari children to boarding-schools, such as the one at Karunagarapuri. In 1947, the author concludes that there was no alternative but to send the Madhari children to boarding-schools, where they could get both food and education. To run schools in the villages for these children was considered both more expensive and less efficient.[71] Reports also indicate that Madhari parents may have kept their children away from the mission schools in order not to provoke their Goundar masters.[72]

However, the Goundar community was not opposed to mission

schools, as such. Many Goundar boys were educated in the mission schools. In some villages, Goundar children were in the majority among the pupils. In Naranapuram in 1936, the Goundar community had informed the missionaries that they were willing to send their children to a mission school if that school was built on common land. On hearing this, the Bishop Sandegren considered the possibility of the Goundar themselves financing such a school and whether the altar of the church could be screened off during school hours.[73]

Throughout the whole period, even until 1970, education does not seem to have involved the Madhari to any substantial extent. When they are mentioned in the reports, attendance is said to have been irregular, and child labour the cause of the lack of schooling. In 1955, the author of a report complained that not a single Madhari boy had passed through the secondary school. But the efforts to provide education should be continued. The concluding comment was that the Methodists already had a Madhari student and two Madhari pastors, so 'it is possible'.[74]

The most organised form of relief distribution by the CSM took shape during the drought from 1946 to 1953. From 1948 onwards, food was delivered from the United States, financed by the Church World Service, to the Madras State. Bertil Envall was the District Convenor in the Coimbatore district, and it was his task to organise the distribution of the food. According to the Government of India's terms, these rations were to be given irrespective of caste and creed and ought therefore not have constituted any reason for conversion. No one had to become a Christian in order to get a share of this food. But, according to Envall, the rations may have given him a good reputation as a distributor of goods.[75] However difficult to measure, the value of a good impression made on people in need should not be underestimated.[76]

The drought relief was exceptional, as the drought itself was exceptional. In day-to-day life, poverty and hunger would direct people to the mission stations. But even though similar, the approaches of the stations were different. Mostly money was handed out as loans. As was discussed in Chapter 2, the missionaries had both economic and social reasons for lending money to the Madhari. In 1940, Stephen reported on a small 'Sakkili-bank'[77] which he kept in order to give loans to Madhari people in distress. He tried to get it affiliated to the Government Co-operative Bank but received a negative reply, as the Government's experience was that such banks had mostly been liquidated.[78] In 1946, the Economic Uplift Committee of the CSM complained that until then loans had been given too easily; they were seldom repaid and often not wisely invested.[79]

At Karunagarapuri mission station itself, Anna Irbe held a different position. The station was started by private means and was intended to be a model farm, both economically and socially. Irbe wanted it to become the 'Lithuanian village in India'. But, during the first few years, the financial resources were meagre. In 1936, she reported that the food was not enough for all who came to Karunagarapuri for help or for the schoolchildren. Beggars were sleeping on the veranda or wherever they could find shelter, and the schoolchildren had to join the evangelist in going to the surrounding villages to sing and collect money for the running of the station.[80]

Until the 1940s, the main aim of the work organised from the Palladam mission station was to form new congregations. Harald Frykholm, just like Mrs. Irbe, brought with him from Sweden the ideals of the work he began in 1931. 'Education' was the guiding star, and the Sigtuna folk high school the ideal institution. Young men were taken from the villages for one or two months of training. Apart from Christian education, hygiene, agriculture, rope-making, gardening, poultry and the weaving of straw mats were taught. Physical exercise was practised on the flat roof of the church.[81]

In 1945, in the midst of the Madhari conversion movement, the need for stricter and more coordinated development work resulted in the proposal of a long-term plan for social and economic uplift. The plan came to have a strong emphasis on the latter. It was presented as a ten-year plan by Stephen and included the organisation of agricultural settlements on a collective basis, the arrangement of living quarters in industrial centres for village Christians, the education of Christian mill-workers to enter business lines, the introduction of savings systems, cooperative banking and saving societies, and providing help both in cash and in kind to start cottage industries and farms. A comment from the meeting was included in the minutes, in which it was remarked that the village Christians in Pandur, west of Madras, had been given land by the German mission in 1894. As a result, these villagers were no longer 'slaves to the caste people'; some of them were also economically independent.[82] Whether the last conclusion was true or not may be left aside. It is interesting to note in this connection that to free 'slaves' was mentioned as a motive for entering into economic uplift work.[83]

In the proposed ten-year plan, the Economic Uplift Committee specified some points about work among Scheduled Caste converts. Among these points, small-scale industries and scholarships for young boys to go to industrial schools came to be an important part of the subsequent work. The minutes were concluded by an argument that was meant to impress the Budget Conference: 'If nothing is done to improve the economic condition of our new converts, we will have strong rivals in the Catholics, who do much for individual young men to bring them forward and who are ever ready to revive disgruntled converts from other Missions.'[84]

When land was bought halfway between Tiruppur and Palladam in 1949, the aim was to build a centre for the village Christians in the area. Institutions were regarded as necessary for the mission work, and Arulpuram was started as a boarding-school for one-year courses of primary education and Christian teaching.[85] The initial years were severely marked by the drought conditions. The budget was weak and almost completely dependent on private funds. Education was still an important part of the work, but small-scale industries were initiated both at Arulpuram and in various villages. The aim was to make the Madhari self-supporting, either by practising different crafts in the home, such as spinning or weaving, or by starting cooperative, small-scale industries. Initially, tanning by the old methods was given support; the agricultural labourers were to take up leather-work as a profession again. But the old methods did not stand the competition from the chemically tanned skins, and from the mid-1960s Arulpuram changed to stitching leather items. When Arulpuram was started, the initiators still had the production of leather bags for the wells in mind as a market for village-based leather-workers. Madhari men were given a sum of money as working capital and could collect material at Arulpuram in order to start or improve tanning cottage industry in their villages. But the installation of electrical pumps and the consequences of the drought eventually forced them to drop that idea. Instead, in the mid-1960s a most profitable enterprise for leather was found when sandals for exports were stitched and sold to Europe and Australia. Therefore, the main emphasis of the economic uplift work at Arulpuram shifted from keeping Arulpuram as an educational centre and supporting village-based craftsmen to building the small-scale industry and farm at Arulpuram itself.[86]

It may be concluded that, when the mission workers were faced with the immediate poverty of the Madhari and with their bonded relationship to the landowners, they chose to go in the direction of more economic involvement. In the case of the drought, resources were simply distributed, but that appears not to have been the rule. Rather than spreading resources around, the economic involvement was basically in the form of providing education and giving initial financial support to make people self-reliant and thereby also more independent of the Goundar landowner. By giving loans, the mission made it possible for the Madhari to repay old debts to the Goundar landowners, and through training and financial assistance, new opportunities for survival opened up. But where lending may have served to untie bonds to the Goundar, the support of cottage industries would rather serve to initiate possibilities for the unemployed to earn incomes.

When the mission workers entered the villages, their financial means may have been scarce. Despite this, they entered as an authority having material resources which they directed towards the Madhari.

### Mediation

Before dealing with the conflicts that arose, there is yet another aspect of the presence of mission workers in the villages to be discussed. This is their role as mediators, not between labourers and landowners, but within the Goundar community itself.

In the mission reports from the 1940s onwards, comments are made about the skills of the Indian pastors in mediating in conflicts between Goundar and Madhari. In several cases, Stephen and Muttiah are mentioned and praised for their ways of talking to the Goundar farmers and for being able to solve problems.[87] In interviews, evangelists are also mentioned as being able to talk with the landowners on behalf of the Madhari.[88] But only in the case of Arulpuram has information indicated that the Indian mission workers were called in by the local Goundar families to mediate in conflicts between families and within the Goundar community. This information was never written down in reports to the CSM in Sweden, most likely because it was not immediately connected with the mission work. The informant is Olle Jonsson, who was in charge of Arulpuram between 1961 and 1976. According to him, the task of mediation was mostly given to one of the staff at Arulpuram who belonged to a high caste. But a highly educated member of the staff was occasionally also entrusted with the task, in spite of being a member of a lower caste. Those mediators were considered as reliable outsiders who represented a respectable institution. Arulpuram had many contacts with local Goundar families; Jonsson mentions the nearby villages of Uppilipalayam and Sekkampalayam. In his words, Arulpuram as an institution was a part of society and existed within it. At the election to the Panchayat, it happened that Jonsson was enlisted in the electoral register.[89]

The ability to mediate appears to have been dependent on the status of the person; caste was important, but education and a trusted position at the institution seem to have compensated for affiliation to a lower caste. As discussed earlier, the pastors Stephen and Muttiah mediated between Madhari and landowners. But their caste affiliations and education would, hypothetically, also have made them good mediators within the Goundar communities. If they did, this was never mentioned in the reports, either, as assumed in the case of Arulpuram, because such information was not passed to the CSM in Sweden or because the CSM in the districts did not have such close relationships with Goundar families before 1954, as described by Jonsson in the case of Arulpuram earlier. Muttiah left his post in Mandiripalayam in 1953, and Stephen was transferred from Karunagarapuri and out of the district in 1954. As will be discussed later, Stephen and Muttiah may have worked in the Coimbatore district at a time when mediation between Goundar families by a representative of the mission was out of the question.[90]

## Integrated Outsiders

If the presence of an outside party, such as the mission, was to influence local social relationships, a certain level of integration into local society was required. Apparently, the mission workers did not remain as complete outsiders to the villagers, either in the case of members of Scheduled Castes or in that of members of the high castes. Being accepted by the Madhari, they apparently met with various levels of acceptance from the Goundar community.

But the different mission workers were not identified with the mission in the sense that they were all uniformly treated. The individual mission worker appears not to have been received as 'the representative' of the mission institution, but rather as an individual with regard to caste, education and mission affiliation in combination. Both Goundar and Madhari villagers appear to have considered this. Simply from the presence of mission workers in the Madhari *cheri*, it may be assumed that the social order was questioned. The presence of Paraiyar bible women or evangelists may not have been sensational, but when European missionaries and high-caste pastors entered the *cheris*, they crossed social borders that the Goundars and members of other high castes in the villages upheld.

The physical manifestation of the conversion of a Madhari community was visible to everyone in the village. Having a building in the holy place, instead of a stone or a wooden image, recalled the rites performed among high-caste Hindus. New rites, ceremonies and festivals, sometimes grand, manifested the presence of an authority that did not originate from the village, but from outside.

The fact that Goundar farmers contributed to the Christian festivals in which Stephen was a driving force in the organisation is particularly interesting. This, and the fact that the agricultural labourers employed by the Goundar participated in them, would indicate that the Christian festivals had reached a level at which they had become accepted by the local society.

However, this situation was exceptional. As will be discussed in the next section, the Goundar community disapproved rather strongly of conversion. The results indicate that the building of a chapel and the presence of pastors conducting services in it was understood by the Goundar as a threat.

The mission also intervened in the villages with material resources. In contrast to other Scheduled Castes, socially and economically placed higher than the Madhari, the latter seem to have been in such a situation of poverty and dependence that they could neither bargain for benefits nor make use of education to any substantial extent. However, material resources were extended to them in the shape of loans and initial financial support for setting up small-scale home industries or other enterprises that were aimed at making them economically self-supporting. Most important to note are the loans that were given to the Madhari for the repayment of debts to the Goundar landowners. Irrespective of whether the aims were ever carried into effect, this form of lending went straight to the core of the formal side of the agreement between a *pannaiyal* and his *pannaiyar*. The loans made it hypothetically possible to repay the advance. They interfered with an important part of the Goundar–Madhari relationship and reveal a deep involvement of the mission in village life.

Becoming a mediator in conflicts within a local caste would certainly be the most obvious sign of a high level of integration of the mission into local society. Unfortunately, no written documents throughout the period give any information about such mediation. But the information in oral material is important and worth bearing in mind when the rural involvement of the mission and the social and economic control and conflicts between the Goundar and Madhari communities are being considered.

## CONTROL AND CONFLICT

It has been unavoidable to touch upon the conflicts that arose in connection with the kinship-based conversions in the previous section. From the time when the mass baptisms began until the mid-fifties, conflicts with the Goundar community followed in the trail of the Madhari conversions. These conflicts were expressed on different levels but were not the only problems that arose. Conflicts followed also upon Paraiyar kinship-based conversions, but, compared with the Madhari conversions, they appear to have been less problematic.

A unique document has been found in the CSM archives that reveals several different types of conflicts that accompanied the presence of mission in the villages. It is the minutes of a discussion held at the Village Leaders' Conference in Palladam in 1936. The meeting was organised during the first bishop's visitation held in Palladam pastorate. The document is unique in the sense that the voices of members of a Scheduled Caste were recorded. In all other documents, Paraiyar or Madhari were referred to as third parties, but in these minutes the words of Paraiyar village leaders were included in the records.

The mission's position was that a system of sextons should be introduced, one person in each congregation in charge of Sunday services and attending to the chapel building. Until then, that task had to a great extent been carried out by the village teachers. By the *kovilppillai* system, as bishop Sandegren explained in 1933, the problem of finding teachers for the numerous Madhari converts that were expected to come would be solved.[91] But the village leaders opposed the proposition strongly. From their point of view, the new system would take resources away from the villages, instead of providing them. The teacher would come less often, as a person from the village would take over part of his job.

In view of the importance of the document, it will be quoted in full. This is what was recorded at the meeting:

*Bishop J. Sandegren* explained the purpose of the Conference as a Conference for discussing the possibility of finding lay voluntary workers to act as kovilpillais or in any capacity when certain villagers are bereft of teachers to guide them.

*Tr.* [teacher] *P. Sebastian* explained the Bishop's words to the villagers in colloquial language.

*Peter, Kallipalayam*: We were climbing the ladder to reach the top and when we are half-way, you pull it off and we fall down. You have given education to our children and spoiled them since they neither get teachers' posts in the Mission nor are willing to do coolie work for 3 or 4 annas a day.

*Tr. Sebastian*: The villagers of this pastorate[92] who are now Christians are still under the sway of the Goundars. Those members who are serving the Goundars who are a party opposed to another party of Goundars under whom the other members of the Church serve, find that they are two opposing parties in their home or Church life also. This results in one party in the congregation being indifferent to Church matters.

*Tr. A.D. Anbaiyan*: There is no vital Church of our Christians with the Goundars after our men have become Christians.

*A.J. Satyanadhan* [evangelist] (to the villagers): What the Bishop wants to know is the possibility of effecting kovilpillai (or any similar) system. The kovilpillai will have to look after the tidiness of the Church and conduct morning and evening prayers daily and look after Sunday worship. This does not prevent him from looking after his coolie work. What is needed is that he be responsible for the spiritual growth of the congregation. In keeping the chapel clean he may be assisted by families in turn for smearing cow-dung etc., once a week.[93] The necessary training for the kovilpillai may be given at Palladam.

*Manasseh, Naranapuram*: Our motives in becoming Christians were the hopes of (1) getting education for our children and (2) getting the support and recommendations of pastor and missionary when necessity arises. But, what has now happened is that we suffer from getting water. When we approach the Goundars they direct us to the missionary and pastor and when we come to you, you say that you don't have money.

*Bishop D. Bexell*: We should be prepared to serve as our Lord Jesus did, night and day. Now, there is no other go but to arrive at a conclusion regarding self-support.

*Tr. A.D. Anbaiyan*: We can even now begin experimenting the kovilpillai system in places where there are no teachers at present.

*Gnanamuthu, Vadugapalayam*: You give us only an honour and nothing else by kovilpillai system. There are parties in our congregations. The paid agent is already criticised—how much more will an honorary man be criticised!

*Bishop J. Sandegren*: One teacher may have to look after 4 or 5 villages. Parties may exist, but if we trust in God, He will lead us on.

*Manasseh, Naranapuram*: We are still in first class, and how can we accept 'Swaraj' at this stage?[94]

*Abraham, Iyampalayam*: Cut down the salaries of the missionaries, pastors and highly paid teachers and give us teachers who are prepared to work on a low scale of salary.

*Gnanamuthu, Iyampalayam*: We have no means to support.

*Bishop Bexell*: Till now you spoke of external things only, but there is faith, all things are possible for him who believes. Begin in faith.

*Gnanamuthu, Iyampalayam*: I have faith. It is easy for a rich man to have faith, but it is difficult for a poor man like me to have influence over his congregation members and gather them for worship to the church.

*Tr. C.S. Manuel*: When the Church which is the mother is on her death-bed and not able to support us, the congregation should look up for supporting itself.

*Abraham, Iyampalayam*: You are 200 years old Christians and can support yourselves, but we are young.

*Manasseh, Naranapuram*: What Tr. C.S. Manuel says is not practicable.

*Bishop J. Sandegren*: The end of planning is the beginning of action. Let us now carry out the new ideas.[95]

It is striking how different interests seem to have collided at the meeting, but also how outspoken the Paraiyar village leaders appear to have been in the faces of two bishops. Several problems, expressed as conflicts by the village leaders, appear in the minutes. Firstly, the children no longer obeyed their parents. The mission had given them education, and now they refused to do low-paid coolie work. Secondly, a conflict between two Goundar parties in the village of Kallipalayam had split the Paraiyar community into two groups, since, as labourers they were expected to give support to the Goundar farmers they worked for. This was a conflict that had roots in local society itself. The presence of the mission had no bearing on the causes of the antagonism. But the division appears to have spread into the Christian congregation and brought church life to a standstill. In Vadugapalayam, the appointment of a paid agent appears to have added to a local conflict. Its village leader, Gnanamuthu, apparently did not think of the *kovilppillai* system as a practical solution to congregational matters but feared that appointing an 'honorary man' would make the conflict even worse. Thirdly, the converted Paraiyar of Naranapuram had had great expectations of education and support from the mission when they converted. They were now paying the price of being prevented from getting water as a punishment for converting to Christianity, but the mission had still not fulfilled the expectations. Their children did not benefit from the education they had been given, and there were no funds for providing water.

Thus, the document indicates (1) conflicts within the Goundar community that had consequences for their labourers; (2) conflicts between the Goundar and Paraiyar communities caused by conversion; and (3) conflicts between different generations among the Paraiyar community caused by mission-initiated education.

A fourth area of conflict represented in the minutes as a whole could also be suggested. How to make ends meet was problematic to the mission when new converts were arriving in great numbers and the mission workers were far too few. In reading the villagers' grievances in the minutes, the mission representatives seem to have been somewhat insensitive to their problems. This impression may be caused by the summary way in which the minutes are written, and even more so as a result of the interest taken in the *kovilppillai* system by the bishops. Both Sandegren and Bexell had long experience of working in India. However, the mission workers' position was that the new system had to materialise.

The teachers' position is interesting to follow. Initially, both Sebastian and A.D. Anbaiyan explained the villagers' point of view to the bishops. There were conflicts and divisions in the congregations and villages. This seems to have been a severely felt problem. But after the bishops had had their say, Anbaiyan and a third teacher, C.S. Manuel, turned the matter around and argued that the villagers should accept the bishops' proposition. This may have reflected the teachers' position and, perhaps, their mixed loyalties, both as being of the villages and as being trained within the mission and the Church.

The Paraiyar had looked to the mission for support. This did not mean support in a vague sense. The converts appear to have looked for assistance to move upward, socially and economically. The pastor and missionary was expected to be there 'when necessity' arose. As related by the author of the document, education, recommendations and other support had motivated the Paraiyar of Naranapuram to convert. 'Support and recommendations' are obligations generally ascribed to a patron. The patron is, to the client, the shield against and the doorway to the outside world. Obviously, the Paraiyar had hoped for this kind of responsibility from the mission. The decision to ask support from the mission had made the Goundars drop at least part of their support for the Paraiyar. Water was no longer given to them. When the teacher Manuel told the village leaders that the congregations should be self-supporting, Manasseh of Naranapuram answered that it was not practicable. Using the Gandhian term 'swaraj', which is foreign to Tamil-speaking people, suggests awareness of current national politics. Most objections and arguments of the Paraiyar were met with a *fait accompli* by the bishops: this is the situation, what we propose is the best of solutions, have faith in God. The relationship between the Paraiyar and the mission does not appear to have been unproblematic.

However, in the main visitation report, in which these minutes are included, Bishop Sandegren related a grave mistake—at least it has been referred to as a mistake—that may explain why the village leaders were so outspoken.

At the conference, the teachers and village leaders had been promised a midday meal. As it turned out, this was served in two different houses, one for the teachers and village leaders and the other for the pastors and other church members. Adding to the segregation was the fact that the food served to the church members was of a somewhat superior quality. Of the forty village leaders, Sandegren noted that not more than ten took their meal at the conference. The others refused to accept the unequal treatment. Sandegren remarked laconically that the fact that several of them stilled their hunger at the liquor shop did not improve the situation.[96] This conference might not have promoted the *kovilppillai* system, though it disclosed deep-reaching conflicts. This situation also points to a strikingly high level of awareness among the Paraiyar reaching far beyond the village level. In spite of the free meal, they walked out and marked their disapproval of hierarchical segregation. When he suggested that salaries should be cut, Abraham challenged all the other parties at the meeting, including the missionaries, pastors and teachers. It is unlikely that a term such as 'swaraj' was put into Manasseh's mouth by the author of the minutes. Had he explained his dislike of self-supporting congregations in Tamil, it would most likely have been translated into English, as in the cases of Bexell and Manuel.

Goundar *versus* Goundar involving the labourers, Goundar *versus* converting labourers, generation *versus* generation, converts *versus* the mission—conflicting parties appear on all levels in the minutes from Palladam and not only in this particular document. As will be shown, reports of conflicts appear in a great number of documents, and from henceforward conflicts involving the Madhari community are given priority.

Some of the results deserve special attention. First of all, the change over time in the occurrence of conflicts caused by conversion needs to be stressed. In spite of continued conversions, reports of such conflicts were numerous before the mid-fifties, to occur thereafter much less frequently. In order to understand the reasons for this change, it has been fruitful to elaborate on the different kinds of conflicts. On the one hand, conflicts in which Goundar stood against Goundar, using their labourers as tools in the combat, can be distinguished. The causes of these conflicts were mainly to be found within the village itself. On the other hand, there were the conflicts that had their origins in conversions among the Madhari, and where representatives of a new authority had entered the village. But, as the subsequent discussion will show, the former type of conflict seems easily to have turned into a conflict between the Goundar and the Madhari communities, when the latter turned to the mission workers for support. This suggests the conclusion that to uphold control over the village was a prime interest of the Goundar community.

As a consequence, conflicts have been analysed from two angles. Firstly, with regard to areas where expressions of social hierarchy can be suspected to have come into conflict with the Madhari's affiliation to the new authority, the mission. Festivals and ceremonies of the village in which a particular part was ascribed to the Madhari community form a good basis for such a discussion. Secondly, the conflicts have been analysed with regard to areas where the economic hierarchy or the division of labour may have conflicted with the presence of mission. As the results will show, the means used by the Goundar to uphold control was primarily boycott. To make the Madhari yield, the labourers were excluded from rights that secured their survival.

The reasons why the conflicts were apparently scaled down after the mid-fifties can fruitfully be understood from this perspective. There is no reason to think that the Goundar farmers feared to lose control over their labourers in a situation in which the need for permanently available labourers was reduced and unemployment rose. It may also be suggested that the Goundar community may have found less reason to fear losing control, whether economic or social, over the Madhari. After three decades, or the period of one generation, of the presence of mission workers and still there had been no social revolution or labour migration, such as that of the Paraiyar in the late nineteenth and early twentieth centuries, conversion may not have seemed particularly threatening.

As previously discussed, the Goundar community held a dominant position in the Tiruppur–Palladam–Pollachi area throughout the period covered by the research. Though not every individual was financially strong, affiliation to the Goundar caste compensated to a great extent for personal lack of resources. Influence and decision-making were also dominated by members of the Goundar community. The means of controlling labour that predominated in the Goundar–Madhari relationship were elaborated and discussed in Chapter 2. Formal and informal contracts acted, in combination with customary law, not only to ensure labour, but also to structure and reproduce social relationships that went beyond the employer–employee relationship.

The following discussion will be structured around two areas of interaction, that of the division of labour and that of the division of social power or domination.

Most striking in the reports from the 1930s, 1940s, and early 1950s in the initial contact between a Madhari group and the mission is the immediate reply from the Goundar community in the village. From the early Madhari conversions in the 1930s to the beginning of the fifties, the reactions of the Goundar communities in the different villages to Madhari conversion showed a very similar pattern. There were exceptions, when a particular Goundar member even welcomed the mission workers,[97] but as a rule they were hostile. Therefore, what in the following discussion may seem like similar examples from different years is rather the result of the fact that no trend of change has been found in the material during this period.

The Goundar reaction to Madhari kinship-based conversion was not directed to the missionary, and mostly not to any of the other mission workers, but to the Madhari community or to those among them who had sought the mission. Often the Goundar community appears not to have had to stage their threats; their words were enough.

To give a few examples, in Kakkadavu, no Madhari came to the inauguration of the chapel in 1937, alleging that the Goundar had forbidden them to do so. In Merkupalladam, twenty out of thirty families withdrew their applications for baptism in 1941 after threats from the Goundar. In an unnamed village near Palladam in 1947, the baptismal ceremony was held in the middle of the night, as the Goundar had tried to stop it by threats and by not granting leave from work on the day of the ceremony. In another unnamed village in 1950, the grown-up men changed their decision to be baptised when the farmers threatened not to give them water and work. In Kallipalayam, the village where the Paraiyar village leader Peter lived, 170 of the Madhari were ready for baptism in 1953, but after threats only 86 participated in the ceremony. These converts were locked out from work for 'a long time' and lived on grants from the mission.[98] The list of cases can be made long.

In another village near Palladam in 1953, the converts went even further. The Goundar had tried to stop the baptismal instruction, and threats had frightened half of the catechumens and caused them to withdraw. The pastor Muttiah, who lived in Mandiripalayam, had stayed in the village and reported that the converts had been locked out from work. In order to get back their work they had prostrated themselves before the Goundar, i.e. fallen down on their faces at his feet to show complete obedience, if he would just let them stay with their new faith and with the mission. But the Goundar was not impressed. At the time when the report was written, the conflict was still on, and the mission was providing food to the converts. The missionary Bror Tiliander commented: 'If all catechumens in the village had agreed to defy all threats from the caste-folk's side, they had been standing powerless since they are dependent on labour power.'[99]

Threats occasionally materialised and changed into punishment. Bertil Envall, who worked in Palladam and Arulpuram between 1947 and 1953, remembers that stones were thrown in almost every village at the place where the bible women were conducting evening classes: not many stones at a time, and they were generally thrown by boys. But Envall himself recalls only a couple of times when he was the target for people throwing stones on the way out of a village.[100] His report from Palladam in 1948 gives a more dramatic picture. 'In Kalinadanpalayam stones were raining over the outcaste's quarters night after night where instruction was given. At the baptism, which was to take place one afternoon and for which we had obtained leave for the baptism candidates, all of the caste youth in the villages gathered to interrupt the festival while most of the candidates had been sent to work in the fields.'[101]

The presence of mission workers apparently made a difference to both Goundar and Madhari. In the examples earlier, when threats and stones dropped or hailed down over the converts, the reaction seems to have stemmed from the situation in which the mission entered a village. The Goundars appear to have been provoked by the arrival of the mission and the decision their labourers had taken. Before entering further into such situations, attention will be given to conflicts that seem to have had immediate roots in the villages, but in which the mission became a part of the situation.

Manickapuram in 1949 and the following years is one such instance. But it is symptomatic of Manickapuram and other cases of local conflicts in which the mission interfered that most likely all the important facts were never given in reports and articles. Bertil Envall confirms this when recalling the situation. Even though he was in the middle of the conflict at the time, he believes that he never really got to know the Goundar understanding of the situation.[102] The example of Manickapuram may be somewhat lengthy, but it is still worth while to relate the event, as it was understood by the mission workers.

### CONFLICTS IN MANICKAPURAM

The first visit to Manickapuram by mission workers was made around 1946 by the missionary Vilhelm Nielsen and an evangelist. Late at night, on their way out of the village, stones had been thrown. When Envall related the situation in 1949, he compared the stone-throwing with the threats and harassment that were staged in almost every village by the high-caste members when the 'out-castes' wanted to convert. The acute situation in late 1949 came up one year after the chapel had been inaugurated, the chapel that had been built without windows in order to prevent the high-caste youths from interrupting the services, as they had previously done. But the conflict was not caused by the presence of the mission, according to Envall. It was rather a situation beginning with the theft of a buffalo. One thing had led to another and, late in the year, all 300 members of the Madhari community of Manickapuram left their village and moved into the mission compound. When Envall reported in 1949, they had been staying in shelters by the wall in front of his house for five weeks.[103]

Already in 1949, the story behind the migration related by Envall lacked some pieces of information essential to the understanding of the underlying causes of the conflict. The information hints at a conflict between members of high castes, probably Goundar. A buffalo was stolen, and a man named Devaraj assisted the thief in causing the animal to 'disappear'. But Devaraj was not the only helping hand in the theft. 'A leading caste man' protected him, and this is what indicates antagonism among the high-caste parties. Devaraj and the thief may not have been out only to make quick money but seem to have been assigned to the task by a leading high-caste person, a Goundar, according to the interview with Envall. In such a case, the latter was most likely not interested in the money that the buffalo would have yielded, but had something else in mind that would have involved the owner of the buffalo. Both the thief and the leading man were said to have previously been sentenced to hard labour for complicity in murder. When he was found to have been involved in the theft, the leading man tried to make Devaraj put the blame on a third person, Vedamuthu. This was where the mission made its appearance on the scene.

Vedamuthu was a member of the Christian congregation, and Envall wrote that, in the presence of all Christians, Devaraj could not blame Vedamuthu. This led the Goundar to stir up his relatives, and violence broke out. Devaraj and Vedamuthu were caught and beaten, and finally, when order was again established, the teacher asked permission to take them to the dispensary. In that way, Devaraj ended up on the veranda in front of Palladam church, where the local pastor, K. Devasagayam, took care of him. Daily visits by a doctor were said to have kept Devaraj alive.

When the same doctor signed a certificate of the assault, and the incident was taken to court, the Goundar began to worry. On the pretext of negotiating compensation, a delegation arrived at the parsonage one evening. But the visit appears to have been only a cover-up for bringing Devaraj away from the compound and making him sign a letter to the court, saying that he did not know who had beaten him and that the pastor had kept him prisoner on the veranda.

Some minor incidents continued to occur, and finally the Goundar turned against the congregation as a whole and demanded reconversion. The report is not quite clear on this point, but it seems that, when Devaraj managed to make his way back to Palladam and the mission compound, the Goundar party served the Christian congregation with their demand. The congregation members refused and were locked out from work. As this was immediately before the *cholam* harvest, when the labourers were receiving their annual shares in kind for months of work, the consequences were severe. All the

Madhari members decided to move from the village and settled in the mission compound in Palladam. When the report was written in 1949, a message had reached Palladam that four of the Christian Madhari's houses had been burnt to the ground, and Envall expressed his desire to reach a peaceful agreement on moderate terms with the Goundar in Manickapuram. Compensation and punishment of the guilty were not necessary, as long as the Madhari were allowed to return to Manickapuram and take up their work.[104] Stephen and the evangelist Masillamani negotiated with the Goundar on behalf of the Madhari.[105]

Half a year later, the Madhari community of Manickapuram had returned, but a division within the congregation was reported.[106] In 1954, the Christians were reported to 'still have been kept away from the church'. And the missionary Jonas Ulrici, who worked in Palladam during the latter part of the time when the conflict was on, recalls that the whole congregation finally reconverted.[107]

Going step by step through the conflict, as it was related by mission representatives, the situation may by elaborated as follows. In the first instance, it appears as a conflict between different Goundar parties or between one Goundar party and another high caste in the village. When some Madhari men were used as intermediaries by one party to steal from the other, members of the Christian congregation became involved and ended up by being severely beaten. But as Christians they had another authority to turn to; they were not totally dependent on the Goundar. When pastors, missionaries and evangelists were called upon, their task was, in a sense, to match the Goundar authority with an authority derived from outside the village. In that way, the mission became a party in the local conflict and, from then on, the conflicting parties described in the report are no longer referred to as individuals and there are no longer indications to the existence of two different Goundar groups, but Goundar *versus* Madhari.

To file a court case on behalf of the Madhari was a strong weapon used by the mission in the conflict, and the Goundar party appears to have acted in order to undo the effects of the case when Devaraj was made to sign a 'counter' letter. The information indicates a situation in which Goundar may have stood against Goundar. But when the Goundar community turned against the whole Madhari congregation, and not only against the Madhari men involved in the theft, the situation had apparently become a conflict between Goundar and Madhari. It seems most likely to have become a conflict for power and influence over the Madhari community, about the authority that the Madhari were to turn to. To reconvert would mean renouncing the mission as an authority and 'returning' to the complete authority of the Goundar community of Manickapuram. By the reconversion of the Madhari, the Goundar would again be able to execute punishment without being questioned or being taken to court.

When the Madhari still refused, the Goundar used an even stronger weapon, that of boycott. A share in the annual *cholam* harvest was a right that the Madhari held; it was their *urimai*, to use the terminology discussed in Chapter 2. By refusing the Madhari their share, the Madhari were locked out, not only from wages and work, but from the system that regulated and distributed resources in the village. The options for the Madhari were to surrender and submit or to migrate. They chose the latter solution.[108]

## BOYCOTT AND LOCK OUT

If we leave Manickapuram and look at the more general situation, boycotts in different forms and lock-outs appear to have been the most common punishments, when threats or being beaten up had no effect on the Madhari. To be locked out from work and prevented from exercising rights, such as that of access to water, meant to be without means of survival. Without alternative means, surrender was the only option. As in one of the cases earlier, the mission was such an alternative. But, for the Paraiyar, there were others. Their seasonal migration to the estates appear occasionally in the reports. From Coimbatore and Dindigul in 1929, the link was clearly spelt out, when it was said that new Christians were often deprived of their livelihoods as agricultural labourers for the higher castes. 'Because of this, many Christians go to the tea plantations.'[109] In 1929, no kinship-based Madhari conversion had yet taken place; the converts were Paraiyar. Migration was never indicated as an option for the Madhari. It seems rather significant of their situation when the Madhari labourers in Kakkadavu were saved by the rains. In 1938, the Goundar of the village were said to have threatened those who participated in the inauguration of the new chapel with being locked out from work. But a heavy rain saved their jobs. Ploughing and sowing had to be done in a hurry, and the farmers needed all the labourers they could get.[110]

In Manickapuram, the mission intervened in a situation in which a local conflict had spilled over into the Christian congregation, and the mission representatives and the local pastor acted on behalf of the Madhari. This happened occasionally but did not always lead to contradictory standpoints, with the mission on one side and the Goundar community of the village on the other. In later documents of the mission, the earlier discussed situation, in which mission representatives mediated and were able to work out compensation for ill-treated Madhari men or women, was more often recorded.[111]

Far more often, conflicts created by the presence of mission workers were set down in the records. In 1940, after seven years in the service of the CSM, the Indian pastor G. Stephen, summarised as follows his understanding of the reasons for opposition and conflicts in the villages where the mission had been called for by the villagers and had entered the village:

> When visiting the surrounding villages I find that religion plays a very small part in the life of the people. They do not object to the Gospel of Christ because of religious fervour. Their opposition has other reasons. One objection is that *Christianity is not the traditional religion* of the place and therefore should not be preached, another is *the levelling influence of Christianity*: caste people do not want that outcastes should become their equals. Still others fear the economical consequences: *who will do the kuli work if all are educated.* Besides these objections there are also deeper going reasons which are unfavourable to the Gospel. One of these reasons is *the group-will*: villagers cannot make individual decisions. Further, there are lots of *factions among the villagers* which cause one party to oppose everything which the other party advocates. Then there is the age-long *communal tension between various castes.*[112] (italics mine)

If we use Stephen's paragraph to structure the following discussion, it falls into three parts.

1. Stephen speaks of the 'traditional religion', which was practised without religious fervour: religion as culture or religion either as structuring the social life or as a social construct. This traditional religion was difficult to replace by Christianity.
2. The social and economic consequences of the presence of mission. Christianity was said to have had a 'levelling effect', and it was feared that education would reduce the number of agricultural labourers.
3. Human action according to caste and kinship not only eased conversion, but also set limits to it. According to 'group-will', individuals did not convert unless the 'group' converted. As in Kallipalayam (see above), factions within a caste could make

> one party convert, while the other, as a consequence immediately refused to have anything to do with the mission. 'Communal tension', like that between Madhari and Paraiyar, would, as a rule, cause divisions in a congregation if both communities were members of the same village. The missionaries were rather proud when this did not happen.

As the third point does not discuss conflicts between the Goundar and Madhari communities, which have been dealt with earlier, it will not be taken up for further discussion.

### Taking Part in Hindu Ceremonies

To begin with, the 'traditional religion', in Stephen's words, was the religion prevalent in the villages before the arrival of the mission. 'Tradition', in this context, would simply mean the religion that people at the time were accustomed to and practised. As has been touched upon, the Madhari did not participate to the same extent in the cults of the high-caste members of the village. They had cult places of their own and worshipped deities different from those of the high castes. But, in the religious ceremonies of the high castes, the Madhari played a role. They were musicians and participated in the procession that, as far as they were concerned, ended in front of the temple, while the high-caste participants entered.

The CSM missionaries in the Coimbatore district appear to have taken a somewhat liberal view of participation in Hindu ceremonies throughout the whole period under survey. The Christian Madhari members were understood to participate because they held the occupation of village musicians. That meant that they did not really participate in the religious ceremony but simply that they played the music because it was their job and they needed the income. They never entered the temple and did not sacrifice to the gods, the missionaries argued. In 1936, Bishop Sandegren observed that economic deterioration had become a marked feature among the Scheduled Caste communities of the Church. He referred this situation to a combination of retrenchments at the estates in Valparai, where 800 to 1,000 of the Lutheran Christians worked, and of congregations in which the members had stopped participating in Hindu festivals and had thereby lost an important part of their income.[113]

In Pottinaickanpatti, in the south of the district, where the Madhari community converted in 1953, they had participated in a local festival three years later but refused to take *vibuthi*, the holy ashes that were to be applied to the forehead. The missionaries interpreted this as a conscious act by the Christians. They played the music, as it was their occupation, but they did not participate in the religious act. The refusal in Pottinaickanpatti resulted in a lockout from work. The missionary assisted by filing a police report and by informing the Assistant Collector. During the two months that the conflict went on, food was distributed by the mission workers, but if there were conditions that accompanied the end of the conflict, they were never mentioned in the report.[114]

There were times when the Madhari refused to participate at all in local ceremonies and when this refusal led to punishment in some form. In all cases, the reason was a refusal to take part in rites and offerings to *Mariamman*, the smallpox or cholera goddess. Several instances are mentioned in different documents, and one is described in detail.

Stephen reported in 1945 that, in twenty villages around Karunagarapuri, all normal life had come to a standstill because of an epidemic of plague. Buffaloes were sacrificed, and old grinding stones and baskets were carried into the fields and thrown away. The Christian Madhari played music at the sacrificial festivals and threw away their stones and baskets as well, as 'they feared both the plague and the Goundars'. In order to control the Madhari, according to Stephen, the Goundar made them erect sheds in their fields. But not all Christian Madhari agreed to participate. In Kondampatti, one out of ten families refused and were deprived of their share of the annual village income—not by the Goundar community, but by their neighbours. The village of Vattaparai had suffered from cholera in the previous year and from smallpox in the present year. Also here, Stephen reported one family who refused to participate in the ceremonies. As a consequence, they were refused water from the common well, and a stillborn baby was buried in a shallow pit in front of their hut. Nevertheless, they did not participate.[115]

These events can be compared to those in Ongole, further to the north-east, north of the present Andhra Pradesh border, in the 1870s. Here, the leather-working caste of Madiga were at the centre of events when a mass-conversion movement spread among them. At the early stage of the movement, converts were baptised in the hundreds, and, as it seems from the description by the American missionary assigned to the work, they came basically for social reasons. Later, at the time of the 1876-8 drought, when thousands of Madiga converts asked for baptism, the reasons appear rather to have merged with the immediate needs of starving people. However, during the earlier years, the missionary Clough observed a difference of attitude on the part of the *Sudra* landlords towards the different commands that he gave the Christians to follow.

The fact that the Madiga Christians worshipped a new Lord was not objected to by the landlords. Many different gods and ways of worshipping already existed side by side, so there was no reason not to tolerate another one, as Clough explained. Much of the teaching from the Christian missionary was also in agreement with several Hindu reformers' messages and did not cause objections from the Hindu village community. As experienced by Clough, it was the commands that interfered with existing labour relations that caused the violent opposition.[116]

Do not work on Sundays, do not eat carrion, do not worship idols—those were the commands that led to conflicts. In this connection, I shall focus on the last and save the other two for a later discussion. Like the Coimbatore Madhari, the Ongole Madiga also performed important functions at religious festivals. For doing so, they were paid in kind 'in accordance with the cooperative system of the village'. As described by Clough, only the Madiga touched drums, and it was by their beating of the drums that the spirits of the land perceived the vibrating din and thus came into touch with the worshippers. When dancing intoxicated in front of the idols taken in processions along the main village road, the Madiga identified themselves with the demons and kept them in check. The drugs gave the dancing men an 'abnormal endurance'. No illnesses were believed to come to the village after such a dance had been performed.

Clough was not as liberal towards this participation in Hindu festivals as were the latter-day Swedish Lutherans. This was considered 'idol worship' and should be abandoned by Christians. Clough explains that, when the Christian Madigas refused to participate, it was not seen by the landlords as a change of religion, but as a 'labour strike' and a rebellion against the village community.[117] Clough describes the measures taken by the landlords to regain control over the Madiga that were both non-violent and violent. When threshing was performed only on Sundays, the Madigas lost their share in the village produce, as this was distributed on threshing-days. In Kanigiri taluk, the Christians who refused to take part in ceremonies were blamed for the outbreak of cattle decease and for dry wells. Five of the leading Madiga were thus forcibly and ceremoniously reconverted.[118]

In Clough's text, labour, on the one hand, and Sudra control or dominance, on the other, are intertwined. The newly adopted, religious symbols or rites are rejected as reasons for conflict. It was a social uprising and a small-scale labour war that the Madigas hoped for and the landlords feared, according to Clough.[119]

It seems reasonable to believe that, as the Lutheran missionaries generally understood the playing and dancing in ceremonies as work assigned to the Madhari and not as an expression of Hindu faith, conflicts like those described did not break out in Coimbatore district. The local religion may have been a stumbling-block to the mission workers when they tried to convince the Hindu Madhari of the superiority of Christianity, as explained by Stephen. What is the use of another religion, when the one that is practised is integrated into the everyday life of all the inhabitants of the village and, so to speak, belongs to the region? But once the Madhari had converted, the Christian faith, ceremonies and rites, as such, do not seem to have provoked opposition from the Goundar community.

The reports indicate that the Christians seem to have been advised not to participate in the religious processions of the high castes, since such refusals among the Christians were mentioned in the most positive terms by the authors of the reports. But it should be kept in mind that the reports were written for the home board, whose members might not have been as understanding of the Christians' participation in Hindu processions as were the missionaries. The Christian villagers do not seem to have been forced to renounce 'tradition' completely, in the sense that they could no longer participate in any local festival. To this extent, they were still part of the 'traditional religion', meaning religion as culture, as long as they were part of and physically participated in the ceremonial expressions of the high-caste cults. Taking part also meant that they carried out their obligations to the village community—and exercised their rights—to play, dance and be remunerated at the village festivals. When the Christian Madhari of Pottinaickanpatti refused *vibuthi*, this indicates a difference between participation in religion as culture and in religion as cult. But what the Madhari congregation members personally believed is a different question, to which there are no answers in the mission documents.

Conflicts with the Goundar arose when the Christian Madhari refused to participate at all. This seems to have happened when participation transgressed their mere role as musicians, as in the sacrificial rites during plague. As one of the castes in a village, the Madhari were 'needed' in the religious ceremonies. In an interview with the Rev. Muttiah in 1951, he related that the Goundar community even offered the Madhari community in their village a compensation of several hundred rupees, in order to persuade them to participate in the ceremony to please *Mariamman*.[120] Therefore, in the cases in which the Christian Madhari refused to fulfil their role, they broke one of their links with the village community. The protector of the order of the village was, in the last instance, the Goundar community, and in particular the *Ur*-Goundar. When the Madhari did not meet their demands, this order was in a sense questioned and the Goundar reacted. The dominance of the Goundar community was manifested also in the temple and its ceremonies and when all the members of the village participated in the festivals according to the roles assigned to them. The presence of Christian chapels thereby represented in themselves a challenge to the authority manifested in the village temple, particularly when the Christian Madhari refused to participate in village ceremonies.

But plague was the exception. In daily life, the Christian Madhari do not seem to have been forced to make a decision as to whether to participate or not, as the mission workers most likely did not demand their complete absence from all Hindu ceremonies.

## The 'Levelling' Effect of Mission

The Rev. Stephen wrote in 1940 that caste people did not want 'outcastes' to become their equals and that they feared the economic consequences of conversion. He believed that the prospects of a social revolution, in which men would respectfully salute each other, irrespective of caste, and labourers with degrees from the schools would leave agriculture, gave the Goundar farming community reasons to oppose the presence of mission workers in their villages.[121] Apparently, the reputation of the mission was enough to cause the Goundar to oppose the mission workers who began to gather people from among the Madhari in their villages. As discussed earlier, often long before the mission had provided money or education to the Madhari in a particular village, the Goundar community showed their hostility and tried to separate the Madhari from the mission workers.

The involvement that may have had a 'levelling effect' appeared in different shapes. Until the mid-1940s, the material aid given to the Madhari was generally in the form of loans. Money was given to repay debts or to purchase a plot of land, a goat or a cow. As it seems that these loans were seldom repaid, the money became more of a gift than of a loan.

In the words of Envall, the missionaries assured the Goundar landowners that the mission had not come to change their relationship with their labourers. Yet it appears that in this matter they were more radical in deeds than in words. Lending may have been on a small scale and randomly given, and the financial support may have reached only a small minority of the large Madhari community in the district. But the act in itself was aimed at the heart of the formal tie between the bonded agricultural labourers and their employers. If the initial advance given to the *pannaiyal* was repaid, there were only the informal ties to keep him at the farm. Lending also kept other agricultural labourers linked to the village, even though an indebted day labourer was allowed to earn money elsewhere to repay his debt.

It should also be remembered that missionaries were of different political or ideological opinions, and attitudes towards the farmer–labourer relationship differed. But, however diplomatically they acted among the Goundar, the missionaries as a rule strongly objected to the loans that kept labourers tied. Following the declarations in the reports of the Economic Uplift Committee in 1945 and 1946, the 'Sakkili bank' was started at Karunagarapuri in 1948.[122] The fact that loans were granted may help to explain the violent reception that Goundar farmers initially gave to mission workers when they entered the villages.

As has been hinted at earlier, hostile and violent reactions from the Goundar side in general became less and less frequent from the mid-fifties onwards and appear to have completely disappeared in the 1960s. Kinship-based conversions, in which a substantial number of Madhari from one or more villages were baptised on the same occasion, still occurred. Though mass conversions became less frequent than in the thirties and forties, they were still a common feature in the 1960s.[123] But from the end of the drought-years onwards, no bible women or evangelists were reported to have been targets for stones, and no Madhari were recorded to have been persecuted during or after baptism. Goundar may occasionally be described as hard or oppressive, and the Madhari as a most underprivileged group, but harsh methods from the Goundar side in their treatment of the Madhari have in no case been found to have been caused by conversion.

In the interviews with the missionaries who worked in the region, Bertil Envall relates examples of violent reactions, while Anders Andrén and Olle Jonsson recall mostly friendly relationships with members of the Goundar community, in which the farmers were quite content with the mission workers, who argued against drinking and made 'decent people' out of their labourers. While Andrén worked in the district between 1953 and 1964, and Jonsson from 1958 to 1977, Envall worked before and during the drought, from 1944 to 1953.[124]

The immediate consequences of borrowing from the missions had most likely no effects that would 'free the slaves' or make large groups of *pannaiyal* repay the money they owed to the *pannaiyar*. The goals that the Economic Uplift Committee had set up in 1945 and 1946 were for the most part never realised.[125] But these aims of the mission workers were most likely as clear to them as they were to the Goundar in the villages, who saw money being distributed among labourers in their own or in neighbouring villages. The act itself—lending to agricultural labourers—may have given reasons to react, but only as long as the Goundar farmers needed those labourers.[126]

When the drought forced labourers into unemployment or to seek work elsewhere, when electricity and mechanical equipment spread into agriculture and gradually replaced the produce of the leather-workers, and when the numbers of *pannaiyal* were reduced, there is no reason to believe that farmers would immediately object to mission workers distributing money or material resources among their labourers. If unemployed labourers found means to support themselves, and if outstanding debts were repaid, so much the better.[127]

It was before these developments, in the year 1940, that Stephen quoted as a typical statement of a Goundar farmer: 'Who would do the kuli work if all are educated?' The farmers were not alone in complaining about education being given to labourers. Also Paraiyar parents complained that their children would no longer do low-paid labour and that they did not want to participate in Hindu religious ceremonies after having attended the mission schools.[128] No such worries of the Goundar concerning the Madhari were reported by the missionaries after the drought, but whether this was caused by the reduced dependence on large numbers of coolie workers or by the fact that very few of the Madhari actually attended school is difficult to say. One reason the missionaries had for sending Madhari children to boarding-schools was to prevent parents from too easily taking them out of school and sending them into the Goundar's fields to watch over cattle. This situation still prevailed in the 1960s.[129] Therefore, the levelling effect that education may have had on the Madhari community appears to have reached only a few of them. Throughout the whole period, Madhari children were needed as workers to add to the family income.

What has been discussed so far is the involvement in which financial or other material resources may have had a levelling effect in the economic sense, and education, as a resource of knowledge, may have served to level out differences, both in an economic and in a social sense. There were also forms of the presence of the mission in the villages that may have served to level out inequalities in a pure social sense, in social interaction. As was discussed in Chapter 2, there were codes of behaviour that acted to enforce the social hierarchy in a village. By their way of acting and talking, the members of one community confirmed their superiority over the other, while the latter would show submission and obedience. The question is, did the presence of the mission workers influence the social codes of behaviour between Goundar and Madhari?

Of course, the possibilities of giving an answer to this question on the basis of the available material are limited. The observations that ended up in the records of the mission are only mere reflections of the complex system of social interaction between the two castes, as it was expressed in each area or village. One example from the Palladam pastorate shows both the benefits and the limitations of the mission reports. The report relates that Christians in the area had stopped eating carrion. These Christians were most likely Paraiyar converts, since this was related in a report from 1936, when only a very few Madhari congregations had been formed in the area. Carrion was considered impure, and eating it was despised by the high castes. A decision to stop eating carrion was thereby a sign of a striving for upward social mobility. But in one village the congregation had run into trouble. They had taken a common decision to abstain from all meat. However, one man had broken the agreement and eaten meat for medical purposes, and now factions had grown up in the congregation. The missionary concluded: 'The caste people sometimes encourage the depressed classes to eat meat in order to keep them in a despised condition. While in itself it is quite permissible to eat meat of cattle, the question arises what attitude we should take to it, considering the general contempt that it carries with it.'[130]

On the one hand, the report shows that the decision to abstain not only from carrion, but from all kinds of meat, was not initiated by the mission. It was a decision taken by the converts themselves. The converts were the party acting to secure higher social status, not the mission. On the other hand, the report does not reveal what effects this had on how they were in fact received in the villages. However, this may give a reason to re-phrase or lay special emphasis on the initial question. To the congregation members, converting and refraining from eating meat may have been two means of achieving a better treatment or higher status in the village. Thereby, the question should not be understood as asking to what extent the mission workers managed to achieve better treatment for their congregation members, but whether their presence had any effect on existing relations.

In the Madiga conversion movement, in Ongole in the 1870s, a decision, as well as a command from the missionary, to refuse to eat carrion led to events taking a different course. As the Madiga were leather-workers, the arrangement for them to get hides was, according to the missionary Clough, an arrangement on a cooperative basis. The members of the village exchanged services. For the leather items produced by the Madiga, the carcass was part of the bargain. Clough remarks that their part of the village was extremely unhealthy. Meat rotted fast in the heat, especially meat from animals which had died of diseases. When the Madiga no longer wanted the carcass, traders had to settle on new rates. The Sudra landlords had to make bargains with the Madiga that concerned only the hide.

Another consequence strained family relations. When not all the members of a family converted, those who remained in the old religion and who ate carrion were looked upon as unclean by the Christians. The Christians, writes Clough, 'instead of being ostracised, they were the ones who ostracised others'.[131]

Interviews may compensate for what mission workers did not grasp or did not consider reporting on. But, more than in other issues, time may have added to the memory of the interrelations between Goundar and Madhari. There is a risk that, for example, an old labourer may remember that his master was always just and good or the other way round, terribly hard, beating him severely for any mistake he made. As a rule, Madhari informants had a tendency to answer that previously 'in the olden days' everything was difficult and the treatment was hard, but after the missionaries had arrived, it all changed for the better. They may have described a changing trend, but their descriptions may also have been coloured, full of contrast, by the distance in time and by the fact that respected people from the outside arrived at their *cheri*, greeted them with the same respectful words as they would have saluted the Goundar with and acted on their behalf.

Two quotations may exemplify and briefly sum up how the Madhari tended to explain the changed behaviour of the Goundar towards them after the arrival of the mission workers at their villages:

When Olle Jonsson met Madhari people in Nallur, near Pollachi, in 1959, he asked if they had observed any difference in their lives after they had become Christians. 'Now the Goundar will say *Vanga Gurusamy* when he speaks to me', came the reply. No longer were these Madhari addressed as *Va Madhari*, in the grammatical form used for children and dogs. They were also addressed by their personal names, and not by their caste names.[132] Madhari was a name that in itself denoted extremely low status in the local social hierarchy. 'Come, you Madhari' was an order that confirmed a low identification of the person addressed. However, among the Madhari community, it has been explained that their name comes from the myth of their origin that relates how they guarded the daughter of a king. According to them, their name means 'pride'.[133] When said by a Goundar, 'Madhari' became deprecatory, but when born by the Madhari themselves, it was a name to be proud of. Ascribed identity and self-identity obviously did not correspond. This will be further elaborated in the following section.

In Uppilipalayam, immediately next to Arulpuram, the Madhari community related how they witnessed the respect the Goundar showed 'Jonsson Aiya'. When a Madhari man was beaten for a trivial reason, or for no reason at all, they would go to Olle Jonsson and he would correct the Goundar. 'Ayyampalayam, Akkanampalayam, Avvarapalayam, Kalinadanpalayam, those were villages where the missionaries went and talked to the Goundar.' 'When a small boy was beaten, . . . the white *Aiya* sued the Goundar in court. That scared the Goundars, so they did not dare to do anything to the Madharis.'[134]

In an interview in 1967 with a barber—who himself was not particularly fond of the Goundars in his village—the man described how the 'Arulpuram Durai' came to the Madharis' rescue in his jeep as soon as he was needed. The man stated that, when the missionary did this, the Goundar had very limited prospects of winning court cases against the Madhari.[135] In Veerapandi, the Madhari explained the difference between being a Christian and being a Hindu: 'If we are Christians, there is one Durai, and if one Goundar beats us, we are protected. For the Hindus, it is not so. . . . Those who are Christians, for them there is material help and protection.'[136]

Similar explanations were given by the Madhari informants at all the interviews in 1995. The different informants may have exaggerated how often the missionary acted on the behalf of the Madhari. Nevertheless, in this case, the reputation of the missionaries may have served just as well as a protection against the arbitrary exercise of power and the use of violence by the farmers towards the Madhari.

Needless to say, for the self-respect and dignity of a Madhari man, to be treated as a human being, respectfully addressed and defended when beaten was important. It is possible that, also in this case, the reputation of the mission and the rumour that ill-treatment of Madhari labourers would not pass unheard, served to improve their treatment by the Goundar.

A project initiated by the mission may have proved a more concrete case where social boundaries were made ineffective. As has been shown earlier, the mission workers documented cases throughout the whole period in which the denial of access to water had been used as a weapon by Goundar farmers to control labourers. Even without conflict, getting water was problematic. Water was sometimes given as part of wages, and the Madhari were not always permitted to use the common well but had to take water from the irrigation canals.[137] In villages where the Madhari had a well of their own, the villagers carefully made a distinction between three wells: one for the Goundar, one for the Madhari, and one for the Paraiyar. Water was sacred in the sense that, if a Madhari drew water from the Goundar well, that water would be polluted by the Madhari vessel, whether that vessel was physically clean or not. In that case, the Madhari community would be immediately punished; 'they would beat us or throw dirty things in our pond if they found us by their water', relates Rajamanickam of Uppilipalayam.[138]

A well may seem a purely material resource but was indeed also a social matter.[139] When Yngve Frykholm took charge of the well-drilling project in 1954, it had come into being both from the realised need for wells in the Madhari *cheris* that would make them independent of the Goundar's permission—their 'benevolence'—to get water and from the acute crisis caused by the drought.[140] Extra funds were collected in Sweden by an appeal from the Archbishop, the *ex officio* chairman of the CSM, in the previous year, arguing for a long-term solution for the poorest people in India, irrespective of religion, to meet their need of drinking water.[141]

In the project's initial year, the local pastor in Arulpuram, A.

Minoson, reported that 'not infrequently I had mediated in the month of Purattasi, [when] people were refused water because in that month no one should give anything!! Even alms will be refused to a dying person!!!' The prime benefit from tube-wells was, according to him, that age-old casteism disappeared.[142] The social advantage of the tube-wells, in contrast to the open dug wells, was simply in their outlet for the water: they had taps. No one had to dip any pots into the water, so it would remain pure and clean whoever used it. In some of the villages, the Goundar community argued for separate taps to keep the segregation visible, but without success. In Sandirapuram, which was the fourth village to get a new well, Frykholm witnessed a happy chaos break out when the water came pouring from the tap. To create some order, Frykholm and the engineer Edervall let the Goundar and the Madhari take turns in distributing water, first to a Madhari woman and then to a Goundar woman. When they could not manage in the heat any longer, two leading Goundar men took over the distribution. According to Frykholm, this was the first time that Goundar men had given water to Madhari women in Sandirapuram.[143]

Where the presence of the mission worked in the direction of levelling out the differences between the Goundar and Madhari communities in a particular place, it implied a threat to the hierarchical structure and the social distance that was upheld between Goundar and Madhari. Materially and financially, its presence appears to have made a difference only to a small number of individuals in the community, whether converted to Christianity or not. Education, which did make a difference to the Paraiyar community, seems to have left the Madhari almost completely untouched.

These results correspond to the findings of Staffan Lindberg, in his survey of the same geographical area in 1967. He chose to make two divisions in his study, one geographical and the other based on the influence of mission, that between Christians and Hindus. Of the two regions, one was under urban influence, situated between Tiruppur town and Arulpuram, and the other completely rural with Mandiripalayam as the nucleus. He concluded that conversion seemed not to have made any difference at all to the Madhari 'position in the economic system'. Differences in income appear rather to have depended on the nearness to Tiruppur.[144] Among Lindberg's respondents, between 80 and 86 per cent had been less than one year at school; the difference in the level of education between Hindus and Christians was marginal.[145]

The social consequences are very difficult to measure. Nothing indicates that the Madhari were able to work their way up in the social structure. They remained at the bottom. But it seems most probable that the mission workers, and in particular the missionaries and high-caste pastors, became an alternative authority for the Madhari to turn to. This authority did not provide alternative means of securing a living, for more than a small number of people who received working capital to set up home industries or who could secure employment at Arulpuram. But it appears to have been sufficient to limit the extent to which the Goundar community was able to exercise its power. It seems reasonable to conclude that members of the Madhari community, or a whole group of Madhari in a village, could obtain better treatment from the Goundar community by relying on the mission workers. The Goundar never lost control over the Madhari, but the exercise of their dominance was questioned.

The actual results of the mission work in terms of financial or material uplift were therefore most likely not decisive to the Goundar's decision to object to the conversions among their labourers, as they did basically before the mid-1950s. In 1940, concrete results that proved to have levelled out the Goundar–Madhari relationship could hardly have been seen. When Stephen concluded that the Goundar objected to a situation in which the Madhari would become their equals, he was rather relating how the Goundar feared their future prospects. They had witnessed the changes for the Paraiyar community and, as long as the Goundar depended on Madhari labourers, no such changes were to come for the Madhari, if the Goundar could prevent them. Many reports relate how the Goundar feared to lose control over their labourers.[146]

## IDEOLOGY AND IDENTITY

When ideology is brought into the discussion, the aim is twofold. On the one hand, it is to open up for a discussion about the role of a dominant ideology, or set of norms, in relation to existing and transforming, social asymmetrical relations. On the other hand, the aim is to focus on ideology as institutionalised practices.

The ideology concept in itself should be understood in a broad sense. It embraces both norms and practices. Ideology in terms of sets of norms, values or ideas may explain how a society should be organised, and how the different members of the society should relate to each other. These norms are mostly, but need not be, systematically coherent. There may be inconsistencies, and all the members of a society do not have to agree on the same norms as just. However, the dominant ideology is the set of norms that the members of the society have to relate to and depend upon.

Ideology as institutionalised practice is manifest in sets of rules, informal law or, more subtly, in behaviour and language. More explicitly, the formalised relationships between castes or rules for the distribution of the village produce may be discussed in terms of ideological praxis. Although these practices are visible, the members of a society need not be able to explain them in ideological terms. These sets of norms may be hidden in everyday language and practices to such an extent that they can be taken for granted. Taking part in a religious ceremony and performing the prescribed tasks may be explained in words such as 'we have always done this, my father played drums and so do I'. People may take such practices as 'natural' as the result of life-long, socialising processes.

This last comment makes the ideology concept border on the concept of 'culture' that is frequently used in anthropological debate. However, there is a risk that this concept may lead us to understand history as formed by long-term, unchangeable or extremely slowly changing cultures carried by concepts and symbols. Sometimes one may find explanations of prevailing ideas that are dated many hundreds of years back in history, still carrying their major meanings intact. To use the term 'ideology' means to emphasise that also norm-systems change and that people are actors with interests, whose actions can be limited or restricted by social structures, but that these structures change by acts of people. In this way, ideology relates closely to identity as well as to social and economic power relations.

In the following discussion, the ideology concept thereby gives room for a discussion about sets of norms and values, as well as about praxis, two different but inseparable aspects of ideology, as it has been defined here.

However, the aim is not to discuss ideology as such, but its *role* and *praxis* with regard to the relationship between the Goundar and Madhari communities within a certain period of time. The focus is on ideology as a mediator of structural contradictions and its influence on social reproduction.[147]

Ideology is used, it has a role, and different ideologies may live side by side in a village or a region. However, there is one set of norms that may be expressed in rules or in informal law that predominates over the others. This ideology expresses and explains the existing hierarchy. It serves to conceal contradictions, whether they are structural inequalities or antagonistic interests. A dominant ideology will, according to this position, work to uphold the status quo and will present the prevailing division of labour and power as the 'normal' situation. To describe the Goundar–Madhari relationship in terms of a set of abstract ideas would thereby mean to speak in terms of master–servant and lord–subject or, in more conceptual terms, patron–client.

However, in the material on which the present study is based, a dominant ideology of the region has never been presented as a credo. It was primarily in its concrete, institutionalised practices that ideology presented itself to the mission workers: in the separate living quarters, in the rules of behaviour and the division of tasks performed at religious ceremonies, in the division of labour, power and resources, as expressed in customary law as well as in the rights that earlier have been termed *urimai*, and in the exercise of control over the same. Also language and address confirmed status and identities, as they expressed by way of grammar how the speaker identified himself and at the same time the person addressed. When the Goundar informants said that they 'kept them [the Maḍhari] low', it was those institutional means, that on the one hand, channelled and, on the other, expressed the dominant ideology that justified the existing division of power.

As regards the present research, the major interest is in the way in which the relationship between the Goundar and the Madhari communities came to express itself. In terms of ideology, praxis is thereby emphasised, as well as people as actors. The relationship between ideology and identity becomes intimate. A group of people carries not only one single identity, but several. In a major division, the role, or identity, ascribed to them by the prevailing norms of local society is different from the identity derived from within the group, the self-identity. They need not be at all coherent. In the case of a group such as the Madhari, ascribed identity and self-identity are rather more likely to be in conflict than in correspondence. Both are changeable and do change. Both can influence each other.

To discuss identity, means to discuss how people perceive themselves and each other. To move further into such a discussion would mean to analyse the inner mind of people. However, even though the ideology concept allows for such a discussion, I shall not attempt to go far in that direction.

As mentioned earlier, ideology as a set of systematic and coherent ideas explaining a whole does not appear in the written documents. When the interviewed informants dwell on the question of why society is organised the way it is, they do not explain an ideological standpoint in what can be called political terms. The answer would rather be in the form of a myth, in which the origin of their own community is given the central place.

Brenda Beck's research into the history of Kongunad has led her to study folk tales and epics of the region. The folk tales, she argues, indicate that there are a great number of stories which explain the history of certain high-ranking communities. Such stories place the Vellalar Goundar community as the lords of the land, defeating their enemies. The stories appear to reinforce an identity of dominance for the Goundar and their allies.[148] In this way, it can be argued that they reflect a set of norms that was embraced by the dominant sections of society and explain the relevance of the Goundar superiority.

The Paraiyar and Madhari communities also relate old stories or myths about their past. But these do not correspond to the tales that give the Goundar community the supreme place in Kongunad. The Paraiyar relate how they were born from evil spirits and thereby came to possess great powers, which others would fear. The Madhari relate a tale of themselves as guardians of the daughter of the sixteenth-century king Tirumalai Naiyak and explain that they have not always been in a downtrodden position. This low position was the result of human action. As explained by the *Amma* Madhari in Mandiripalayam, the Madhari guarded the princess during the rites performed after she had had her first menstruation. When the ceremony is described, it is seen to be a replica of the rites performed among the Madhari community. In these rites, the maternal uncle has a central place that can be compared to being a 'guard'. Keeping this in mind, the Madhari thus describe themselves as related to supreme power in the myth that they carry of their own origin. This is a powerful myth.[149]

Understood as parts of the self-identities of the two communities, these myths do not correspond to an ideology that ascribes low places in the social hierarchy of a village to the Paraiyar and in particular to the Madhari. They rather contradict such explanations of asymmetrical relations and seem to fulfil the purpose of reinforcing an assertion that: 'Certain power belongs to us', 'We were protectors of supreme power' or simply 'We are real human beings, just like anyone else.'

In Chapter 2, the Pandaram priest in Palayakottai explained the relationships, rights and duties as between the different castes in the local region in a strictly hierarchical scheme. Even more relevant in this connection, and as was pointed out in Chapter 2, the information he gave to Brenda Beck appears as an ideal-type description of the order of society, and not as a description of reality itself. Reality generally turns out to be much more inconsistent than the given scheme. The information given rather reveals a set of norms regulating the distribution of the produce and the duties of labour ascribed to the different castes according to rank and affiliation to right- or left-hand divisions. The Goundar community is found at the top of the hierarchy. All other right-hand castes, together with the left-hand Madhari community, are supposed to carry out different forms of labour for the supreme Goundar family and be remunerated by them. The Madhari are found at the bottom end. The scheme is the image of an asymmetrical, social power structure, however, explained in terms of reciprocity between the castes.[150]

When the mission workers appeared in the villages, they represented an authority deriving from outside the village. As has been discussed, this authority came to have influence when there were Madhari villagers who chose to rely on the mission for assistance, whether material assistance or protection. When such assistance was given, its presence was in itself a challenge to the authority of the Goundar community in those particular villages, since the Goundar were the 'protectors' of the Madhari. This is not to say that the mission took over the role that the Goundar had in relation to the Madhari. As previously stated, such a situation was in effect impossible. The mission did not have the means and did not aspire to such a position. Nor do the Madhari appear to have sought a complete alternative to the Goundar community when they turned to the mission workers. But, in ideological terms, the presence of the mission and the kinship-based conversions came to interfere with an ideology that declared the Goundar to be the rulers and explained their dominance in local society. As a result of the conversions among the Madhari, the Goundar were no longer an unquestioned authority.

The role of the dominant ideology may have been questioned and also weakened in situations of conflict, depending of the outcome of the conflict in each particular case. A general conclusion from the interviews is that there is not only one explanation of the order of society and life that exists in the Madhari community in a particular place. Together with tales of a better past and with political ideologies of conflicts and unjust oppression, also explanations of reciprocity between castes and a low position given by God or Fate prevailed. An old Madhari woman in Arulpuram explained that they were Madhari because of God's plan.

> God has given different duties to the people, everyone could not do the same thing. God thought that all human beings should share the responsibility. Some had to do the cleaning, some the sowing, the weaving, and so on. God did not want caste, but wanted the whole human race to work hard and do different things. It was God's plan that I should do the cleaning work, but God did not mean that I am a lower person.[151]

According to such a conception, everyone should be treated with equal human dignity. But that should not be confused with equal rights or socio-economic equality. The young men standing by disagreed and intervened loudly. However, in the statement by the old woman, also a low position in the social and economic hierarchy is explained as being only natural and just.

Where the ideology served to conceal structural contradictions, such as the unequal relationship between the Goundar and Madhari communities, these contradictions came to the fore when the status quo was disturbed. In cases in which new converts were punished by being shut out from their means of livelihood, the structurally uneven relationship that had been hidden behind conceptions of a society functioning smoothly, in which all participated with different abilities to the benefit of everyone was suddenly laid wide open. In their relationship to the Madhari, the Goundar farmers possessed all important means of survival. They controlled the material resources and often also the access to water, gave work and had the power to judge over the Madhari's lives. When the Goundar withheld water and work, they exercised the power deriving from their high social and economic position in the social hierarchy of the village in relation to the Madhari. When the Madhari were locked out from their place as agricultural labourers and from their rights to water and food, their only power lay in their refusal to yield. When conflicts arose, the dominant ideology was hardly powerful enough to hide the structural contradiction between the two.

The fact that some Madhari village communities that converted were threatened by the Goundar community and maybe also punished and yet sided with the new authority meant that the ability of the Goundar community to exercise its power to punish disobedience was in effect circumscribed. The Madhari had found a way out. The examples given earlier show how the Goundar farmers had to yield to the influence of this new authority.[152] The point is not the extent to which this situation occurred, but that it did occur.

Underlying conceptions of everyday language change only slowly. When Stephen related that villagers objected to Christianity by saying that it was not the 'traditional religion ... and ... should not be preached', it was most likely the expression of a wish to protect the prevailing religion as a form of culture that structured social life.[153] In the prevailing understanding of social life, the position of the Madhari in relation to the Goundar was taken as given. Occasionally, such conceptions can be observed but can hardly be measured in this type of material. However, it should be noted that a situation in which the Madhari community of a village repeatedly complained to the mission about ill-treatment and the mission workers interfered may mean that in that village an understanding of the Madhari as a group of people who could be treated roughly and who lived at the mercy of the high-caste people had turned into a situation in which milder treatment was 'normal'.

When the Madhari chose to turn to the mission, they acted along lines that transgressed the role ascribed to them in local society. The Madhari were known as leather-workers, agricultural labourers and labourers for the Goundar farmers. To this, a new identity was added, that of being Christian.

This was an identity that they mostly did not share with anyone else in the village, and an identity that did not have roots in local society. But it was clearly manifested, both in personal visits of mission representatives, in new places of worship, and in new ceremonies and rites. The converted Madhari members appear to have participated to a large extent in the ceremonial life of the whole village, but the example from Pottinaickanpatti shows that the Christian Madhari of that place set a limit to their participation. This and other examples give the impression that the converted Madhari were willing to risk threats or boycotts to uphold their new identity and loyalty.[154]

The question of conversion naturally leads into discussions about how this new identity was constructed, how old ceremonial practices slipped into Christian rituals, and how some converts came to be open to both their old and their new religious affiliations. However, this is not the issue here. The important conclusion in this connection is rather that the Madhari who chose to convert found an additional place outside the village and its hierarchical relationships to anchor themselves in. The identity ascribed to them by local society had to carry a new component.

## NOTES

1 For two different examples, see Tharakan 1984 and Mosse 1986.

2 As a result of an organisational union of the Wesleyan Methodist Missionary Society, the Primitive Methodist Missionary Society and the United Methodist Society, the Methodist Missionary Society was formed in 1933. For the sake of simplicity, the abbreviation for the latter will be used throughout the discussion. Bickers and Seton 1996, p. 250.

3 The first MMS missionary, James Lynch, arrived in Madras in 1817. Negapatam, the place-name that occurs in Manickam (1977), is another name for Nagapattinam. Manickam 1977, p. 47; Dorairaj 1990:2, p. 10.

4 Sandegren 1924, p. 69.

5 The mission station in Coimbatore was founded in 1856, during the Leipzig mission era. Swedish missionaries worked in the district from 1872 to 1901, and again from 1914, as a consequence of the repatriation of German missionaries who were not allowed to work in the country from 1915 as a result of the war in Europe. The Swedish missionaries considered it 'their field', a position that was often contested by the Germans. In Dharapuram, the MMS began work in 1881. Sandegren 1924, pp. 104-5, 164; CSMA, MBa 1948:585, p. 1; Dorairaj 1990:2, p. 11; Grafe 1990, p. 51, 75.

6 Foreign Field 1927, July, p. 232.

7 See, for example, Dick Kooiman (1989) on the conversions to the London Missionary Society, Sundararaj Manickam (1977) on the conversions to the Wesleyan Methodist Missionary Society, and Henriette Bugge (1994) on the conversions to the Danish Missionary Society. See also Khan (1983) for a mass-conversion movement to Islam. These movements took place in the twentieth century. Susan Bayly (1992 (1989)) discusses conversions during an earlier period to the Roman Catholic Church, in the sixteenth century. For an early contribution to the debate, see Pickett 1933. See further Forrester (1991) for a general discussion on conversions among the depressed classes to Christianity between 1860 and 1960.

8 CSMA, MBa 1924:141; Tiruppur Baptismal Records.

9 Some pastors worked in 'Pioneer pastorates' administered by the CSM, while others worked in TELC pastorates. However, this distinction is not relevant to the scope of the present study and all pastors will be called mission workers.

10 Guha 1994 (1983), pp. 1-17.

11 According to Dorairaj, these were the Morasar Madhari, the Athai dialect, the Aiya and Avva sections. Dorairaj 1990:2, pp. 13-14. For a more detailed

overview of Madhari kinship relations, see Appendix.

12 In the MMS Trichinopoly Mass Movement Report of 1935, statistics have been collected and categorised according to kinship groups. For each of the groups, the villages are counted and summed up in three categories: completely received, partly received, and no Christians yet. Obviously, the author considered it only a matter of time before all members of the same kinship group converted. The following castes are mentioned: Sangu Pariah (Paraiyar); Thottiya Chakklis (Madhari); Kongu Murasar (Madhari); Pachavalayal Pariah (Paraiyar); Koravas; Samban Pariah (Paraiyar). The name *Sangu* derives from the conch-shell that was used as a horn to blow at funerals. MMS, Annual Report 1925, p. 45; MMS, Annual Report 1926, pp. 34-5; MMS, Report of the Trichinopoly Mass Movement Commission 1935, in South India Provincial Synod 1936, App. IX, p. 101; Thurston 1909, Vol. 6, p. 77.

13 CSMA, MBa 1927:243, p. 8.

14 In reports from 1935, there was an outcry at the 'state of emergency' that the MMS missionaries experienced in the Dharapuram region. With an increase of more than 2 000 new members from untouchable castes in each of the recent years, the mission had had to close down schools in the eastern part of the mission district which remained untouched by the conversion movement and redirect teachers to Dharapuram. At the same time, grants had been cut from England by 12 per cent. MMS, Annual Report 1935, pp. 14-18; MMS, Report of the Trichinopoly Mass Movement Commission 1935, in South India Provincial Synod 1936, App. IX, p. 62. See also Ulrici 1993, interview; Envall 1995, interview; Andrén 1993, interview.

15 MMS, South India Provincial Synod 1940, p. 113.

16 The Methodist missionaries appear to have been conscious of caste and sub-caste in all the fields of their activities. The missionary W. Lillie pointed to a well-known problem when he published *Some Customs and Ceremonies of the Karur and Dharapuram Areas* in 1956. The missionaries strove to wean the converts from Hindu customs and ceremonies; the problem was to get a clear picture of these ceremonies. If the reader wanted to know more about the Hindu festivals, Lillie recommended works by Abbé Dubois. His own contribution was a detailed study of the different *rites de passage* of the following castes and sub-castes:

Paraiyar: Paccavalai, Samban, Sangu, and Sholiyar; Madhari: (Telugu-speaking) Thottiyar, Kollan, Koyyan, and Retti, (Kannada-speaking) Anuppa, and Morasar with the sub-groups Marutha Morasar, and Konga Morasar of the Athai and Enai dialects.

It is interesting to note what seems to be the missionary's deep knowledge of the *rites de passage* that obviously came to conflict with Christian rituals practised by the Methodists. In contrast, whoever sought information about the cosmology embraced by the Madhari and Paraiyar communities was referred to Dubois. Dubois' *Hindu Manners, Customs and Ceremonies* gives a rather detailed overview of the South Indian population. Also untouchable castes and tribes are included in the descriptive text. However, the main subject is the Brahmins, and in the subsequent parts Dumont discusses their life and religion. What is remarkable is that Lillie obviously had the religious life and ceremonies of the Paraiyar and Madhari under his eyes, a cosmology and worship that differed from the Brahmin worship. Yet he referred to Dubois.

See Dubois 1825 or the English translation by Henry K. Beauchamp 1906.

See also MMS, Correspondence, Trichinopoly Chairman, Minutes of the Standing Committee, Dharapuram, 6.4.1938, §4.

17 As a rule, only members of one kinship group lived in one particular village. CSMA, MBa 1941:362, p. 2.

18 Stephen explained his method in a report of 1940: 'I am trying more and more to get first into touch with the people in the villages where I have to work. I try to find out what they think, what their social relations are, who are the influential people amongst them, who are those who are likely to oppose the Gospel and which factions there are in the village. I try to find out all I can about the economic life and interdependence of the villagers, about their relationship with other villages, etc. Thus I may visit a village several times before I actually begin to sow the seed. These preliminary investigations have been very useful in paving the way for the Gospel message. . . . [These experiences] convinced me that it is useless to baptise one village here and another there without following any definite plan. . . . it is most essential to choose the villages where we are to work along community lines. . . . hence it is essential to get hold of a whole interrelated group. Only then will the new Christians be able to face the problems which confront them when they change their religion. Having begun with the Murasar group of the Sakkilis, I have tried to approach all Murasars in the area, leaving alone other Sakkili groups such as Ammas, Avvas and Anuppars.' CSMA, MBa 1941:362, pp. 1-2. See further Hård af Segerstad 1967, p. 22, for a detailed report on the conversion movement written by G. Stephen in 1950.

In correspondence between the Rev. Paul Sandegren and the Rev. Sigfrid Estborn, Sandegren writes that he has come to realise that he had unconsciously begun to use the method of arguing according to kinship relations with Hindus to try to persuade them to convert. But these were late events. The letters are dated 1963 and 1968. CSMA, Paul Sandegren Collection, 1:1*b*, Sandegren to Estborn 29.3.1963 and 27.12.1968. CSMA, MBa 1948:508.

19 The circuit was an administrative subdivision of the MMS mission districts in India. Trichinopoly district, in which the conversion movement

directed to the MMS took place, comprised 21 circuits. See further MMS, South India Provincial Synod.

20 MMS, Annual Report 1926, pp. 34-5; MMS, Annual Report 1935, pp. 14-15; MMS, Report of the Trichinopoly Mass Movement Commission 1935, in South India Provincial Synod 1936, App. IX, pp. 68-9, 101.

21 See also Oddie (1991) on the importance of kinship ties for the spread of Christian conversions in the Tanjavur and Tiruchirapalli districts in the 1880s and 1890s. Oddie 1991, p. 156.

22 MMS, Annual Report 1925, p. 45. For further details about the Madhari kinship-groups involved in the conversion movement, see Appendix, 'Madhari Kinship Groups'.

23 CSMA, MBa 1932:145, p. 3; CSMA, MBa 1932:146, p. 3; CSMA, Unsorted documents, Correspondence, Coimbatore 1929-1933, J. Sandegren to the Church Council, draft; Palladam pastorate, Baptismal Records, Vol 1.

24 SKMT 1931:22, extract from letters by Frykholm dated 24.7.31 and 3.9.31; CSMA, MBa 1932:145, p. 3.

25 MMS, Correspondence, Trichinopoly General, 10.12.1933, J. J. Ellis to 'Dear Noble'.

26 CSMA, MBa 1932:145, p. 3; MMS, South India Synod Minutes, Meeting of the District Synod of the Trichinopoly District, 2-10.1.1935, App. E, 'Mass Movement Report', p. 5.

27 While the missions had striven to convert members of high castes, thereby hoping that the Christian faith would trickle down to reach their labourers or dependants among the untouchables, the CSM missionaries expressed the opposite view after having admitted numerous Paraiyar converts. Good behaviour among the Christian Paraiyar was believed to impress the high-caste members of the villages and the congregation would work as an evangelising agency. However, Indian members of the Lutheran Church, the majority of whom were high caste and in particular Vellalar, argued against admitting large numbers of untouchable-caste converts. Not only were they considered an economic burden, but within the Church caste conflicts had begun to grow. In the early 1930s, Christian Paraiyars, organising as Adi Dravida, had joined the South Indian Depressed Classes Society and protested against discrimination within the Church and the requirement of reservation quotas for admission to theological seminaries. CSMA, MBa 1936:146, p. 3; CSMA, MBa 1931:221, p. 2; Grafe 1990, pp. 217-19.

28 MMS, Report of the Trichinopoly Mass Movement Commission 1935, in South India Provincial Synod 1936, App. IX, p. 67; MMS, Annual Report 1926, p. 34.

29 CSMA, Unsorted documents, CSM in India 1946, pp. 7-8. In 1930, not only Madhari members were kept at a distance from the CSM, but also a large number of the Paraiyar were not admitted for lack of resources.

However, the populations statistics do not reveal any stagnation in the growth of the Christian population between 1931 and 1941. They rather show a substantial increase. Thus, it is more likely that the Palladam report of 1946 related a situation where there was a certain growth but a lack of resources made a much larger increase impossible. Cf. Table 5.1 and CSMA, MBa 1931:221.

30 Ellen Söderström, who worked in Arulpuram between 1952 and 1961, describes a written petition handed over by a group of Madhari to the missionary, requesting baptism and signed by all the persons' thumbprints. CSMA, Holmåsen Collection, Franzén-Söderström 1960, p. 6; CSMA, MBa 1933:181; CSMA, MBa 1934:166; Ulrici Collection, 1, p. 8.

31 CSMA, MBa 1933:181.

32 *Cheri* refers to the segregated area where a particular untouchable caste lived, in this case the Madhari. Envall 1995, interview.

33 Ulrici 1993, interview.

34 Svenska Kyrkans Missions Årsbok 1934, p. 96.

35 MMS, Annual Report 1926, p. 40; MMS, South India Provincial Synod 1943, p. 112.

36 MMS, South India Provincial Synod 1936, p. 132.

37 Envall 1995, interview. See also Frykholm 1995, interview, and Ulrici 1993, interview.

38 There were exceptions from this general description. For example, a well-known bible woman, Mrs. Pushpam, was of a high caste. In the late 1960s, the Rev. Anders Andrén estimated the proportion of Adi-dravida (i.e. Paraiyar) pastors in the Tamil Evangelical Lutheran Church at 70 per cent of all pastors. Andrén Collection, Manuscripts, 'Kristen kastkyrka', no date, probably 1967 or 1968; Jonsson 1996, interview.

39 CSMA, MBa 1951:520*a*; Jacob 1996, interview.

40 A.S. Muttiah was stationed in Mandiripalayam from 1948 to 1953.

41 Jacob 1996, interview.

42 Lindberg Collection, Lindberg Field Diary, Vol. 1, pp. 28, 31.

43 The Rev. E. Jacob was brought up at Karunagarapuri mission station, which is situated near Kinnathukadavu. Lindberg Collection, E. Jacob Field Diary, 8.5.1967.

44 Lindberg Collection, Lindberg Field Diary, Vol 1, p. 31; Lindberg Collection, E. Jacob Field Diary, 9.5.1967.

45 Mandiripalayam 1995, Ramasamy Goundar.

46 Envall 1995, interview.

47 *Toottiram* is an honourable greeting, often used between Christians. Jacob 1996, interview.

48 Aḍi-dravida equivalent to Paraiyar in the highlands. Envall 1995, interview.

49 Kuppandampalayam 1995, interview; Jonsson 1996, interview.

50 TELC—Tamil Evangelical Lutheran Church. Stephen worked at

Karunagarapuri mission station from 1934 to 1955, while periodically having responsibility for other pastorates in the highlands. KMs, Karunagarapuri Annual Report 1934; CSMA, MBa 1956:155/56, p. 6.

51 See, for example, Andrén Collection, Biskopsvisitation, Karunagarapuri 16-18.3.1937; SKMT 1938:4, pp. 86-7; Andrén 1993, interview.

52 SKMT 1947:7, pp. 150-2; SKMT 1951, pp. 256-7.

53 CSMA, MBa 1925:192, p. 3.

54 KMs, Karunagarapuri Annual Report 1934.

55 CSMA, MBa 1952:547, p. 7. As a rule, the Goundar farmers in the surrounding villages contributed to the Christian festivals. See CSMA, Unsorted documents, CSM in India 1941, p. 22.

56 Foreign Field 1927, July, p. 231.

57 CSMA, Unsorted documents, CSM in India 1946, p. 8; CSMA, MBa 1949:489, p. 3; CSMA, MBa 1956:155/56, p. 6.

58 CSMA, MBa 1952:553, p. 2.

59 CSMA, Unsorted documents, CSM in India 1947, pp. 7-8. The antagonistic feeling of the CSM towards the Catholics did not derive only from when Catholics began to baptise Valayar who were under or waiting for Lutheran baptismal instruction. The Rev. Stephen dates it back to 1896, when David Bexell had taken up work in the district. The general criticism of the Roman Catholics in the CSM reports concerned what they understood as a violation of the geographical boundaries between churches and missions. The Catholics did not keep outside of the CSM domains. CSMA, MBa 1947:393; CSMA, MBa 1948:508, p. 1; KMs, Karunagarapuri Annual Report 1948.

60 CSMA, MBa 1952:553, p. 2.

61 See, for example, the villages of Devanampalayam and Kuppandampalayam. See also the problems as described by Anna Irbe at Karunagarapuri boarding, where parents of Paraiyar and Madhari pupils refused to let them live together. KMs, Karunagarapuri Annual Report 1936.

After a journey to the Coimbatore district, the Rt. Rev. Ysander reported to the CSM Board that in one of the villages two Christian communities lived on either side of the chapel, one Madhari and the other Paraiyar. Ysander went to greet them both, but when the service began in the chapel, only one of the communities showed up (unfortunately Ysander does not tell us which one). The community that was last to receive the bishop stayed away and asked for a church and a service of their own. CSMA, MBa 1956:152/56, p. 2.

62 Mandiripalayam 1995, interview, Ramasamy Goundar; Ganesamurthi 1935, p. 270.

63 In 1956, the paragraph was qualified by the addition of 'Sikh' to the text, and in 1990 also Buddhists could be classified as a Scheduled Caste. Massey 1995, p. 134.

64 CSMA, MBa 1952:539, p. 2; Jonsson 1996, interview.

Even before the constitution was changed, reports indicate a different treatment of Christians, as compared with Hindus. From the villages of Kodavadi and Singarampalayam, Stephen reported that the president and members of *grama sangams* (village organisations) and group committees, who had been appointed by the Government to distribute food and cloth among poor villagers, delayed the distribution, arguing that the applicants were Christians and should turn to Christian missionaries for benefits. CSMA, Unsorted documents, CSM in India 1946, p. 3; CSMA, MBa 1947:393, p. 1. See also KMs, Karunagarapuri Women Work, Annual Report 1955.

65 CSMA, MBa 1947:393, p. 1.

66 KMs, Karunagarapuri Annual Report 1948.

67 CSMA, MBa 1949:489, p. 2.

68 SKMT 1936:24, p. 270.

69 KMs, Karunagarapuri Annual Report 1948, p. 2.

70 KMs, Karunagarapuri Annual Report 1946, p. 5.

71 CSMA, Unsorted documents, CSM in India 1947, p. 8.

72 Andrén Collection, Karunagarapuri Annual Report 1937. See also CSMA, MBa 1953:545, p. 1.

73 CSMA, MBa 1936:146, p. 2.

74 CSMA, MBa 1955:155/56, p. 4.

75 In India, the relief was organised by the National Christian Council, Famine Relief Committee. TNA, Food, Famine Relief, G. O. 976, 28.10.1948; CSMA, MBa 1949:489, p. 5; CSMA, MBa 1952:544; Envall 1995, interview.

76 Dick Kooiman discusses the relationship between famines and conversion in South Travancore between 1860 and 1881, a period that included three famines. He concludes that just as famines may lead to a change of religion as a strategy for survival, reconversion and a return to the old beliefs was just as possible. The three famines show different behaviours among the untouchables. A common feature was that famines created a kind of 'rush hour' in the existing 'religious boundary traffic'. Kooiman 1991, pp. 290-1, 298-9.

77 Sakkili = Chakkiliyar, i.e. Madhari.

78 CSMA, MBa 1941:362, p. 3.

79 CSMA, Sorted documents, box 9:A, Appendix. The Minutes of the Meeting of the Economic Uplift Committee 22.8.1946.

80 KMs, Karunagarapuri Annual Report 1936; KMs, Karunagarapuri Annual Report 1936, hand-written manuscript that later came to be revised; Hård af Segerstad 1967.

81 SKMT 1931:17, pp. 246-52; CSMA, MBa 1932:145, p. 3; Frykholm 1937, pp. 190-1; See also CSMA, MBa 1952:554, p. 3.

82 CSMA, Sorted documents, box 9:A, Proceedings of the Budget Conference of the Church of Sweden Mission 10-11.10.1945, §9.

83 On a visitation of Pandur pastorate in 1922, the situation was described

as 'deplorable'. The Christians were said to have converted for 'worldly motives', when the missionary helped them to get loans in a situation of famine. These loans were understood to have been the reason why people converted in great numbers. But, after that, the work was left to agents, who signed on when they were promised high wages, and reconversion followed. CSMA, MBa 1922:320, p. 6.

84 CSMA, Sorted documents, box 9:A, Appendix. The Minutes of the Meeting of the Economic Uplift Committee 22.8.1946.

85 CSMA, MBa 1950:551, p. 3.

86 CSMA, MBa 1951:545; CSMA, MBa 1952:544; CSMA, MBa 1962:158*b*; TELC, Annual Reports, A:1*a*, Palladam Annual Report 1954, Minoson; TELC, Annual Reports, A:1*b*, Project connected with the work of the Rural Centre, Arulpuram, Tamil Nadu, 1974; Envall 1995, interview; Jonsson 1996, interview.

87 Andrén Collection, Biskopsvisitation, Karunagarapuri 16-18.3.1937; SKMT 1938:4, pp. 86-7; CSMA, Unsorted documents, CSM in India 1941, p. 23; CSMA, MBa 1953:547, p. 7.

88 Mandiripalayam 31.1.1995, interview.

89 Jonsson 1996, interview. See also Uppilipalayam 26.1.1995, interview, where elderly Madhari members relates how the Goundar sought advice from 'the white *Aiya*'.

90 CSMA, MBa 1954:320, p. 4; CSMA, MBa 1956:155/56, p. 4.

91 CSMA, Unsorted documents, Correspondence, Coimbatore 1929-1933, Johannes Sandegren to the Church Council 3.4.1933. *Kovil*—temple or church; *pillai*—son.

92 That is, the Palladam pastorate, which included the villages from where the village leaders came.

93 Cow-dung with water added was spread over the sandy ground to give it a hard surface, easy to keep clean.

94 *Swaraj*—self-rule or home rule.

95 CSMA, MBa 1936:146, Appendix to minutes of visitation of the Palladam pastorate 14.3.1936. Caste affiliations of congregations in the Palladam pastorate were recorded in CSMA, MBa 1947:391, Appendix to Palladam Annual Report 1946.

96 CSMA, MBa 1936:146, pp. 4-5.

97 CSMA, MBa 1932:154, p. 2; Envall 1995, interview.

98 Andrén Collection, Karunagarapuri Annual Report 1937; CSMA, Unsorted documents, CSM in India 1941, p. 24; SKMT 1947:7, pp. 150-2; SKMT 1950:19, pp. 236-8; CSMA, MBa 1954:320, p. 5.

99 SKMT 1953:22, pp. 302-5.

100 Envall 1995, interview.

101 CSMA, MBa 1949:489, p. 2.

102 Envall 1995, interview.

103 SKMT 1949:25, pp. 336-9; CSMA, MBa 1949:488, p. 2.

104 SKMT 1949:25, pp. 336-9.

105 Envall 1995, interview.
106 CSMA, MBa 1950:551, p. 3.
107 CSMA, MBa 1954:320, p. 5; Ulrici 1993, interview.
108 There are other examples in the reports of similar conflicts, but they do not give as many details as in the Manickapuram case. One such report of a conflict is from Vadugapalayam, near Palladam, in 1953. A Madhari congregation member was beaten 'almost to death', and the mission filed a case against 'a caste Hindu' (possibly a Goundar or a Naicker). The caste man filed a counter-suit against the mission 'and others' for theft. The conflict was still on at the time when the report was written. CSMA, MBa 1954:320, p. 5.
109 CSMA, MBa 1930:249.
110 CSMA, Unsorted documents, CSM in India 1938, p. 20.
111 CSMA, MBa 1953:547, p. 7.
112 CSMA, MBa 1941:362, p. 1.
113 The Rt. Rev. Torsten Ysander reported to the CSM Board after a journey in 1956 that the experience he had come to value most on his journey was the visits he had made to village congregations in the Coimbatore district. On arriving at the villages late at night, he had been met by hundreds of villagers. A group of musicians, whom he believed to be Hindus (he may certainly have been mistaken), had led the party, playing drums and trumpets and, together with other villagers, dancing backwards all the way to the chapel up to its altar. This was Ysander's first experience of dancers in church processions, and his feelings seem to have been bewildered and confused. CSMA, MBa 1936:146, p. 5; CSMA, MBa 1956: 152/56, pp. 2-3.
114 CSMA, MBa 1946:357, p. 1; CSMA, FaR, A IV:4, Jothipuram 1956; Jonsson 1996, interview; Envall 1995, interview.
115 CSMA, MBa 1946:357, p. 1. See also SKMT 1946:19, pp. 435-438; CSMA, MBa 1956:155/56, p. 5.
116 John Everett Clough worked for the Telugu Mission of the American Baptist Mission Society from 1864. Clough 1914, pp. 159-60.
117 Clough 1914, pp. 166-8.
118 Clough 1914, pp. 162, 168-71. A. T. Fishman, who worked for the American Baptist Telugu Mission from 1920 to 1944, has discussed the conversion movement of the 1870s in *Culture Change and the Underprivileged.* He emphasises the conflicts that were caused by refusal to play drums in religious ceremonies. The drums were not completely banned; missionaries were often greeted by drums when they arrived at the villages. The Christian Madigas continued to play and dance among themselves. However, eventually the missionaries realised that *chindu*, a dance often performed, expressed Madiga superiority over the Malas. This enmity between the two communities was carried on within the Church. Fishman 1941, p. 5, 184.
119 Clough 1914, p. 160.

120 SKMT 1951:24, p. 340. The compensation was said to have been equal to 70 Swedish *kronor.*

121 CSMA, MBa 1941:362, p. 1.

122 CSMA, MBa 1948:508, p. 5. See also CSMA, MBa 1931:224, p. 14, for early arguments against the indebtedness that tied labourers.

123 Mandiripalayam and Tiruppur baptismal records.

124 Jonas Ulrici worked in the area during two periods, from 1941 to 1958 and from 1960 to 1969, but relates in rather more general terms that there were sometimes conflicts, but generally no problems when permission had been asked from the Goundar community of the village in advance. Ulrici 1993, Andrén 1993, Envall 1995, Jonsson 1996, interviews.

125 CSMA, Sorted documents, box 9:A, Proceedings of the Budget Conference of the Church of Sweden Mission 10-11.10.1945, §9; CSMA, Sorted documents, box 9:A, Appendix. The Minutes of the Meeting of the Economic Uplift Committee 22.8.1946.

126 This situation resembles the conclusions by Geoffrey Oddie in his article on missionaries as social commentators. Oddie states that the Protestants spent most of their time among people who tended to represent a challenge to the power and status of the traditional, landed and commercial classes. Conflicts between missionaries and landlords occurred as the missionaries regarded landlords as 'an obstacle to the spread of the Christian Gospel', but also because conversions among the labourers made the landlords fear to lose control over them. Oddie 1996, p. 200.

127 Duncan Forrester emphasises how the conversion of untouchables to non-Hindu faiths became politically controversial in the 1930s, when Gandhi opposed untouchables leaving the Hindu fold. These, the lowest of society, were to be included and upgraded as *Harijans* and were to be given opportunities to advance within the nationalist movement as Hindus. But there are no indications that any such motives supported the Goundars' strong objections to Madhari conversions in the 1940s. Forrester 1991, p. 79.

128 CSMA, MBa 1936:146.

129 CSMA, Unsorted documents, CSM in India 1947, p. 8; Jonsson 1996, interview; Lindberg Collection, Field Diary, Vol. 2, p. 42, Kullampalayam 23.6.1967.

130 CSMA, MBa 1936:146.

131 Clough 1914, pp. 163-6.

132 'Please, come.' Jonsson 1996, interview; Jonsson 1994, lecture.

133 Mandiripalayam 31.1.1995, interview.

134 Uppilipalayam 26.1.1995 and 29.1.1995, interviews.

135 Lindberg Collection, E. Jacob Field Diary, 25.5.1967.

136 Lindberg Collection, Lindberg Field Diary, Vol. 2, 15.6.1967, pp. 11-12.

137 SKMT 1951:24, p. 340; Mandiripalayam 31.1.1995, interview, Abraham;

Semmipalayam 1995, interview, Narayana Goundar.

138 Arulpuram 26.1.1995, interview; Frykholm 1970, p. 136.

139 P. Solomon relates from 1967 how the women in Muruganpalayam village had to place their pots on the ground by the Goundar's well, so that a Goundar could draw water and pour it into their pots and in this way protect the water from being polluted. Sometimes the women had to wait for a long time by the well or return without water, as no Goundar had come to assist them. Lindberg Collection, Field Notes, Vol. 2, pp. 6-7.

140 CSMA, MBa 1952:544, p. 1; CSMA, MBa 1952:550, p. 1; CSMA, MBa 1954:320, pp. 2, 5.

141 CSMA, MBa 1953:218; Frykholm 1970, p. 135.

142 The fact that villagers of all castes could use the new pumps was often emphasised as the major benefit of the project, besides making more water available. TELC, Missionaries, M:1*b*, Memorandum regarding the Future of the Well-Drilling Project, 1956; TELC, Annual Reports, A:1*a*, Palladam Annual report 1954, Minoson.

143 The project continued under the CSM management for five years. Sixty-one of the approx. 170 wells giving water were drilled in villages where the CSM worked, another 20 in villages where other missions had established work. All wells in the villages were located on *poramboke* or common land. After the initial years, the project continued in cooperation with the Government of Madras, and the Government covered the major part of the costs, while the CSM staff ran the project. Frykholm 1960, pp. 40-1, 77; Frykholm 1995, interview.

144 Lindberg 1969, pp. 104, 109. Comparing Christian and Hindu Madhari hamlets in the area near Tiruppur turned out to be difficult. In the selection that Staffan Lindberg made, the Christian lived closer to Arulpuram (which was more rural), while the Hindu hamlets were nearer to Tiruppur.

145 Lindberg 1969, p. 118.

146 See, for example, CSMA, MBa 1941:362, p. 1; CSMA, MBa 1949:489, p. 2.

147 Nicos Mouzelis 1992 (1990), a sociologist arguing for a post-Marxist standpoint, has developed the concept of ideology in a way fruitful to this discussion. See also Mouzelis 1992, pp. 68-73.

148 Beck 1972, pp. 29-40.

149 Washbrook 1993, p. 78; Mandiripalayam 31.1.1995, interview. See also Lillie 1956, pp. 17-18.

150 Beck 1972, Table 1.2.

151 Arulpuram 26.1.1995, interview.

152 Andrén Collection, Biskopsvisitation, Karunagarapuri 16-18.3.1937; SKMT 1938:4, pp. 86-7.

153 CSMA, MBa 1941:362, p. 1.

154 CSMA, MBa 1930:249; CSMA, FaR, A IV:4, Jothipuram 1956.

CHAPTER 6

# Bonds Lost

Over the century, the rural Coimbatore district had changed. The young Assistant Collector who was impressed by the 'blowing and panting' buffaloes pulling water outside Coimbatore town in 1937 would now have had difficulties in recognising the place. The *kavalai* water-lifts that brought water out of the wells and had been praised for their simple and efficient technique were by 1970 regarded as a complement to the electrical pump sets. In the late 1960s, the old technique was still necessary for profitable farming, but it was soon to be entirely superfluous. The *kavalais* were no longer a distinguishing feature of the rural Coimbatore district. For an outsider who had been able to observe the agricultural transformation, this was one of the most obvious changes. But beneath the disappearing *kavalais* lay a more fundamental change.

The major question addressed in the present study is how rural social relations between landowners and labourers were linked to the deep-reaching, economic and structural changes that took place in agriculture during the greater part of the twentieth century. The Goundar farmers and the Madhari agricultural labourers and leather-workers played key-roles in this process. To study their mutual history has been found to be a most useful way of analysing the changing rural relations.

To approach this question from the view-point of the supply of and the demand for labour and agricultural produce and of the farmers' urge to maximise their profits, may take the analysis deep into the understanding of rural relations. As was discussed in the 'Introduction', the historical change can be understood in the light of a growing, market-oriented class of farmers making efficient use of the labour market. However, there are also problems with such an approach. The results of the present study show that rural relations cannot be studied fruitfully without an understanding of the close relationship between labour relations and local power hierarchies. Equal importance has to be given to both economic and social rationality or logic.

In the preceding chapters, rural social relations in the Coimbatore highlands have been studied in very different aspects. Chapter 2 was aimed at reconstructing the Goundar–Madhari relationship and at relating it to the local or village society. Earlier research on the Coimbatore district that has dealt with rural social relations has arrived at results that differ from those of the present study in some important respects. The difference in method and the type of material used may partly explain this. The mission material has proved very useful in finding traces of existing labour contracts and the social aspects of the Goundar–Madhari relationship. The findings in this material can fruitfully be related to Government surveys and commissions, the interpretations of the separate materials mutually benefiting from the analysis. Oral sources contribute to deepen the understanding of written documents, but they have to be used with much caution because of the distance in time.

However, not until the findings are seen in the light of the nineteenth-century history of the Kongunad region does the role of the Madhari community in agriculture become clear. Therefore, some of the documents that Christopher Baker refers to in his *An Indian Rural Economy* have been read and interpreted in a different way.

In Chapters 3 and 4, the process of industrialisation with regard to agriculture and the effect of the sudden drought have been discussed. Here, the interplay of social and economic logic in keeping or dismissing permanent agricultural labourers is essential for the analysis.

Finally, in Chapter 5, the conversion movement, in which four of the Madhari sub-groups participated, is analysed. In this chapter, the mission material is primarily matched by interviews. To distinguish different authors and actors in the mission material from each other has proved important to the understanding of the information provided in the different documents.

In all these aspects of rural relations and agricultural transformation, the Goundar–Madhari relationship remains in the main focus. Each of the chapters gives an understanding of the relationship between Goundar farmers and Madhari labourers with regard to the topic discussed. However, when the findings of the different aspects are put together, a new pattern emerges. Studying how they concurred provides a deeper understanding of the process of transformation of the Goundar–Madhari relationship during the twentieth century until the late 1960s. The most interesting findings can be organised into three main fields of discussion. Before going into detail, these will be briefly introduced.

### 1. ADJUSTING SOCIAL RELATIONS TO ECONOMIC CHANGE

Firstly, the study of the period up to the depression in the 1930s reveals a process in which the number of controlled labourers grew side by side with increased industrial and market involvement in agriculture. This may seem to suggest that feudal relations subsisted within a transition to capitalism. However, the issue needs to be problematised much further.

The most important conclusion is that, during this fundamental economic transition, existing social and labour relations were adjusted and made use of in order to meet the immediate needs for labour in agriculture and to uphold the relations of local dominance. The *pannai* (or farm) system of employing labour seems to have worked well in meeting these interests. A *pannaiyal*, or permanent farm labourer, formally entering into a one-year employment with a farmer, received advance payment to sustain him and his family throughout the year. These advances were to be deducted from his remuneration by the end of the year. In effect, this system of advance payments served to make him indebted and came to restrict his mobility. While indebted, the labourer had to remain with the same farmer, a situation that could last more than a generation. Nevertheless, also the labourers could find benefits in staying within the relationship. However low their position, they could rely on a secure livelihood and a certain protection from the Goundar farmer. During the first few decades, the results indicate that, when cash-cropping grew in importance and industrial processing of agricultural produce developed, this form of labour increased on the farms.

### 2. SOCIAL CONSTRAINTS ON ECONOMIC CHANGE

Secondly, on studying the Goundar–Madhari relationship throughout the whole period and observing how social and economic logic interacted, the relationship shows an interesting change. In the period up to the 1930s, both the economic efficiency of farm management and the social logic of relations of dominance in the villages served to support the growth in the number of permanent farm labourers.

Sufficient labour was scarce and had to be secured. These labourers needed to possess certain skills. Securing labour was possible through the *pannai* system. At the same time, by this system, the existing power relations that placed the Goundar community in the superior position were reinforced.

At the beginning of the 1940s, the preconditions for replacing a large and permanent labour force by industrially produced, technical equipment were established. It had thereby become both economically and technically possible to introduce labour-saving techniques into agriculture. However, although economic logic would suggest replacement, permanent labourers were still employed in the villages. Mobilisation among the Madhari labourers to break with village control by conversion to Christianity met with a violent reply from the Goundar community.

The arrival of the great drought of 1946-53 changed this situation. With only very little rain for six years in succession, the *pannai* system of employing labour could not be maintained. After the drought, unemployment had risen among the Madhari labourers and only a small number of them were taken on as *pannaiyal*. After this, it is no longer possible to speak of a *pannai* system of labour. To be a *pannaiyal* had changed its meaning. The bond had become a privilege—the privilege of securing an income. However, this bond was now lost to most of the previous *pannaiyal*.

Thus, the 1940s appears to have been a crucial decade. Though farming could be made more efficient by replacing permanent labourers by day labourers and by reducing the labour force, the Goundar farmers prevented such a development by strong measures. When labour relations did not exist separately from the social power relations of the village, labour relations could not be changed without affecting the local power hierarchies. Having stated this, it is reasonable to conclude that a situation implying reduced control over the Madhari labourers was seen as a threat to the dominant position of the Goundar community. Thus, a striving to uphold power relations served to constrain plain economic rationality in agriculture.

### 3. QUESTIONING LOCAL POWER

Thirdly, mobilisation among the Madhari to convert to Christianity carried some specific characteristics that reflect the Goundar–Madhari relationship and the position of the Madhari in the local context.

Contrary to what has been emphasised in other studies of mass-conversion movements, the mobilisation among the Madhari was not based on the caste, or *jati*, within the larger region for the purpose of achieving common goals. Mobilisation was village-based and a result of local, village-based, structural conflict. Since geographical mobility and social interaction outside the village were to a certain extent limited to the kinship group, conversion spread along those lines.

The results indicate two principal aims that could be achieved by turning to the mission. On the one hand, the authority of the mission and the mission workers invoked by the Madhari could give protection from the arbitrary exercise of local power. On the other hand, by becoming Christians, the Madhari community in different villages was able to develop an identity that was acknowledged in the village where they lived and that linked the Madhari to an authority and a context outside the village. Both the aspect of protection and that of identity called into question the subordinate position of the Madhari in the social hierarchy of the village.

## ADJUSTING SOCIAL RELATIONS TO ECONOMIC CHANGE

To return to the first argument, the change in agriculture to cultivating cash-crops for the market resulted in profound consequences for labour relations and for cultivation itself. The subsequent development affected both Goundar farmers and Madhari labourers. However, they acted within and responded to the changes in very different ways.

The cultivators who benefited most from agricultural change have been found among the medium and the wealthiest farmers. These were cultivators who had been able to invest in cash-cropping from the early twentieth century. Cotton was soon considered the most profitable cash crop which paid well, provided the land was watered and labourers were employed in sufficient numbers. In spite of depression and drought, there were farmers who managed to repay their debts and who invested in new technology on the farms and in units for the initial industrial processing of cotton.

Nevertheless, a permanently available labour force was essential and had to be employed until a new and labour-saving technique was available and there were economic possibilities of making use of it. Because agriculture competed for labour with urban factories and estates in the hills at a time when agriculture was expanding into cash-cropping, measures were taken by the farmers to secure a sufficient labour force. Within the *pannai* system, agricultural labourers, preferably Madhari, were given advance payments that in fact served to tie them to the farms. In spite of the low status attached to the labourers, they had to be skilled. The farm labourers had to manage the whole process of irrigation, including working the wells, stitching and repairing leather bags and handling draught animals. This explains the preference for taking on the leather-working Madhari as *pannaiyal*. Considering the prevailing cattle economy during the major part of the nineteenth century, the role of the leather-working community becomes even more evident. The Goundar–Madhari relationship can be assumed on firm grounds to have had much deeper roots than the agricultural change from growing food crops to growing cash-crops.

As mentioned earlier, controlled mobility was part of the *pannaiyal* contract. Thus, the contract in itself was not entirely formal, as would have been the case had it been a one-year employment of labourers who by the termination of the contract were free to earn wages elsewhere and to repay any debt they may have had to their former employer. Day labourers who became indebted to a landowner were free to choose any employment, on the estates if they preferred this, in order to return with money and repay debts. But pre-paid remuneration for a *pannaiyal* carried restrictions. Hence, debt bondage is a slightly misleading term with which to characterise *pannaiyal*.

The bond that a *pannaiyal* worked under does not seem to have been added to the form of employment in the shape of a loan, but to have been a part of the agreement as such—unless the advanced remuneration could be deducted from the annual share of the harvest, the *pannaiyal* was not allowed to leave. It may therefore be assumed that in its initial stage the arrangement was a formal contract, but informal law exercised the restriction. Poverty may make a man conclude that entering into a *pannaiyal* contract is the only way of making a living. But no landowner could force a labourer to become *pannaiyal*, and no one was obliged to enter into such a labour contract as a result of belonging to a certain caste. However, as a rule, by the end of the year the *pannaiyal* seems to have ended up in a situation in which he was indebted to the landowner. Exercise of local authority and power by the Goundar farmers could thereafter restrict the mobility of the labourer. The results indicate that such restrictions did not originate from the labour contract, but from local relations of power and domination.[1]

An important conclusion of the present study is that most likely this labour contract did not only serve to keep a sufficiently large labour force within agriculture, but was also an integral part of the local hierarchical relationships. Thereby, keeping labourers in the village as *pannaiyal* served to confirm further the dominant position of the Goundar farmers in local society.

Thus, while agricultural production was increasingly directed to the market, the labour market did not become 'free' to the same extent. The agricultural labour-force appears rather to have become increasingly controlled by extra-economic means, by a complex combination of contract, informal means of control and customary law. When labour relations were intertwined with hierarchies of power, they were made to adjust to them, and could not easily be abandoned and exchanged for the employment of casual labour in free labour market relations.

Looking into labour relations in some detail has served to further clarify the dynamics of the Goundar–Madhari relationship. Focusing on the form of remuneration given to a *pannaiyal* has revealed a relationship between the labourer and the landowner in which labour was a part of the ascribed roles in the village and part of the system of sharing the resources of the village between its members. Such ascribed roles are generally given an explanation that emphasises caste. A Goundar performs certain tasks, a Madhari others. However, judging by the evidence brought out in the present study, these ascribed roles seem to have gone beyond the *jati* level of caste. One and the same task, for example, bringing messages of death to other villages, was carried out by members of different castes in different villages. No doubt, there are many general features that must be acknowledged, but generalisations for a larger region of caste and work performed should be made with much caution also for this early part of the century. In the present study, no clear and detailed pattern for the whole of the studied area has been possible to observe.

All the Madhari in the whole of the Coimbatore district obviously did not carry out the same tasks or claim the same rights. From the information gathered, the individual and concrete local situation seems to explain the differences in praxis. If no Paraiyar lived in a certain village, no one went to the neighbouring village to ask the Paraiyar community who lived there to come to act as messengers. Madhari members could decorate wedding halls, as well as bring messages to Goundar relatives. This was the case, for example, with

Mandiripalayam village. Another example can be given from the Palladam region where the evidence indicates that, while the Madhari acted as messengers for the Goundar in family matters, this was a task for the Paraiyar further west and south-west.[2] However, the people in the villages do not themselves explain the division of particular tasks performed in their village by practical circumstances, but by caste affiliation. Locally, or village-wise, this explanation makes sense. However, it is not valid for the larger region but rather explains local hierarchical relations.

The remuneration of an agricultural labourer was basically given in shares of the village produce. The major part was a share of the harvest. However, for a Madhari *pannaiyal*, only part of what he lived on was given to him for the work he carried out as a *pannaiyal*. Another part of what formed the basis for his survival was given to him because he belonged to the Madhari community. Both were *rights* that the Madhari could claim as members of the village, without the Goundar farmer being present on the occasion, distributing the share. As *pannaiyal*, they had fixed shares of the harvests. As Madhari, they could claim the carcasses of animals that had died of natural causes. Other necessities, from water to clothes, were also often rights that they could claim. The ways in which these rights were expressed in the different villages could vary. The rights in dead animals show some local differences. While the Madhari community in one village had to pay the owner of the animal for the skin and could thereafter themselves sell what they produced from it, the procedure in another village did not allow the Madhari to buy the skin. Instead, they had to prepare and stitch items from it for the village community, for which they were given customary (*mamool*) remuneration.[3] But whatever the practice, unless the meat was poisoned, it was an important additional food besides the grains they received as payment for labour and it added to the security of their livelihood.

Eating meat, taking care of dead animals, and tanning and stitching leather all carried a social stigma. Such an 'unclean' life had to be segregated from the main village and its inhabitants. The skills of a leather-worker, skills that members of the Madhari community were proud of, thus did not raise the status of their community. However much needed by the farmers, the Madhari community was controlled by more than financial ties. Rules of behaviour and living marked the subordination of the Madhari in relation to the inhabitants of the main village and in particular to the Goundar community.

## SOCIAL CONSTRAINTS ON ECONOMIC CHANGE

By studying labour relations, the interaction between the economic and social interests that simultaneously formed the Goundar–Madhari relationship becomes clear. As emphasised earlier, it is when the interplay between social and economic aspects is observed that the tension which arose between the Goundar and Madhari communities in the 1940s finds a reasonable explanation. Until the 1930s, the social and economic interests of the Goundar farmers seem to have merged in the *pannaiyal* form of labour. From the 1940s, however, the economic efficiency of farm management pointed to the replacement of the *pannaiyal* labour force by casual labourers in agriculture.

To begin from the 'economic' point of view. When electricity and mechanical equipment were introduced on the farms, the skills of the Madhari community, and the immediate need for them, became technically redundant. Electricity connections for agricultural purposes were made in the district from the early 1930s onwards. From the 1940s, installations were made not only in the immediate vicinity of the main transmission lines, but also in villages where new lines had to be erected. The government promoted the shift to electric operation of the wells and subsidised loans were made available to farmers. The government argued that, in the long-term perspective, and in order to make the most effective use of the labour market, labour costs could be reduced by changing to electrical pump sets. However, though it was possible during the forties to make investments and achieve more efficiency in farming, the results of the present study show that the Madhari *pannaiyal* were not immediately replaced by casual labourers.

Moreover, when the Madhari made attempts to gain a certain freedom of mobility, the Goundar farmers reacted forcefully to stop it. When groups among the Madhari community mobilised on kinship lines to convert to Christianity and thereby to be able to approach mission workers and invoke an authority different from that of the Goundar, there were immediate conflicts and tension was high between Goundar and Madhari in the late thirties and during the forties. Nothing indicates that *pannaiyals* were dismissed and that the farmers decided to loosen the ties with their permanent labourers to rely on a casual work force. Not until the six years of drought made farming difficult and the remuneration of *pannaiyal* in shares of the village produce impossible did the farmers decide to begin replacing the old *kavalai* by electrical pump sets and change from relying on permanent labourers to employing casual labourers on a daily or a weekly basis. Subsequently, the conflicts caused by conversions ceased.[4]

The drought arrived at a crucial period of time. Agriculture on the larger farms continued to move in the direction of further capitalisation. But failing rains made irrigation by the *kavalai* impossible. The wells that did not dry out did not have the capacity to provide enough water for the crops. Since the Government had approached farmers over the last decade with information about the benefits of electric pump sets and continued to give subsidised loans for agricultural implements, this new technology was willingly adopted by the farmers during the drought years. Interestingly, the peak years for the installation of electrical pump sets coincided with the period of the drought. It was primarily the medium and the wealthiest landowners who could find a way to maintain profitable production in spite of the drought.[5]

Thus, whereas there were farmers who benefited from the drought, it proved disastrous for the Madhari labourers. While, before the drought, the Goundar had reacted violently against all signs of loosening ties between them and their Madhari labourers, the labourers returning to the villages with the arrival of the rains found themselves taken on as casual labourers. As leather-workers, they had been indispensable to the farmers, their skills being their bargaining power. Now those skills had faded in importance, and the position of the Madhari in agricultural production was weakened. Unemployment grew among the agricultural labourers, and a substantial part of the production that had depended on cattle-breeding and leather-work began to disappear. Tanning had become an industrialised process, and the Goundar had increasingly begun to sell the hides to the leather industry.

*Pannaiyal* were still employed on the farms. However, it is no longer reasonable to speak of this as a system of employing labourers for farm work. By the 1960s, the *pannaiyal* had become an overseer, tied by what he owed the farmer and still having to be available from early morning until night, but to some extent envied by those who earned their income from one day to another.

The drought was a lengthy experience of hardship. However, six years is a short period of time, considering the severe consequences for the Madhari labourers. Formerly, the greater part of the agricultural labourer's remuneration was a share of the harvest. This was the situation also for the casual labourers. Payment was given in kind and was secure as long as there were crops to harvest. From the 1950s, payment in kind was still an important part of remuneration. However, cash payment came to be increasingly practised.

Previously, after threshing, the harvest was divided into shares. Threshing days were thereby important days. A threshing machine in place of manual labour would challenge the old system of remuneration. (The strategy of the farmers in Ongole in the 1870s, which was discussed in Chapter 5, of forcing Christian converts to reconvert by threshing only on Sundays and thereby preventing Christian labourers from getting their annual share, may be kept in mind.) Apart from the annual share of the harvest given for agricultural labour, the labourers had rights to the village produce also as members of the Madhari community. But apparently, by and by, those rights were made ineffective. For example, a reduced number of cattle on the farms, together with the new technology in agriculture, not only reduced the demand for leather-work only to the stitching of sandals, but also meant less meat in the Madhari diet.

The bonds that tied *pannaiyal* to labour on the farms had also implied security. Now these bonds were lost.

## QUESTIONING LOCAL POWER

Finally, attention will be paid to the mobilisation within the Madhari community. This was an important movement that needs to be understood in the light of the processes of change discussed earlier. It followed upon the mass, or kinship, conversion movement within the other main Scheduled Caste community in the Coimbatore district, the Paraiyar. But no immediate correlation between the two communities should be concluded from this. Both movements originated from outside the highlands and spread into the district via the relatives of converted Paraiyar and Madhari communities in Tiruchirapalli and Ramnad districts.

For both castes, these movements can fruitfully be understood by considering the growing mobility among untouchable or Scheduled Castes in the Madras Presidency from the late nineteenth century onwards. For the Paraiyar, the connection is fairly obvious, while in the case of the Madhari it may have come about in a more indirect way.

If we consider the growth in the numbers of *pannaiyal* in the Coimbatore district up to the 1930s, this does not seem to have been only a matter of tying labourers in a situation of competing interests.

It is reasonable also to conceive of such an act in the light of the growing political awareness among the untouchable castes during the last decades of the nineteenth and most of the twentieth century. This was to a large extent an awareness of new opportunities to advance socially and economically and to gain influence, of being conscious of dignity and self-respect.

Growing organisation following caste affiliation was a common feature. It should not be understood as purely a caste phenomenon. Nevertheless, caste mattered.[6] It was particularly the Paraiyar community that began to mobilise in various parts of the Presidency. At an early stage, caste-based organisations argued for the rights of the 'Pariah'. Spokesmen were even sent to London to propagandise against the oppression of the Paraiyar.[7] Later, Paraiyar labourers formed the major element in the uprising to protect the *pannaiyals'* rights in the movement that had Tanjavur district as its nucleus.[8] Furthermore, as was discussed in Chapter 5, Paraiyar kinship groups were deeply involved in conversion movements, mainly in different Protestant missions. Increasing numbers of people coming from this community formed organisations, were educated and found employment with the government or in private companies. Of all the migrant labourers from the Presidency, members of the Paraiyar community formed a substantial part.

In the Coimbatore district, a difference between the Madhari and the Paraiyar communities is apparent. In contrast to the Madhari, the Paraiyar had managed to break away from village control by different means. Sub-groups of the Paraiyar community were the first to convert on community lines. Large parts of the community were also seasonal migrants to the tea estates in the Nilgiri and Anamalai hills. In the villages, the Paraiyar community could easily amount to half of the potential agricultural workforce. But the Paraiyar had become 'fussy' about what work to take on, in the words of the older Goundar. They would not do 'anything', as would the Madhari.[9] The farmers had witnessed the Paraiyar being offered money by labour contractors from the estates and thereafter repaying their debts in the villages and making the estates their home for up to ten months in a year. Such a situation would not have passed unnoticed.

Hence, the Paraiyar community, or groups within it, had mobilised both in political and religious forms. They had organised as labourers, as well as received education and employment outside the villages. They had thereby got out of reach of the enforcement of local power and of the Goundar. In a situation in which labour became scarce around the turn of the century, the Madhari were obviously not to have the same opportunities to break with village relations, if the Goundar farmers could prevent it. The Paraiyar community had broken away from the village control in which the Goundar community held the dominant position. Most likely, the Goundar did not want this to happen with the Madhari. Thus, the ties inherent in *pannaiyal* contracts served to control more than a labour force; they were also part of the control of the Madhari community in the village. The most likely development was therefore that any mobilisation among the Madhari would be met by strong Goundar opposition.

The general situation of the Scheduled Castes in many parts of Tamilnad was that one particular caste outnumbered the others. However, in the Coimbatore district, both the Paraiyar and the Madhari were large communities. The Paraiyar community proved to be the most active of the two, but they never joined forces. Their mutual antagonism was deep. The results of this study thus point to the importance not only of the particular economic situation and the division of labour in agriculture, but also to that of caste and kinship in rural mobilisation among the Scheduled Castes.

When members of the Madhari community approached either the Methodist mission or the Lutheran mission from the mid-1910s onwards to ask for baptism for their community in the village where they lived, this was an act that stirred up tension and caused conflicts. Missionaries could observe how mobilisation took place on kinship lines, involving the whole or most of the Madhari community of a village. This movement had both material and social aims, which have been discussed in Chapter 5. However, in this connection, the mobilisation process, as such, needs looking into. In contrast to the organisation among the Paraiyar, the Madhari mobilisation was strictly village-based. From the material presented in Chapter 5, it may be concluded that this was not a movement which involved the whole of the Madhari caste, or *jati*, in the highlands. Conversions spread within particular sub-groups and were rather a consequence of and a reaction to the immediate conflicts experienced by the Madhari community of a certain village, whether open and violent or structurally hidden. Thus, they cannot be compared with social movements organised to achieve common goals in a larger region. A more thorough comparison between the different forms of mobilisation among the Madhari and Paraiyar communities would contribute to a better understanding of how people of the lowest sections in Indian society organised themselves to achieve social, economic and political goals. However, this is beyond the scope of the present study, in which the main focus remains on the relationship between the Goundar and the Madhari in the rural Coimbatore district.

The kinship character of mobilisation among the Madhari can fruitfully be discussed by considering the narrow geographical mobility allowed to them. Also their limited interaction with members outside the kinship group is an important factor. An immediate conclusion would be that it was a result of an urge among the Madhari belonging to one and the same kinship group to turn to the same god. However, at times, this urge appears to have been stronger among the mission workers than among the Madhari. The missionaries always made strong efforts to baptise a Hindu bridegroom who married a Christian bride.

Religious conviction is, of course, a central feature of a conversion movement. However, it can only be part of the explanation of why this movement spread only along kinship lines. The limited possibilities which the Madhari had of interacting with people outside the village would rather have acted as more obvious limits to the spread of the conversion movement. Of course, Madhari members were not locked up in the villages but went to local markets and sometimes seasonally went for harvest work to nearby places. However, most of the contacts with people outside the home village were in marriage and family relations, which were kept strictly within the sub-group of Madhari to which they belonged. Conversion therefore spread along these lines.

The difference between the Madhari and the Paraiyar communities in their possibilities to organise is also reflected in the apparent lack of interest shown by political parties in the Madhari throughout most of the studied period. In the later part of the period, party representatives arrived in the major villages in time for the elections. However, there is nothing to indicate that there was a strategy to treat this community as a presumptive 'vote bank', with promises to improve their situation.

In the late 1950s and 1960s, Christian Madhari had realised the effects of the constitutional order of 1950, by which Christians, among others, were excluded from the Scheduled Caste category. Thereby, in principle, positive discrimination in a system of quotas did not reach Madhari members known to be Christian. However, during the first 25 years of conversions among the Madhari, no such considerations would raise obstacles to their decision to convert, and after the promulgation of the constitutional change, the application of this law in the district was mild, in the sense that being included in the

Scheduled Caste category appears to have been more a matter of using a Hindu name than of having to reconvert, though it needs to be said that Christian 'untouchables' thereby had to depend on an arbitrary application of the law. To conclude, mobilising village- and kinship-wise for conversion was apparently the only possible way for the Madhari to organise.

A major change, which was also discussed in Chapter 5, resulted from inviting into the Madhari *cheri* an outside authority that came to question the exercise of Goundar power. However, questioning the power of the Goundar was almost always done in an indirect way or was a consequence of establishing Christian congregations among the new converts. The mission workers themselves seem to have been keen not to provoke the Goundar community. But, by the very presence of the mission, this seems to have been unavoidable.

By conversion, the Madhari realised the possibility of breaking up the firm links tying them to the Goundar community. By turning to the mission workers, the Madhari, in effect, not only questioned the complete control exercised by the Goundar over them, but in fact challenged it. To find protection and support in an authority that could match that of the Goundar appears in some respects to have been an important reason for turning to the mission workers. When court cases were started by missionaries on behalf of the Madhari, the case was to be judged by an outside authority and not by the village panchayat or by the Goundar farmer himself. In most cases, the missionaries did not take such strong measures but were able to influence the Goundar's decision and settle the matter by mediation. However, in cases in which Madhari labourers chose not to turn to the mission or ask for conversion, this should not be interpreted as indicating passivity on the part of the Madhari community. Interpreting such behaviour as 'backwardness' is a mistake. When the aim was to find protection and the means of survival, remaining in the village under the superiority of the Goundar certainly was a most rational decision.

Becoming a Christian was a decision far more visible than the change of mind of a number of individuals. The link with the outside world established by the Madhari community of a village became manifest in ways that counteracted the local society's expressions of Madhari inferiority. The physical segregation between the Madhari and members of high castes with superior status was transgressed by visiting pastors and missionaries. New ceremonies and places of worship manifested the presence of outside authority. Also, the one and only authority hitherto experienced by the Madhari was questioned and sometimes even challenged when mission workers approached the Goundar farmers to speak on behalf of the Madhari labourers.

The Madhari were thereby no longer 'just Madhari', identified by their labour and social position within the village, but were also Christian. This added a new identity that was observed and eventually acknowledged by local society. This identity did not derive from within the village but from an outside context that was not controlled by members of local society. It was a link with the outside world that the Madhari could establish without leaving the village.

## TO CONCLUDE

The present study has been aimed at shedding light on the complexity of rural social relations over a period of historical change. When capital grew in importance in agriculture at the beginning of the twentieth century, the existing relations of labour and relations of social power were adjusted and made relevant in the new situation. However, it would be as incorrect to say that feudal relations persisted and continued unaltered as to state that a dramatic shift to market-determined relations occurred. Relations were rather moulded by fundamental economic changes and by interests articulated within it, at the same time as they served to limit and influence the course of that change in the Coimbatore district.

By the end of the studied period, during the 1960s, when the social and economic logic of keeping large numbers of permanent labourers on the farms had largely disappeared, there were still special tasks in local society to be carried out by its members. These tasks still carried high or low status. However, the *pannai* system was no longer necessary to uphold the local power relations that made enforcement of these tasks possible. As long as the Madhari were unemployed or in need of an extra income, they did not refuse to carry out any task demanded. Some of the tasks they carried out also marked a certain status of the Madhari and were 'rights' that they guarded that operated to reinforce the position of the community as a necessary part of the village.

In all the interviews, a double-edged explanation was given by the Madhari of their carrying out unclean work and being disrespectfully treated. Yes, they were held in low regard by the other villagers, living segregated and placed at the bottom of local society. But, with a laugh, the Madhari men and women immediately reversed these values and ridiculed the Goundar, who 'always ate the food the Madharis had touched when we gathered the harvest'.

## NOTES

1 Baker and Breman, along with other researchers, describe a situation in which labourers were tied by a debt. Thereby, the question of interest immediately appears. However, by distinguishing advances from loans, this question becomes less problematic. The question is no longer whether *pannaiyal* were excluded from interest payments as a privilege they held in contrast to casual labourers. The main difference comes from whether that which was owed derived from an advance or from a loan. See also the Introduction.

2 Lindberg Collection, E. Jacob Field Diary, Vavipalayam 16.5.1967. See Chapter 2.

3 Gopalaratnam 1931, p. 523; Arulpuram 26.1.1995, interview. See Chapter 2.

4 These results resemble broadly the logic of the results presented by Amit Bhaduri, though, for a much earlier period. He argues that landowners in West Bengal in the 1970s gave priority to keeping political and economic control over share-croppers rather than to achieving higher profits in agriculture and risking losing control. See the 'Introduction'.

5 In this connection, Table 5.1, showing population statistics, can be considered. For the period 1941-51, the Christian population shows a net decrease. During this period, it had a lower increase than the total population of the district. The reasons for this trend cannot easily be stated and the exactness of the figures can always be doubted. However, it is interesting to note that this was a period when conflicts caused by conversion were numerous and the effects of the drought caused congregation work in the most affected areas to come to a standstill.

6 In his work on the politics of south India, Christopher Baker writes that agitation for political representation among the depressed classes (Scheduled Castes) increased during the 1920s to peak in 1933. Together with David Washbrook, he argues that caste-based organisations were founded in the Presidency for instrumental purposes. They were functional groupings that were organised to achieve political goals, and not ritual communities. Being geographically spread over a large region, only a few castes possessed a unity strong enough to act as a political power. A common 'south Indian' or 'Tamilnad' ritual identity was not developed. Political aims had priority within this kind of organisation. Baker 1976, pp. 181-2, 195; Baker and Washbrook 1975, pp. 162, 191-2.

7 Pandian 1895.

8 See Chapter 2.

9 See, for example, Mandiripalayam 2.2.1995, interview.

APPENDIX

# Madhari Kinship Groups

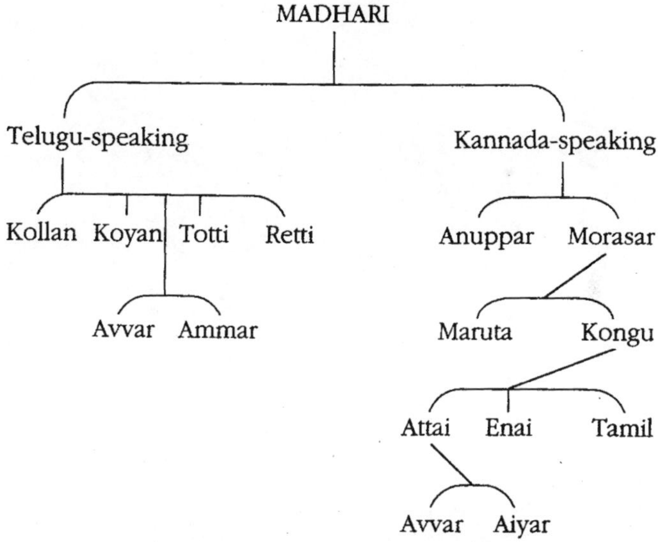


KINSHIP GROUPS IN THE CONVERSION MOVEMENT TO CHRISTIANITY IN THE COIMBATORE DISTRICT

Source: Dorairaj 1990:1, p. 26. Dorairaj bases his diagram on Lillie 1956.

Of the many different Madhari kinship groups, four are mentioned by different authors as being involved in the conversion movement. These four are the Avvar and Ammar of the Telugu division and the Anuppar and Morasar of the Kanadam division. See further Lillie 1956, p. v; Hård af Segerstad 1967, p. 22 (referring to a report by G. Stephen in 1950); Manickam 1977, p. 31 (referring to Lillie 1956 and to MMS, Report of the Trichinopoly Mass Movement Commission 1935, App. II, p. 43); Dorairaj 1990:1, pp. 13-14 (referring to Lillie 1956; however, his diagram is a copy of Manickam 1977, p. 32, but isolates the Madhari community in the diagram and supplements it by qualifying the Avvar and Aiyar division among the Morasar of the Attai dialect).

The Rev. I. Manuel distinguishes between different villages where communities of the different kinship groups live in a larger area around Kinnathukadavu. Nowhere was there a village where members of more than one kinship group lived. (Manuel 1992, interview).

# Glossary

| TERMS USED IN THE TEXT | TRANSCRIBED TAMIL | |
|---|---|---|
| *adimai* | *aṭimai* | slavery |
| *asuttamaka* | *acuttamāka* | impure, unclean |
| *cheri* | *cēri* | hamlet, the part of a village where members of certain low castes live (particularly the Scheduled Castes) |
| *coolie* | *kūli* | daily wage labourer (also *kūliyāḷ*) or the pay for work performed by this labourer |
| *devasam* | *tevacam* | payment in kind for the contracted labour |
| *dhoti* | *tōti* | male clothing |
| *Inam* | — | grant of land, often in return for service, with revenue discount |
| *kanakkuppillai* | *kaṇakkuppiḷḷai* | accountant having responsibility for the land registers in a number of villages (also *kaṇakkappiḷḷai*) |
| *kangani* | *kaṅgāṇi* | labour contractor |
| *karnam* | *kārṇam* | village accountant |
| *karudu* | *karuṭu* | payment for day labour (colloquial) |
| *kasbah* | — | revenue village (Persian) |
| *katralai kilangu* | *kaṟṟāḻai kiḻaṅku* | aloe root |
| *kavalai* | *kavalai* | water-lift for deep, open wells, where water was drawn from the well by two bullocks |
| *kovilppillai* | *kōvilppiḷḷai* | sexton (literally: temple boy) |
| *lungi* | *lūṅki* | male clothing |
| *mamool* | *māmūl* | customary right |
| *mundi* | *maṇṭi* | wholesale trade |
| *padiyal* | *paṭiyāḷ* | hired agricultural labourer paid with a measure of grain (*paṭi*), working on contracts |

| | | |
|---|---|---|
| *panchayat* | — | local court or council |
| *pangan* | *paṅkaṉ* | one who shares |
| *pannai* | *paṇṇai* | farm |
| *pannaiar* | *paṇṇaiyār* | holder of a large farm, landlord |
| *paṇnaiyal* | *paṇṇaiyāḷ* | farm labourer, 'attached' or 'permanent farm servant', working on one-year contracts |
| *parai* | *paṟai* | a drum resembling a tambourine |
| *pari* | *pāri* | part of the leather equipment of the *kavalai* |
| *patta* | *paṭṭā* | land deed |
| *ryotwari* | — | land-revenue system in which a title to the land is given in return for annual payment of revenue |
| *seruppu* | *ceruppu* | sandal |
| *salperi* | *cālperi* | part of the leather equipment of the *kavalai* |
| *Sangu* | *Caṅku* | conch shell, name of one of the Paraiyar sub-castes |
| *siraipanam* | *ciṟaippaṇam* | slave money |
| *siraisoru* | *ciṟaiccōṟu* | slave rice |
| *taluk* | *tāluk* | administrative area below the district |
| *tandal* | *taṇṭal* | a large drum for messages, used in the Coimbatore district (generally translated: collection (of revenue) or loan carrying interest) |
| *tandalkkaran* | *taṇṭalkkāraṉ* | in the Coimbatore district: messenger, a village official (generally translated: tax collector, usurer) |
| *tootiram* | *tōttiram* | salutation, greeting |
| *totti kanji* | *toṭṭi kañci* | gruel from mixed seeds, *totti* in the local dialect meaning 'coconut shell' |
| *urimai* | *urimai* | rights, privilege, claim to ownership, see Chapter 2 |
| *vanga* | *vāṅka* | Please, come (*vāruṅkal*). A polite way to address somebody. Second-person, plural |

| | | |
|---|---|---|
| | | form, *vāṅka* in colloquial Tamil. |
| *va* | *vā* | 'Come'. Second-person, singular form. |
| *valavu* | *vaḷavu* | housing area, a cluster of houses |
| *vallam* | *vaḷḷam* | measurement of dry volume |

| | |
|---|---|
| k | க் |
| ṅ | ங் |
| c | ச் |
| ñ | ஞ் |
| ṭ | ட் |
| ṇ | ண் |
| t | த் |
| n | ந் |
| p | ப் |
| m | ம் |
| y | ய் |
| r | ர் |
| l | ல் |
| v | வ் |
| ḻ | ழ் |
| ḷ | ள் |
| ṟ | ற் |
| ṉ | ன் |

# Bibliography


## ARCHIVES

### India

Tamil Nadu Archives, Madras (TNA).
District Record Centre, Government of Tamil Nadu, Coimbatore (DRCC).
Tamil Evangelical Lutheran Church, Tiruchirapalli (TELC).
The Pastorates of Tiruppur, Palladam and Mandiripalayam.
Karunagarapuri mission station, Kinnathukadavu (KMs).

### England

India Office Library and Records, London (IOR).
South Asian Archives, Cambridge (SAA).
Wesleyan Methodist Missionary Society, School of Oriental and African Studies, London (MMS).

### Sweden

Church of Sweden Mission Archives, Uppsala (CSMA).
Collections in private hands.

## UNPUBLISHED SOURCES

### Tamil Nadu Archives

Department of Food (Food)
*Civil Supplies*
*Famine Relief*
Department of Public Works, *Indexes*

### District Record Centre, Coimbatore

*Re-survey and Re-settlement Registers*, 1912, Coimbatore district , Palladam Taluk, nos. 30, Thongattipalayam; 33, South Avanashipalayam; 35, Vadamalaipalayam; 47, Kamanaickenpalayam Krishnapuram;

48, Puliyampatti; 49, Anuppapathi; 50, Kettanur; 51, Elavanthi; 52, Velarasikallipalayam; 53, Pongalur; 54, Madapur; 56, Vadugapalayam; 58, Kasbah Ayyampalayam; 59, Sembipalayam; 61, Palladam; 62, Naranapuram; 63, Velampalayam; 64, Peruvayi; 81, Kangayampalayam 83, Ichipatti; 84, Kodangiripalaiyam; 86, Karadibavi; 87, Mallekavundanpalayam; 88, Jalakkarisal; 89, Appanayakanpatti.

TAMIL EVANGELICAL LUTHERAN CHURCH, CHURCH DOCUMENTS

*Annual reports*
*Missionaries*

THE PASTORATES OF TIRUPPUR, PALLADAM AND MANDIRIPALAYAM, CHURCH DOCUMENTS

*Mandiripalayam Baptismal Records*, Vol. 1.
*Palladam Baptismal Records*, Vols. 1–2.
*Tiruppur Baptismal Records*, Vols. 1–3.

KARUNAGARAPURI MISSION STATION, CSM, MISSION DOCUMENTS

*Annual reports*
*Manuscripts*

INDIA OFFICE LIBRARY AND RECORDS

*The Baramahal Records*, Captain Read's Further Report on the Baramahal and Salem Districts, 1794.
*District Officers' Collection*

SOUTH ASIAN ARCHIVES

*Gwynn Papers*

WESLEYAN METHODIST MISSIONARY SOCIETY

*Annual Reports*
*Correspondence*
*South India Provincial Synod*
*Report of Secretarial Visit to Burma, India and Ceylon*, Sept. 1936 to March 1937.
*Report of the Trichinopoly Mass Movement Commission 1935*, also included

in South India Provincial Synod 1936, App. IX.
*Synod Minutes, South India*

CHURCH OF SWEDEN MISSION ARCHIVES

*Field annual reports* (*Fältens årsberättelser*) (FaR)
*Mission Board minutes appendixes* (*Missionsstyrelsens protokollsbilagor*) (MBa)
*Mission Director's correspondence* (*Missionsdirektors korrespondens*) (MDc)
*Holmåsen Collection*
*Sandegren,* Paul, *Collection*
*Sorted documents,* not catalogued
*Unsorted documents*

COLLECTIONS IN PRIVATE HANDS

*Andrén,* Anders, *Collection,* Uppsala
*Lindberg,* Staffan, *Collection,* Lund
*Ulrici,* Jonas, *Collection,* Göteborg

ORAL SOURCES

Interviews (tape recordings and notes with the author):

*Anders Andrén,* 15.10.1993, Minister and missionary for the Church of Sweden Mission 1946–64 in India. Stationed in the Coimbatore district in 1953–64. Has held positions as Asia Secretary, Prodirector and acting Mission Director.

*Durai, A.M.R.* , 21–22.1.1992, MA in Social Work, Social worker for the Tamil Nadu Christian Council and the Tamil Evangelical Lutheran Church, 1965–71, in Palladam pastorate, Coimbatore district.

*Envall, Bertil and Ingefrid,* 12.10.1995, Bishop Bertil Envall was a missionary for the Church of Sweden Mission 1939–74. Stationed in the Coimbatore district in 1944–53.

*Frykholm, Yngve,* 11.10.1995, Minister and missionary for the Church of Sweden Mission 1948–60. Stationed in the Coimbatore district during the whole of the period.

*Jacob, E.,* 7.3.1996, Minister in the Tamil Evangelical Lutheran Church, Madras. Born in Nallakalipalayam, near Arulpuram.

*Jonsson, Olle,* 25.3.1996, Minister and missionary for the Church of Sweden Mission 1955–79. Stationed in the Coimbatore district in 1958–77.

*Manuel, I.,* 14.1.1992, Minister in the Tamil Evangelical Lutheran Church, Kinnathukadavu. Born in K. Iyampalayam, near Palladam.

*Samuel,* 11.1.1992, shoemaker (80) in Palam (north-east of Arulpuram). Born in Naripatti in Jothipuram pastorate, converted to Christianity at the time when the Rev. Tage Holmberg was assigned to the pastorate. Lived and worked on Arulpuram farm when the Rev. Olle Jonsson was stationed there.

*Ulrici, Jonas*, 12.12.1993, Minister and missionary for the Church of Sweden Mission 1939–69 in India. Stationed in the Coimbatore district in 1941–69, except for the period 1958–60, when he was stationed in Tranquebar.

Village field study, interviews (tape recordings with the author):

*Arulpuram, 26.1.1995*
Gnanasigamani, 38
Jeyaraj, 45, sexton or *kovilpillai*
Rajamanickam, 51, evangelist
*Arulpuram, 29.1.1995*
P. Natarajan Goundar, 43
*Uppilipalayam, 26.1.1995*
Vedamani, 62
Rajamani, 40
Mary Muthamma, 48
Arumaiyamma, 45
Eyamma, 70
Ramatta Goundar, 60.
*Uppilipalayam, 29.1.1995*
Eyamma, 70
Duraisami, 80
Karunayammal, 70
*Kuppandampalayam, 27.1.1995*
Kanakaraj, 78
Selvam, 60
Stephen, 41
Chellamuthu, 39
*Mandiripalayam, 31.1.1995*
Abraham, 102
Subban James, 82
*Mandiripalayam, 2.2.1995*
Ramasamy Goundar, 83
*Semmipalayam, 1.2.1995*
Narayana Goundar, 74
*Semmipalayam, 1.2.1995*
Sivasubramaniyan Goundar, 58, advocate and Panchayat President an older relative of S. Goundar

OTHERS

*Jonsson, Olle*, 23.3.1994, 'Skomakare bli vid din läst', lecture given at Svenska Kvinnors Missionsförening, Mikaelsgården, Uppsala. The Rev. Olle Jonsson was a missionary for the Church of Sweden Mission 1955–79. Stationed in the Coimbatore district in 1958–77. (Notes with the author.)

## PUBLISHED SOURCES

### Government Files

GOVERNMENT OF INDIA

*Agricultural Labour Inquiry. Report on Intensive Survey of Agricultural Labour Employment, Underemployment, Wages and Levels of Living*, 1954, Government of India, Ministry of Labour, Vol. 1, All India (TNA).

*Royal Commission on Agriculture in India, Vol. III, Evidence taken in Madras*, London 1927 (TNA).

*The Famine Enquiry Commission. Final Report*, 1945, Govt of India (TNA).

GOVERNMENT OF MADRAS

*Annual Statistical Abstract for the Madras State* (DSC).

*Department of Electricity*, Administration report (IOR).

*Department of Hydro-electric Development*, Administration report (IOR).

*Department of Industries*, Bulletin (IOR).

*History of Land Revenue Settlements and Abolition of Intermediary Tenures in Tamil Nadu*, 1976, Finance Department and Board of Settlement of Estates (IOR).

*Quinquennial Statistical Abstract for the Madras State*, 1949–50 to 1953–4, Director of Statistics, 1958 (DSC).

*Report of the Economist for Enquiry into Rural Indebtedness*, 1946, B. V. Narayanaswami Naidu (TNA).

*Report of the Land Revenue Enquiry Committee*, 1937, Revenue Department (IOR).

*Report on the Operations of the Department of Agriculture* (IOR).

*Royal Commission on Labour in India*, 1931, Evidence, Vol. VII, Madras and Coorg (TNA).

*Season and Crop Report of the Madras State*, Department of Statistics (TNA, IOR).

### Census, Gazetteers, Manuals

*Census of India*

Cox, A. R., ed., 1933, *Gazetteer of the Coimbatore District*, Vol II, Madras.

Ramaswami, A., ed., 1966, *Madras District Gazetteers, Coimbatore*, Madras.

Nicholson, F., 1887, *Manual of the Coimbatore District*, Madras.

JOURNALS, BOOKS

Hård af Segerstad, 1967, *Den 'lettiska' byn i Sydindien. Minnesblad*, Växjö: Smålandspostens Boktryckeri AB.

Lillie, W., 1956, *Some Customs and Ceremonies of the Karur and Dharapuram Areas*, Tiruchirapalli : St. Therese Printing Works (MMS).

*Svenska Kyrkans Missionstidning*, Appelbergs Boktryckeri AB, Uppsala (journal, SKMT).

*Svenska Kyrkans Missions Årsbok* (Church of Sweden Mission Yearbook).

*The Foreign Field. Of Wesleyan Methodist Church* (journal).

## SECONDARY WORKS

BOOKS AND ARTICLES

Appadurai, A., 1981, *Worship and Conflict under Colonial Rule: A South Indian Case*, Cambridge: Cambridge University Press.

Appadurai, A., and Breckenridge, C., 1976, The South Indian temple: Authority, honour and redistribution, *Contributions to Indian Sociology*, Vol. 10, pp. 187-211.

Arokiaswamy, M., 1956, *The Kongu Country: being the history of the modern districts of Coimbatore and Salem from the earliest times to the coming of the British*, Madras.

Athreya, Venkatesh B., Djurfeldt, Göran, and Lindberg, Staffan, 1990, *Barriers Broken. Production Relation and Agrarian Change in Tamil Nadu*, London: Sage Publications.

Baker, C.J., and Washbrook, D.A., 1975, *South India. Political Institutions and Political Change 1880-1940*, Madras: Macmillan.

Baker, Christopher John, 1976, *The Politics of South India 1920-1937*, Cambridge: Cambridge University Press.

———— 1984, *An Indian Rural Economy 1880–1955. The Tamilnad Countryside*, Oxford: Oxford University Press.

Bayly, C. A., 1990 (1988), *Indian Society and the Making of the British Empire*, Cambridge: Cambridge University Press.

Bayly, Susan, 1992 (1989), *Saints, Goddesses and Kings. Muslims and Christians in South Indian Society, 1700-1900*, Cambridge: Cambridge University Press.

Beauchamp, Henry K., 1906, *Hindu Manners, Customs and Ceremonies*, Oxford: Clarendon Press.

Beck, Brenda E. F., ed., 1972, *Peasant Society in Konku. A Study of Right and Left Sub-castes in South India*, Vancouver: University of British Columbia Press.

———— 1979, *Perspectives on a Regional Culture. Essays about the*

*Coimbatore Area of South India*, New Delhi: Vikas Publishing House.

Bhaduri, Amit, 1973, A Study in Agricultural Backwardness under Semi-Feudalism, *Economic Journal*, March.

Bickers, Robert A., and Seton, Rosemary, eds., 1996, *Missionary Encounters. Sources and Issues*, Surrey: Curzon Press.

Breman, Jan, 1985, *Of Peasants, Migrants and Paupers. Rural Labour Circulation and Capitalist Production in West India*, Oxford: Oxford University Press.

Buchanan, Francis, 1807, *A Journey from Madras through the Countries of Mysore, Canara and Malabar*, Vols. I, II and III, London.

Bugge, Henriette, 1994, *Mission and Tamil Society*, Surrey: Curzon Press.

Cederlöf, Gunnel, (forthcoming) 1997, Power and Dependence: Social and Labour Relations in Rural South India, 1900-1930, in Kortteinen, Timo, and Said, Ikmal, eds., *Classes, Strata and Hierarchies—Social Organization in Contemporary Asia*, Surrey: Curzon Press.

Clough, John Everett, 1914, *Social Christianity in the Orient. The story of a man, a mission, and a movement*, New York: Macmillan.

Diehl, C. G., 1974, *Arvet från Tranquebar. Kyrka och miljö i södra Indien*, Stockholm: Verbum/Studiebokförlaget.

Dirks, Nicholas B., 1979, *The Hollow Crown: Ethnohistory of an Indian kingdom*, Cambridge: Cambridge University Press.

Dubois, Abbé J. A., 1825, *Mœurs, institutions et cérémonies des peuples de l'Inde*, Paris. Translation into English by Henry K. Beauchamp, 1906, titled *Hindu Manners, Customs and Ceremonies*, Oxford: Clarendon Press.

Duraiswami, S. V., 1934, Low Prices and the Plight of the Lowly Ryots, *Madras Agricultural Journal*, Vol. 22, No. 4.

Estborn, Sigfrid, 1959, *Our Village Christians: A Survey of the Life and Faith of Village Christians in Tamilnad*, Studies in the Indian Church and Theology, No. 3, Mysore: Christian Literature Society.

Evans, Barbara, 1990, From agricultural bondage to plantation contract: A continuity of experience in southern India, 1860–1947, *Journal of South Asian Studies*, Vol. 13:2.

———— 1995, Constructing a plantation labour force: The plantation–village nexus in south India, *The Indian Economic and Social History Review*, Vol. 32:2.

Fishman, A. T., 1941, *Culture Change and the Underprivileged: A Study of Madigas in South India under Christian Guidance*, Madras: Christian Literature Society.

Forrester, Duncan B., 1991, The Depressed Classes and Conversion to Christianity, in G. A. Oddie, ed., *Religion in South Asia*, New Delhi: Manohar Publishers.

Frykholm, Harald, 1937, *Harald Frykholm. Mannen och missionären.*

*Självbiografiska anteckningar med tillägg av hans maka*, Stockholm: Svenska Kyrkans Diakonistyrelses Bokförlag.

Frykholm, Yngve, 1960, *Vatten ur torrt land*, Uppsala: Wretmans Boktryckeri AB.

Ganesamurthi, N., 1935, Economic Survey of a South Indian Village—Perumanallur, *The Madras Agricultural Journal*, Vol. .23:7.

Gardner Cassels, Nancy, 1988, Social Legislation under the Company Raj: The Abolition of Slavery Act V 1843, *Journal of South Asian Studies*, Vol. 11:1.

Gleig, G. R., 1830, *The Life and Correspondence of Major-General Sir Thomas Munroe*, London, 3 vols.

Gopalaratnam, P., 1931, Rural Studies — Madathupalayam Village, Coimbatore District, *Madras Agricultural Journal*, Vol. 19:12.

Gough, Kathleen, 1977, Agrarian Change in Thanjavur, in K.S. Krishnaswamy *et al.*, eds., *Society & Change*, Oxford: Oxford University Press.

———— 1978, Agrarian Relations in Southeast India, 1750–1976, *Review*, Vol. 2:1.

———— 1981, *Rural Society in Southeast India*, Cambridge: Cambridge University Press.

———— 1989, *Rural Change in Southeast India*, ,Oxford: Oxford University Press.

Grafe, Hugald, 1990, Tamilnadu in the nineteenth and twentieth century, *History of Christianity in India*, Vol. 4, part 2, Bangalore: Church History Association of India.

Guha, Ranajit, 1994 (1983), *Elementary Aspects of Peasant Insurgency in Colonial India*, Oxford: Oxford University Press.

Hardiman, David, 1995 (1987), *The Coming of the Devi: Adivasi Assertion in Western India*, Oxford: Oxford University Press.

Harriss, Barbara, 1983, *The Process of Commercialisation of Agriculture in India*, Discussion Paper No. 108, University of East Anglia, School of Development Studies, March.

Harriss, John, 1982, *Capitalism and Peasant Farming. Agrarian Structure and Ideology in Northern Tamil Nadu*, Oxford: Oxford University Press.

Harriss, John, Kannan, K.P., and Rodgers, Gerry, 1990, *Urban Labour Market Structures in India: A Study of Coimbatore*, Research Series No. 92, ILO, Geneva.

Hjejle, Benedict, 1967, Slavery and Agricultural Bondage in South India in the Nineteenth Century, *The Scandinavian Economic History Review*, Vol. 15:1,2.

Hunt, Roland, and Harrison, John, 1980, *The District Officer in India*, London: London Scholar Press.

Khan, Mumtaz Ali, 1983, *Mass Conversion in Meenakshipuram*, Madras: Christian Literature Society.

Kooiman, Dick, 1983, Untouchability in India through the Missionary's Eye, *Itinerario*, Vol. 7:1.

——— 1989, *Conversion and Social Equality in India. The London Missionary Society in South Travancore in the 19th Century*, New Delhi: Manohar Publishers.

——— 1991, Mass Movement, Famine and Epidemic. A Study in Interrelationship, *Modern Asian Studies*, Vol. 25:2.

Kumar, Dharma, 1984 (1982), *The Cambridge Economic History of India, Vol. II, c. 1757 to c. 1970*, Hyderabad: Orient Longman/Cambridge University Press.

——— 1992:1, *Land and Caste in South India. Agricultural Labour in the Madras Presidency during the Nineteenth Century*, New Delhi: Manohar Publishers.

——— 1992:2, Caste and Landlessness in South India, in Prakash, Gyan, ed., *The World of the Rural Labourer in Colonial India*, Oxford: Oxford University Press.

Kurien, C. T., 1989 (1981), *Dynamics of Rural Transformation. A Study of Tamil Nadu 1950-1980*, Hyderabad: Orient Longman.

Ludden, David, 1989 (1985), *Peasant History in South India*, Oxford: Oxford University Press.

Mahadevan, R., 1992, *The Process of Manchesterisation in Colonial South India: A Study of the Pattern of Textile Investment and the Growth of Indigenous Capitalists in Coimbatore in 1914-45*, Paper presented at the 12th European Conference on Modern South Asian Studies, Economic and Demographic History of South Asia, Berlin, September 1992.

Manickam, Sundararaj, 1977, *The Social Setting of Christian Conversion in South India. The impact of the Wesleyan Methodist missionaries on the Trichy–Tanjore diocese with special reference to the mass movement area 1820–1947*, Wiesbaden: Frans Steiner Verlag.

Massey, James, 1995, *Dalits in India: Religion as a Source of Bondage or Liberation with Special Reference to Christians*, New Delhi: Manohar Publishers.

Moffatt, Michael, 1979, *An Untouchable Community in South India, Structure and Consensus*, Princeton: Princeton University Press.

Mosse, C. D. F., 1994, Idiom of subordination and styles of protest among Christian and Hindu Harijan castes in Tamil Nadu, *Contributions to Indian Sociology*, Vol. 28:1.

Mouzelis, Nicos P., 1992 (1990), *Post-Marxist Alternatives. The Construction of Social Orders*, London: Macmillan.

Mukherjee, Nilmani, 1962, *The Ryotwari System in Madras 1792 – 1827*, Calcutta: Firma K. L. Mukhopadhyay.

Oddie, Geoffrey A., 1991, *Hindu and Christian in South East India*, London: Curzon/Riverdale.

———— 1996, Missionaries as Social Commentators: The Indian Case, in Bickers and Seaton, eds., *Missionary Encounters: Sources and Issues*, Surrey: Curzon Press.

O'Hanlon, Rosalind, 1988, Recovering the Subject: *Subaltern Studies* and Histories of Resistance in Colonial South Asia, *Modern Asian Studies*, Vol. 22:1.

O'Hanlon, Rosalind, and Washbrook, David, 1992, After Orientalism: Culture, Criticism, and Politics in the Third World, *Comparative Studies in Society and History*, Vol. 34, pp. 141-67.

Pandian, M.M.S., 1990, *The Political Economy of Agrarian Change. Nachilnadu 1880-1939*, New Delhi: Sage Publications.

Pandian, T. B., 1895, *Pandian and the Pariahs*, Madras: Madras Britannia Press.

Patel, Surendra, J., 1952, *Agricultural Labourers in Modern India and Pakistan*, Bombay: Current Book House.

Peel, J.D.Y., 1996, Problems and Opportunities in an Anthropologist's Use of a Missionary Archive, in Bickers and Seaton, eds., *Missionary Encounters: Sources and Issues*, Surrey: Curzon Press.

Pickett, J. Waskom, 1933, *Christian Mass Movements in India*, Lucknow.

Ponniah, J. S., 1934, The *Kapas* Market at Dindigul: A Study in the Local Factors that Influence the Prices, *Madras Agricultural Journal*, Vol. 22:11.

Prakash, Gyan, 1990, Writing Post-Orientalist Histories of the Third World: Perspectives from Indian Historiography, *Comparative Studies in Society and History*, Vol. 32:2.

Price, Pamela G., 1996, *Kingship and Political Practice in Colonial India*, Cambridge: Cambridge University Press.

Rothermund, Dietmar, 1992, *India in the Great Depression 1929–1939*, New Delhi: Manohar Publications.

———— 1993 (1988), *An Economic History of India. From pre-colonial times to 1991*, London: Routledge.

Sandegren, Herman, 1924, *Svensk Mission och Indisk Kyrka*, Stockholm: Svenska Kyrkans Diakonistyrelse.

Sivanappan, R.K., and Aiyasamy, P.K., 1978, *Land and Water Resources of Coimbatore District*, Coimbatore: Tamil Nadu Agricultural University.

Sivaswamy, K.G., 1948, *The Ryotwary Tenant*, Madras: South Indian Federation of Agricultural Workers' Unions.

Spate, O.H.K., and Learmont, A.T.A., 1967 (1954), *India and Pakistan: A General and Regional Geography*, London: Methuen & Co. Ltd.

Spear, Percival, 1992 (1958), *The Oxford History of India*, Oxford: Oxford University Press.

Srinivas, M.N., 1955, The Social System of a Mysore Village, in Marriott, McKim, ed., *Village India*, Chicago: University of Chicago Press.

Stein, Burton, 1980, *Peasant State and Society in Medieval South India*, Oxford: Oxford University Press.

Tharakan, Michael, 1984, Socio-Economic Factors in Educational Development: The Case of Nineteenth-Century Travancore, *Economic and Political Weekly*, Vol. 19:45-6, pp. 1913-28, 1959-67.

Thompson, Paul, 1988 (1978), *The Voice of the Past: Oral History*, Oxford: Oxford University Press.

Thorner, Alice, 1982, Semi-Feudalism or Capitalism? Contemporary Debate on Classes and Modes of Production in India, *Economic and Political Weekly*, Vol. 17; 4, 11 and 18 Dec.

Thurston, Edgar, 1909, *Castes and Tribes of Southern India*, Vols. II, IV and VII, Madras: Government Press.

Tyabji, Nasir, 1995, *Colonialism, Chemical Technology and Industry in Southern India 1880–1937*, Oxford: Oxford University Press.

Wadhwa, D.C., 1973, *Agrarian Legislation in India (1793-1966)*, Vol. I, Hyderabad: Orient Longman.

Washbrook, David, 1993, Land and Labour in late Eighteenth-Century South India: The Golden Age of the Pariah?, in Robb, Peter, ed., 1993, *Dalit Movements and the Meanings of Labour in India*, Oxford: Oxford University Press.

Yanagisawa, Haruka, 1996, *A Century of Change. Caste and Irrigated Lands in Tamilnadu 1860s-1970s*, New Delhi: Manohar Publishers.

## Unpublished Dissertations

Brimnes, Niels, 1996, *European Authority and Caste Disputes in South India 1650-1850. British and Danish Perspectives*, PhD thesis submitted to the Faculty of History, Cambridge University.

Dorairaj, J., 1990:1, *M.Th. Thesis no. 609A*, Tamilnadu Theological Seminary, Madurai.

——— 1990:2, *A Study of the Post-Conversion Developments among the Madharis Community of the Karur-Dharapuram Area between 1913-1973. Summary of the Thesis submitted for the M.Th. studies degree History of Christianity) to the Senate of Serampore College*, Tamilnadu Theological Seminary, Register No. 470/88, Madurai.

Frykholm, Yngve, 1970, *Christian Churches as Agents of Socio-Economic Development in India with Particular Reference to Action for Food Production (AFPRO)*, Licentiate dissertation submitted to the Department of Theology, Uppsala University.

Jeyaranjan, J., 1993, A *Village Economy in Transition. A Study of the Process of Change in Iluppakkorai, Tamil Nadu, 1960-1985*, PhD thesis submitted to the University of Madras, Madras Institute of Development Studies.

Lindberg, Staffan, 1969, *The Madharis. An Ex-untouchable Caste in South India. Socio-economic and religious aspects of conversion into Christianity and urbanization-industrialization*, course diss. (3 points) submitted to the Department of Sociology, Lund University.

Mosse, C. D. F., 1986, *Caste, Christianity and Hinduism: A Study of Social Organisation and Religion in Rural Ramnad*, PhD thesis submitted to the University of Oxford.

Washbrook, David A., 1974, *The Society and Politics of the Madras Presidency 1880-1920*, PhD thesis no. 8901, submitted to the Faculty of History, Cambridge University.

## Dictionaries

*An English-Tamil Etymological Dictionary*, 1911.

*Tamil Lexicon*, University of Madras, 1936.

*Winslow's Tamil and English Dictionary*, 1979.

*Dictionary of Contemporary Tamil*, Cre-A, Madras 1992.

# Index